The Ethical Dimension of the *Decameron*

MARILYN MIGIEL

The Ethical Dimension
of the *Decameron*

UNIVERSITY OF TORONTO PRESS
Toronto Buffalo London

© University of Toronto Press 2015
Toronto Buffalo London
www.utppublishing.com
Printed in the U.S.A.

ISBN 978-1-4426-3188-5

Printed on acid-free, 100% post-consumer recycled paper with vegetable-based inks.

Toronto Italian Studies

Library and Archives Canada Cataloguing in Publication

Migiel, Marilyn, 1954-, author
The ethical dimension of the Decameron/Marilyn Migiel.

(Toronto Italian studies)
Includes bibliographical references and index.
ISBN 978-1-4426-3188-5 (bound)

1. Boccaccio, Giovanni, 1313–1375. Decamerone.   2. Boccaccio, Giovanni,
1313–1375 – Criticism and interpretation.   3. Ethics in literature.
4. Italian literature –To 1400 – History and criticism. I. Title.
II. Series: Toronto Italian studies

PQ4293.P4M54 2015   853'.1   C2015-903101-X

University of Toronto Press acknowledges the financial assistance to its publishing
program of the Canada Council for the Arts and the Ontario Arts Council, an agency
of the Government of Ontario.

**Canada Council
for the Arts**

**Conseil des Arts
du Canada**

ONTARIO ARTS COUNCIL
CONSEIL DES ARTS DE L'ONTARIO
an Ontario government agency
un organisme du gouvernement de l'Ontario

Funded by the   Financé par le
Government   gouvernement
of Canada   du Canada

For Andrea Kavaler and Michael Migiel-Schwartz

Contents

Acknowledgments

In the course of writing this book, I had the great pleasure of interacting with a good many people who generously commented on my work in progress and who helped me articulate my arguments more effectively and, I hope, more elegantly. Kathleen Long, who commented on more versions of the manuscript than seems fair to have asked her to read, deserves special recognition and thanks in this regard; for many years, she has been a wonderful colleague, co-teacher, and friend. William J. Kennedy, John Najemy, Hannah Chapelle Wojciehowski, and Anna Paparcone have been staunchly supportive interlocutors, and for this I am grateful. I am appreciative of the input given by so many Boccaccio scholars at conferences and in informal conversation: Guyda Armstrong, Susanna Barsella, Dino Cervigni, Rhiannon Daniels, Irene Eibenstein-Alvisi, Martin Eisner, Elsa Filosa, Disa Gambera, Tobias Foster Gittes, Eugenio Giusti, Jason Houston, Ashleigh Imus, Timothy Kircher, Millicent Marcus, Simone Marchesi, Stephen Milner, Roberta Morosini, Victoria Kirkham, Christopher Kleinhenz, Kristina Olson, Michael Papio, F. Regina Psaki, Michael Sherberg, Janet Levarie Smarr, and Thomas Stillinger. I extend my thanks also to the many students who have participated in discussions relevant to this book.

To Telluride Association and to all those who participated in its projects alongside me, from 1971 on, I owe a debt of gratitude for the way that Telluride and its associates helped form my intellect, my character, and my temperament, by setting high standards for excellence, by creating opportunities for leadership and hard work, and by repeatedly offering occasions to reflect on and to debate what we wanted for ourselves and for others in our communities. I do not believe this book could have been written if I had not had the experiences I have had in Telluride.

I am indebted to anonymous readers of my book manuscript, engaged by my editor Suzanne Rancourt at the University of Toronto Press, for their generous readings and commentary. To those readers and to Suzanne, I express heartfelt thanks.

Several chapters of this book are revised versions of previously published essays. For chapter 1, see "Wanted: Translators of the *Decameron's* Moral and Ethical Complexities," *Heliotropia* 6.1–2 (2009), http://www.brown.edu/Departments/Italian_Studies/heliotropia/06/migiel.pdf; for chapter 2, which now bears a different title, see "Figurative Language and Sex Wars in the *Decameron*," *Heliotropia* 2.2 (2004), http://www.heliotropia.org/02-02/migiel.shtml; for chapter 4, see "Some Restrictions Apply: Testing the Reader in *Decameron* III, 8," in *Boccaccio in America*, ed. Elsa Filosa and Michael Papio (Ravenna: Longo, 2012), 191–207; and for chapter 5, see "New Lessons in Criticism and Blame from the *Decameron*," *Heliotropia* 7.1–2 (2010): 5–30, http://www.brown.edu/Departments/Italian_Studies/heliotropia/07/migiel.pdf.

As the book was in production, I had the good fortune to work with Matthew Kudelka, a supremely efficient and gracious copy editor, and with Ashleigh Imus, an expert freelance writer and editor who created the index and proofread with an eagle eye.

In dedicating this book to my friend of some forty years, Andrea Kavaler, and to my son, Michael Migiel-Schwartz, I take the opportunity to thank two individuals who proved influential, in ways I would not have originally foreseen, to the writing of this book.

Andrea was there to witness my first encounter with the *Decameron*, when she and I were roommates in Telluride House at Cornell University, and I, as a twenty-year-old with two semesters of Italian language study under my belt, undertook (ambitiously and irrationally) to read Boccaccio's *Decameron* and Dante's *Comedy*. Andrea has always represented for me a commitment to wide-ranging intellectual curiosity, to ethical inquiry, to thinking that is sharp and nuanced, to clear writing, and to good-humoured intolerance of foolishness. Dedicating the book to her is a way of thanking her for modelling these qualities.

If Andrea is associated with my first encounter with the *Decameron*, Michael provided the stimulus that brought *The Ethical Dimension of the "Decameron"* to a close. One might say that it was friendly competition with a son who wrote a 181-page Wesleyan University honours thesis in a single year that made me realize I should stop lingering over the manuscript and get this book in print. And while Andrea, who is of my own generation, was a key person who modelled for me the kind of careful and creative reflection that I have tried to cultivate in my own life, my son, who belongs to the next generation, is the person I most often had in mind in writing this book. This is not because I have ever expected him to read the *Decameron* or to learn from my specific analyses here, but rather because I believe that the habits of mind and character that brought me to write this book in this particular way, with constant attention to the ethics of reading, speaking, and writing, could serve him well in all aspects of his personal and professional life. Dedicating the book to Michael is a way of expressing my ardent hope that, on all those occasions when he will have to interpret what others say and write, he will judge patiently and carefully, and that when he himself speaks and writes, he will remain mindful of the potential impact of his own narrative and rhetorical choices.

Note on Citations of the *Decameron*

All citations from the Italian text of the *Decameron* are drawn from Giovanni Boccaccio, *Decameron*, ed. Vittore Branca, 2 vols. (Turin: Einaudi, 1992). Italian passages from the *Decameron* are identified not by page number but by Day, novella, and section (i.e., *comma*). Thus "2.9.67" should be understood as *Decameron*, Day 2, novella 9, comma (or section) 67.

All English translations of passages in a foreign language are my own, unless otherwise indicated.

In citing the following widely used translations of the *Decameron*, I often identify them by the translators' last names.

Giovanni Boccaccio, *Decameron*, trans. Guido Waldman (Oxford: Oxford University Press, 1993).

Giovanni Boccaccio, *Decameron*, trans. G.H. McWilliam, 2nd ed. (New York: Penguin Books, 1995).

Giovanni Boccaccio, *The Decameron*, trans. Mark Musa and Peter Bondanella (New York: New American Library [Signet Classics], 2002 [1982]).

Giovanni Boccaccio, *Decameron*, trans. J.G. Nichols (New York: Everyman's Library, 2009).

The Ethical Dimension of the *Decameron*

Introduction: The Ethical Dimension of the *Decameron*

The aim of ethics ... is not to "teach the difference between right and wrong" but to make people more comfortable facing moral complexity.

– Robert C. Solomon[1]

One of the great innovations of Giovanni Boccaccio's *Decameron* is that it aims to complicate our moral views and our ethical responses. If one believes, as I suspect many of us do, that the *Decameron* is neither immoral nor amoral in its stance, and if one believes, as I suspect many of us do, that the *Decameron*'s purpose is not solely to entertain, this claim won't strike us as earth-shaking. Precisely *how* the *Decameron* complicates our moral views – how it goes about teaching us about moral reasoning, how it leads us to reflect on what we find praiseworthy or blameworthy, and above all how it demonstrates the value of literature to this enterprise – is a matter unlikely to be resolved any time soon. It must continue to be discussed.

The interplay of reading, writing, and ethics is highlighted in the very first lines of the *Decameron*. The book greets us with this *incipit*: "Comincia il libro chiamato Decameron cognominato prencipe Galeotto, nel quale si contengono cento novelle in diece dì dette da sette donne e da tre giovani uomini" (Here begins the book called Decameron, surnamed Prince Gallehault, in which are contained one hundred novellas told over the course of ten days by seven women and by three young men [*Proemio*, 1]). Lest we forget how important this characterization of the *Decameron* is, we are reminded in the *explicit* that "[q]ui finisce la Decima e ultima giornata del libro chiamato Decameron cognominato prencipe Galeotto" (Here ends the Tenth and final Day of the book called Decameron, which is surnamed Prince Gallehault [Conclusione dell'Autore, 30]). The double-reference to Prince Galle-hault (who brought together Lancelot and Guinevere in an illicit rela-tionship) is manifestly linked to the peremptory judgment offered by Dante's Francesca in *Inferno* 5.137 as she blames a book and its author for having led her to damnation among the lustful: "Galeotto fu 'l libro e chi lo scrisse" (A Gallehault was the book and he who wrote it). Read-ers, understanding that they are thus called upon to respond to ques-tions about the ethics of reading, writing, and interpretation that Dante had raised in *Inferno* 5 and that the Author of the *Decameron* raises when he notes that his book can also be called "Prince Gallehault," have sought to understand exactly how they should judge Boccaccio's inten-tions. By citing Dante, what is Boccaccio saying? Should we understand this to be a condemnation of the book's project? Robert Hollander has cogently argued against a moralizing, condemnatory response to the book as Gallehault and likewise has argued against the refusal to see the seductive, erotic push of the book.[2] Reading the *incipit* and the Author's Proem, Hollander reveals a Boccaccio who always wants it both ways. On the one hand, as Hollander notes, "the persona [Boccaccio] knows he has apparently assumed is that of Dante, whose fifth canto is resolute in putting even the most sympathetic of carnal sinners into the pit."[3] On the other, as Hollander takes care to emphasize, the Author of the *Decameron*, in his presentation of himself and his work, repeatedly aligns himself with Ovid. Importantly, however, this is not the Ovid who apparently teaches lascivious pleasure in the *Amores*, nor is this the Ovid who apparently condemns the pleasures of love in the *Reme-dia amoris*. Rather, Hollander brings forth an Ovid who writes ironi-cally, whose message is not as univocal as some readers have taken it to be.[4] This is an Ovid who, while teaching love in the *Amores*, reveals how foolish lovers are, and who, while denouncing love in the *Remedia*, offers his pronouncements selectively, "as a police action on behalf of those lovers who are unhappy, while those who are joyful in their ardor are urged to continue in their pleasure."[5]

Among the things I especially like about the path Hollander has forged in his commentary on the *Decameron* as Galeotto and the *Decam-eron* as positively useful is the way it encourages a dialogue about the ethical choices involved in the creation of meaning. When scholars like Hollander seek to gauge Boccaccio's subtle positioning of himself as Author of the *Decameron*, they are engaged in work that is ethical. This might not seem immediately apparent, because these kinds of

readings do not ask us to see Boccaccio as virtuous and morally uplifting, they do not ask us to censure the author or the work, and they do
not try to wrench towards clarity and resolution those moments when
the *Decameron* remains problematically indeterminate. Rather, they ask
us to recognize that the meanings we find in the *Decameron* must be
subjected to constant scrutiny and refinement, and that this can happen
only if we remain in constant dialogue with this literary work and with
other texts and contexts that could help us read it better.

The Ethical Dimension of the "Decameron" is about the dialogue about
ethical choices that the *Decameron* creates with us and that we, as individuals and as groups, create with the *Decameron*. Examining this dialogue
grants us insight into our values, our biases, and our decision-making
processes.

The dialogue is born of stories: the one hundred stories told by the
ten Florentines who escape the Black Death of 1348, the stories the
Author tells about those ten Florentines, the stories the Author tells
about himself, the plague, the denizens of his home city, his detractors, his supporters, and the book itself. We respond. We take these
stories and we "retell" them, even if only in the moment of reading
them. We receive the stories and understand them in our own way, in
frameworks that are sometimes shared with other readers and sometimes distinctively our own; we focus on certain details and not others;
we respond by agreeing and disagreeing and questioning. Moreover,
because the *Decameron* is constructed so as to undermine facile judgments, our conclusions prove ever so contingent: contingent upon the
evidence we have selected from this multifaceted work, contingent
upon our understandings of the *Decameron*'s linguistic and rhetorical
textures, contingent upon our willingness to hear stories we had not
counted on hearing, and contingent upon our willingness to rethink
our own perceptual schemas.

A cautionary word: My book (like the *Decameron* itself) will not tell
anybody what course of action we should pursue or whose behaviour
we should imitate. To rephrase: I do not care to pronounce, for example, on whether it is better to be like Madonna Filippa (the adulteress
of *Decameron* 6.7 who successfully defends her adultery in court) than
like Griselda (the supremely long-suffering and patient wife in the final
story of the *Decameron*). Rather, I examine how Boccaccio's narrators,
translators, and readers establish the ethical questions about how we
ought to live, and I ask readers to consider the implications of such
choices. How do we select the questions, deliberate about them, and

use logic and good evidence (or not) to support our views? What sort of "moral language" do we construct, and what do our rhetorical and stylistic choices reveal about us as moral and ethical beings? Do we report information selectively or comprehensively? Do we restrict views or invite a plurality of them? Do we strive to make clear the intellectual and emotional biases that generate unjust practices, or do we cement injustice?

One might wonder why I, having written *A Rhetoric of the "Decameron,"* didn't move on to think about other matters.[6] It is a question I myself have repeatedly asked, since I hadn't planned on this turn of events. I discovered, as apparently Pier Paolo Pasolini did as well, that I hadn't chosen the *Decameron*, the *Decameron* had chosen me. The questions the *Decameron* posed weren't easy to lay to rest. And they kept multiplying.

In the work I have done on the *Decameron* – indeed, in all the work I have done over the past three decades – questions about what stories we tell about ourselves and others have remained constant. What has shifted is the organizing principle. In *A Rhetoric of the "Decameron,"* I was concerned with offering alternatives to the question, "Is the *Decameron* feminist or misogynist?" Choosing to make the figure of woman central in my analysis, because the figure of woman is central to Boccaccio's work, I studied how messages about women in the *Decameron* were the product of gendered voices, how narratives that trumpeted women's empowerment also delineated the limits on women's power, how rhetorical instruments such as figurative language were distributed along gender lines, and how the *Decameron* explored the nexus of women's empowerment and violence against women. In studying the ethical dimension of the *Decameron*, I am training my focus on another question in the debate: "How does the *Decameron* teach?" – a question that has also been formulated as "What sort of moral and ethical orientation does the *Decameron* offer?" – and I am offering some alternative ways of thinking about the lessons we could take away from our reading of this work.

It seems hard to imagine that only a quarter-century ago it was not fully accepted that Boccaccio's goal in the *Decameron* was other than to entertain.[7] In "To Teach or Not to Teach: The Moral Dimension of the *Decameron* Reconsidered," published in 1989, R.W. Hastings writes that "until comparatively recently few critics were prepared to allow that Boccaccio actually had an educative purpose."[8] Hastings then carefully documents the various critical positions. First he describes those readers for whom moral reflection in the *Decameron* is entirely lacking, or without substantial importance, or troubled by Boccaccio's ideological inconsistency and lack of coherent moral criteria.[9] He discusses at some length the view of Glending Olson, who maintains that the educative value of the *Decameron* lies in the "therapeutic effects of literature as entertainment" and who supports his hypothesis by citing evidence from both the *Decameron* and the *Genealogie deorum gentilium libri* (*Genealogy of the Gentile Gods*).[10]

"Is the *Decameron* immoral?" Nobody asks that question anymore. Given that there is no religious or legal outcry about how the *Decameron* could threaten morality, scholars no longer need to defend the *Decameron* and its author. Likewise, given that we no longer subscribe to the view of Boccaccio as a man untroubled by serious thought, nobody asks, "Does the *Decameron* participate in serious reflection about moral issues, or is it simply for entertainment?" Now that these debates have been put to rest, scholars are divided over *how* the *Decameron* engages with ethical and moral issues. Emerging from the scholarship are questions such as these: Does a literary text such as the *Decameron* support a moral, rational order? Do its descriptions of reprehensible behaviour condone that behaviour? Where in it are we to find the voices of moral authority (if any)? And how do we orient our own moral compasses as we read a book that showcases conflicting moral and ethical claims?

The name that probably first comes to mind when we think about the *Decameron*'s moral and ethical lessons is Victoria Kirkham. Her scholarship has long engaged with the question of moral virtue in Boccaccio's works, and she is the author of a key entry bearing the Italian title "Morale" in the *Lessico critico decameroniano*.[11] The fundamental question for Kirkham remains this: How does the *Decameron* teach us to avoid vice and pursue virtue? According to her, Boccaccio draws on Cicero, Seneca, the Church Fathers, Brunetto Latini, and Dante, but his ideas about moral virtue are based principally on Aristotle's *Nicomachean Ethics*, which Boccaccio knew well, given that he had transcribed Thomas Aquinas's text and commentary on this Aristotelian treatise, as well as ideas about virtue in his *Summa Theologica*.[12] The moral message of the *Decameron* emerges in the narrators themselves (personifications of virtues and vices), in the attention Boccaccio pays to civic and political values, in the programmatic design of the *Decameron*, which highlights moral and family values, and in the war of virtue and vice throughout that culminates in a reflection on magnanimity.[13] Kirkham takes care to point out that Boccaccio expects us to regard the novellas not as discrete units but as interconnected parts within a framing tale.[14] Along with Fernando Neri and Vittore Branca, she sees the novellas moving from the most wicked of beings (ser Ciappelletto) to the height of virtue (Griselda, who represents the highest Christian virtue, humility).[15] As Robert Hollander notes, Kirkham's *Decameron* is a "conventionally moralizing text which champions reason in its battle against the appetitive soul."[16]

While Kirkham does not lack allies,[17] numerous voices have risen with alternative understandings of the *Decameron*'s moral and ethical vision. Adopting a framework that is less strictly tied to a Christian (and specifically to an Aristotelian–Thomistic) world view, they turn down the volume on Boccaccio's didacticism. They suggest that the literary achievements of the *Decameron* are in themselves ethical achievements. Most important, they emphasize the *Decameron*'s conflictual multiplicity, which makes it difficult to affirm a single interpretative stance.

When, for example, R.W. Hastings explores how the *Decameron* guides us to pursue happiness and virtue, he emphasizes Boccaccio's rejection of didacticism.[18] Instead, he finds Boccaccio's moral vision in a new understanding of human emotions, in the relativity of our points of view, in tolerance, in a secular rather than transcendental perspective, in the respect for nature, in the role of reason, in a more permissive view of love and marriage and women's place, in his criticism of religion, in his celebration of intelligence and of the ability to face the challenge posed by Fortune, in his respect for the medieval values of courtesy and nobility (modified, of course, given the demands of a different age).[19] Of greatest importance, Hastings claims, is "simply the message of the author himself to his readers: the declaration that to be at ease with life and with oneself, to find fulfillment in the responsible exercise of one's natural function, is the means to achieve the happy and virtuous life to which all men are entitled."[20]

Mario Baratto also emphasizes what Hastings calls the "responsible exercise of one's natural function," but he does so in order to speak about the *Decameron*'s moral vision as structured by man's relation to Fortune and Nature (the former being an external force that humans must constantly deal with, the latter defined as the instincts and drives that must be recognized and directed toward a better end).[21] Recognizing the importance granted to language and to eloquence in the *Decameron*, and recognizing that the work of rhetorical construction is a "product typical of the intellectual," Baratto both privileges the role the *Decameron* offers for the intellectual (i.e., to articulate the fundamental values of human existence and to be the new "wise man" of earthly virtue) and opens up that role so that it is available at diverse levels to diverse individuals.[22]

Millicent Marcus is one scholar who has shown how the *Decameron* calls attention to how we use language to represent our world and to negotiate our place in it. As Marcus sees it, the *Decameron* offers a variety of authorial and audiential role models, some seemingly reliable, some far less so, some puzzlingly uncertain; it also invites us to reflect on what it means to speak, to listen, to write, to read. Marcus writes: "Boccaccio embodies his teachings in the very mode of his narration, offering successful and unsuccessful examples of the storytelling art which will serve as models for the perspectives he would have us adopt as his reading public."[23] According to Marcus, "Boccaccio teaches us to read the text" by portraying "internalized artist figures" and a variety of "internalized publics."[24] For her, figures of the artist such as ser Ciappelletto (1.1) and Frate Cipolla (6.10) alert readers to the "untrustworthiness of all human discourse," and the gullible audiences in these and other novellas alert us to the "dangers of too literal a belief in both the spoken and the written word."[25] The Florentine narrators' responses to the novellas become a platform that readers are invited to use in order to consider what their own responses should be. Marcus shows how Boccaccio, in his exploration of narrative genres (romance, tragedy, comedy), elects comedy as the one most congenial to his moral message. And finally, in a sustained discussion of the final story of the *Decameron* – that of Griselda, which has so often served as the linchpin for scholars who proclaim the *Decameron*'s lofty moral content – Marcus demonstrates how "with this story, which resists all univocal interpretation, the author challenges his public to entertain a multiplicity of perspectives at once."[26]

Robert Hollander makes a crucial point regarding the complexity of the debate about the morality of the *Decameron*, a point worth reiterating here:

If most students of the *Decameron* agree that it does have a "moral" purpose, I need hardly report that there is sharp disagreement between those who see it as championing the "new morality" that it so amply portrays (surely the majority opinion) and those who argue that it is a work promoting traditional religious and moral values. This description of the broad and general contours of the continuing debate does not do (nor does it attempt to do) justice to its layers of partial agreement and disagreement, the differences over the moral tone of one form of behavior or another, in short over the manifold complexities of what all can agree is an extraordinarily subtly-woven literary fabric. Indeed, one has to look only as far as the first *novella* to find behaviors and situations which are considered in very different lights by those who agree on a basic interpretive position. For example, is Cepparello's self-creating "confession" to be condemned or admired? Does he go to heaven or hell, or are we not supposed to attempt such judgment? Does the fact that gullible Frenchmen pray to him confirm God's mercy in allowing intercession through even such flawed vessels as he, or does it call into question the very efficacy of prayer? Such questions are invited by the text; answers to them are virtually impossible to confirm in the text. The author of the *Decameron* prefers to formulate questions rather than to answer them perhaps aware that the first generation of Dante's enthusiastic readers would find his work a hard nut to crack.[27]

Responding to scholars like Victoria Kirkham and Marga Cottino-Jones, who see a "moral and spiritual heightening" in the final day of the *Decameron*, especially in the final story of Griselda, Robert Hollander, writing with Courtney Cahill, calls into question the celebration of virtuous behaviour on the final day of storytelling and reaffirms that "the magnanimity exhibited in Day Ten is always problematic and never the sort that Boccaccio himself describes in the *Esposizioni*."[28]

The perspectives on the *Decameron*'s moral and ethical dimension do not come solely from Italianist literary scholars. Kurt Flasch, a German historian of medieval philosophy, argues that we should see the *Decameron* as a work of practical moral philosophy written in a language available to women, a work that rejects "*our* distinctions" between literature and philosophy."[29] He affirms that Boccaccio "conceived of a philosophy that, like the philosophy of the wise ancient Greeks, was a lesson on how to live, and therefore was ethics, politics, poetry, and theology."[30] Focusing in particular on the Author's Proem and on Day 1 of the *Decameron*, Flasch portrays a Boccaccio who, as he was thinking about moral philosophical reflections that were communicated by a new kind of literature, was also engaged with the ethical and epistemological reflections of Aristotle, Aquinas, and Ockham.[31] Perhaps most compelling is Flasch's candid and thoughtful assessment of how he found moral philosophy where he least expected it – in a book that offered pleasure and useful lessons but not the kinds of moral and philosophical reflections one would find in Dante.[32] His book thus

contradicts one common accusation against moral responses to literary texts – that they suffer from cognitive triviality (meaning that we
"learn" in literature only what we already know).[33]

The historian Timothy Kircher, in the course of examining the tension
between medieval and Renaissance cultures, has studied the *Decameron*'s
"modality of moral communication" to show how it diverges from
the approach taken by medieval Tuscan preachers.[34] Distancing himself from scholars who see the *Decameron* as "preaching moral truths
as knowledge," Kircher reaffirms that the *Decameron* "attends to the
process of becoming aware of the human capacity for goodness and
wickedness, a process buoyed by time's potentiality, rather than to the
certain measurement of moral goodness, which is the aim of the *exemplum*."[35] He investigates how the *Decameron* offers a "new way of nar-
rating moral problems to a more sceptical readership" by "project[ing]
the *exemplum* tradition through the lens of irony."[36] In the *Decameron*
there is no clearly defined moral spokesperson; the process of discerning moral and ethical lessons falls to readers, who must rely on their
own personal experience rather than the dictates of external authorities.
This proves to be a "liberating, anxious moment."[37]

In the most recent contribution to the debate about the moral
communication of the *Decameron*, Michaela Paasche Grudin and Robert
Grudin – who come from different disciplinary traditions (literary
studies and political science, respectively) – have argued that the moral
and aesthetic basis of the *Decameron* is founded on a key Ciceronian
concept: *ingenium*, meaning "genius, imagination, inventiveness."[38] In
the *Decameron* they see "the first coherent expression of moral principles
that scholarship has come to associate with the Renaissance."[39]

Obviously, how we respond to this debate that has emerged over the
past forty years will depend on the principles that gird our approaches
to reading literature, on the kinds of questions we find most illuminating, on our assumptions about the values Boccaccio held dear, and on
how we perceive these values emerging in his work. I myself tend to
align with those readers who see the *Decameron* as questioning moral
authorities, transcendental messages, and traditional didacticism
(e.g., Hastings, Baratto, Marcus, Hollander, Flasch, Kircher), but it is
important to note that all of the critical approaches I have discussed
above have merits. While I am of the mind that the final day (especially
the final story) of the *Decameron* does not offer the kind of positive
summary lesson that a scholar like Kirkham sees in it, I would still
argue along with her for the relevance of Aristotelian and Thomistic

reflections about virtue. While I find that the Grudins' readings of individual moments in the *Decameron* tend to be too thin to support their assertions about a unified Ciceronian reading of the work, I do believe that their argument about the relevance of Cicero to Boccaccio is illuminating and should be taken seriously.

With the present book, I hope to contribute to the ongoing debate about the way the *Decameron* engages us in ethical reflection. My own view is that the *Decameron* is sticky and thorny: It catches us as we move through it, compelling us to reveal who we are as well as how we relate to it and, by extension, to the world outside us. My focus remains unabashedly on the experience of readers, on the meanings they find in the *Decameron*, and on their ideological assumptions about the way a literary text such as the *Decameron* – not to mention the world itself – works. I respectfully reject the notion that considering how readers process the meanings generated by the *Decameron* is a less valid approach than studying the meanings generated by the *Decameron* in its social and cultural context, as if it were possible for readers to isolate Boccaccio's intentions from what, at a subsequent historical moment, readers are able to perceive and express.

Before I provide an overview of the specific analyses I will offer in the following chapters, I want to clarify for readers how I think about the act of reading, the act of translation, the possibility of ethical improvement, and the thorny question of authorial intentionality. In doing so, I hope also to clarify what areas of investigation remain outside the scope of my project.

Throughout this book, I work with a wide selection of readings of the *Decameron* – not only those offered in scholarly publications, but also those found in published translations and in the many readings and commentaries I have heard in classrooms and during conference presentations and informal conversations. I am especially interested in the variances among readings provided by translators of the *Decameron*. Variances among translations have allowed me to understand better how the *Decameron* baits readers with subtle indeterminacies. In other words, the text is capable of generating meanings that can be perceived and articulated differently by different readers. Translators are thus a distinct category of reader, because in responding to a source text in order to generate an alternative text for a destination audience, they are required to make choices that bind them, choices that must stand on their own, typically without supplementary explanations.[40]

Given that I use other translators' choices to help identify what I earlier referred to as the "thorny moments" in a text, moments that catch us as we move through and force us to reveal ourselves, one might well ask how I view my own translations of the *Decameron* in this book, especially where I offer my own translation as a way to push back against alternative versions. I admit that I do at times offer my translations as better, though it is important to clarify that I see them as better in a very restricted sense, which is to say, better because my translations help me get at very specific instances where I see that the text is generating meanings that other translators do not capture or do not capture to the greatest extent possible. I will be the first to admit that my translations are not always optimal, given that, unlike many other readers, I am willing to tolerate unusual diction and unusual syntactic contortions in the interest of understanding the ways the *Decameron* challenges us.

Throughout this book, I will frequently speak of the *Decameron* as inviting us to engage in ethical reflection, as encouraging us, reminding us, asking us to consider certain questions, fostering debate, challenging us, testing us. Students who have studied the *Decameron* with me often come to our discussions assuming that the *Decameron* will tell them which virtues to espouse and how to make ethical decisions about complex social and political matters. My response to such expectations is to reaffirm that it is possible that the *Decameron* could bring a reader to be more caring and more just in her life but that since there is no guarantee this will happen, and since the only thing I myself am able to observe first-hand is the relationship between the student and the text of the *Decameron*, my primary concern is to help the reader be more caring and more just in her reading of the words on the page. It is to try to make sure that to the extent humanly possible, the reader approaches the text with openness as to what the text might be saying, that the reader is willing to engage in questioning and dialogue with the text in order to see where it could be resisting her readings, taking her in another direction and offering a lesson other than the one she wishes at first to recognize.

I also wish to clarify what assumptions I make about Giovanni Boccaccio and how he might have wanted us to read the *Decameron*. Even as I prioritize what readers are able to perceive over an attempt to identify authorial intention, I – like every other reader, I would venture to say – come to the text with working assumptions about how Boccaccio would position himself in relation to his authorial persona and to the ten narrators of the *Decameron*. One could, of course, analyse and evaluate what the authorial persona and the narrators say without reference to a historical author at all. Still, as we certainly have learned from reading the *Corbaccio* – a Boccaccian work that has sometimes been read as an expression of Boccaccio's misogyny but that readers now tend to perceive as a Boccaccian critique of misogyny – we are never entirely free of our assumptions about this author's intentions even if we keep firmly in mind that his intentions are impossible to pin down precisely.[41] The important thing, I believe, is for my assumptions about Boccaccio's purposes and methods to be clear enough throughout this book that my readers can decide whether they share my assumptions.

With this, let me introduce briefly the matters I will be investigating in the following chapters.

I begin by reflecting on the importance, in translating the Italian of the *Decameron*, of respecting Boccaccio's interest in ethical matters. Many readers and translators cling to deeply entrenched ideological views of the *Decameron* that hinder an accurate understanding of its ethical project. In chapter 1, "Wanted: Translators of the *Decameron*'s Moral and Ethical Complexities," I retranslate a key passage from the Introduction to Day 1 of the *Decameron*, where Dioneo and Pampinea offer divergent views of how to set up their communal project. Counter to other translators, I see Boccaccio using Pampinea's speech to encourage the reader to reflect on how to live well. Also, he uses it to foster debate about the roles men and women play in such reflection and to ask us to consider how speech acts can achieve multiple objectives – and not always the ones we first expect.

In chapter 2, "He Said, She Said, We Read: An Ethical Reflection on a Confluence of Voices," I return to a central claim from my *A Rhetoric of the "Decameron"* – that "multiple contributions from multiple subjects with presumably independent agendas, combined with factors that could be purely casual or random, can produce a 'text' that no individual authorial subject could have produced."[42] I bring to light the gender schemas that readers rely on when they respond to passages in the *Decameron* where the desires of men and women are in conflict. Examining how readers of *Decameron* 1.10 (the story of Maestro Alberto, who puts a woman in her place) have responded to the language of this story by undoing its logical contortions and presenting it as clear where in many cases it is not, I reflect on the ethical consequences of such reductive readings, and I exhort us to recognize our responsibility for the stories we may unwittingly construct about men and women.

In chapter 3, "Can the Lower Classes Be Wise? (For the Answer, See Your Translation of the *Decameron*)," I turn from issues of gender to issues of class and consider a question the *Decameron*'s upper-class narrators pose implicitly through their storytelling: Is it possible for people who are not of the upper class to be prudent and wise? Offering a detailed textual analysis of *Decameron* 3.2 (the story of the stablehand who impersonates king Agilulf to lie with queen Teudelinga), I demonstrate how our unconscious schemas about class – especially schemas we have inherited from Aristotle and Thomas Aquinas – influence our readings and translations. I exhort us to recognize our own responsibility for perceptual distortions about class status, intellect, and judgment.

Although many readers have asked how the *Decameron* "teaches," the evidence I present in chapter 4, "Some Restrictions Apply: Testing the Reader in *Decameron* 3.8," suggests that we should ask instead how the *Decameron* "tests" us. Relying on a close reading of the story of Ferondo in Purgatory (3.8), I show how the *Decameron* offers us alternative propositions about our world in ways that bring to light how unwilling we can be, even when faced with overwhelming evidence, to modify our original frameworks for understanding. By testing the reader in this way, the *Decameron* does ethical work that is absolutely vital, because it brings us (assuming we are at all willing) to see how complex human behaviour and motivation is, and it constantly reminds us that our conceptualizations of the world, if they are to be true and accurate, must be as finely tuned as humanly possible.

In chapter 5, "Rushing to Judge? Read the Story of Tofano and Ghita (*Decameron* 7.4)," I reflect on the peremptory judgments encouraged by stories in the *Decameron*, and I propose that the *Decameron* helps us see how readers process textual information in order to arrive at their conclusions. Showing how the story of Tofano tricked by his wife Ghita (*Decameron* 7.4) is constructed – like so many stories in the *Decameron* – so as to encourage a rush to judgment even while revealing the precarious framework on which that hurried judgment is based, I ask what we need to do in order to remain open to the multiple possibilities suggested by the text. I contend that we need to decide *before we begin reading* what our objective in reading is and that we need to be clearer about what our stated objective will or will not achieve for us.

In chapter 6, "New Lessons in Criticism and Blame from the *Decameron*," I continue to discuss our responsibility to think critically about the assumptions we make, the evidence we cite, the judgments we proffer. Drawing attention to the "ethics of reporting," I focus on specific reported events – moments when a wife criticizes her husband for behaviour a reader could objectively find blameworthy. I show that multiple voices come together to tell a story about how "good women" in the *Decameron* should speak when they have been aggrieved. The situation I describe has broader implications: How do we assign praise and blame? Can the less powerful ever speak truth to power? Can they ever really name blameworthy behaviour as such? The *Decameron*, which steadfastly refuses to tell an uncompromised story about what to praise and what to blame, invites us to reflect on how we form our opinions. It describes situations that will elicit a range of responses (often contradictory ones); then, as a great and innovative literary text, it invites us to examine how we might be encouraged by its (often contradictory) rhetorical formulations to accept certain judgments and to discard others.

Most readers recognize that Boccaccio's *Decameron* uses ironic distance to encourage the reader to respond wisely to less than noble behaviour. Chapter 7, "He Ironizes, He Ironizes Not, He Ironizes ...," focuses on how willing we are (or not) to respond with irony when we believe the *Decameron* is offering valuable lessons about how we should conduct ourselves. My textual evidence is drawn from the tenth and final day of the *Decameron*, where the Florentine storytellers proclaim their protagonists to be noble and generous even when they have portrayed actions that strike some readers as ignoble. Focusing on the story of Gentile de' Carisendi (10.4), I reveal how the English translators have encouraged us to renounce irony and to accept an edifying lesson in virtue. Using medieval responses (such as Francesco Mannelli's marginalia in his 1384 copy of the *Decameron*) and contemporary ones (such as those by Stephen Colbert of *The Colbert Report*), I remind readers that we recognize utterances as ironic only if we judge that praise or blame has been wrongly assigned and only if we accept that the topic, the audience, and the situation are appropriate for ironic commentary. Analysing the rhetorical strategies that function so as to elicit widely divergent views – that is, affirmations of virtue on one hand and ironic responses on the other – I ask why Boccaccio would have constructed the storytelling of his *Decameron* to end in this way, and I emphasize how the stories of Day 10 oblige us to reveal what sort of moral and ethical vision we wish to embrace.

In my closing statement, "To Conclude: A Conclusion That Is Not One," I focus on how scholars have read the Author's presentation of himself, and in particular on how, in order to wrap up on a secure note, readers must necessarily elide questions that propel discussion beyond their conclusions. In a final gesture of ethical allegiance to the complexities of Boccaccio's work, I invite us to ask what sorts of questions have been set to one side in order to produce the illusion of stability and finality.

1 Wanted: Translators of the *Decameron*'s Moral and Ethical Complexities

As readers of Boccaccio's *Decameron*, we need to cultivate our ability to recognize – and to articulate in all their complexity – the moral and ethical concerns that emerge in this work. To this one might counter: Haven't we been doing precisely this? Thanks to those scholars who have long recognized Boccaccio as an author with sustained interests in moral and ethical discourse,[1] we have transcended the view of Boccaccio and his *Decameron* that Francesco De Sanctis promulgated in his *Storia della letteratura italiana* (*History of Italian Literature*): a Boccaccio who was superficial, a Boccaccio about whom De Sanctis would write "Le rughe del pensiero non hanno mai traversata quella fronte e nessun'ombra è calata sulla sua coscienza" ("The wrinkles of thought never crossed that brow and no shadow fell on his conscience").[2] We no longer see the *Decameron* as a book without "serietà di mezzi e di scopo" ("seriousness of means or objective") where "i racconti non hanno altro fine che di far passare il tempo piacevolmente, e sono veri mezzani di piacere e d'amore" ("the stories, real brokers of pleasure and love, have no other goal than permitting one to pass the time pleasurably").[3] Increasingly, readers recognize that the *Decameron* complicates a landscape of blacks and whites, that it calls into question the world of established authorities, and that it shows the tensions between conflicting systems of values – that things commonly held to be virtues may not always be so laudable and that things we thought of as reprehensible are not necessarily to be excluded from our moral palette.[4]

Still – and sometimes despite explicit statements to the contrary – many readers cling to deeply entrenched ideological views of the

Decameron that hinder an accurate understanding of its ethical project. Among these deeply entrenched ideological views are the following:

- that the *Decameron* focuses on entertainment
- that the *Decameron* focuses on formal questions (about order and organization) rather than substantive ones
- that the *Decameron* makes no distinctions along the lines of gender and sex
- that speech acts in the *Decameron* are focused so as to achieve a single purpose

We need to question ideas such as these. I say this not because I want to argue that there is no entertainment, no order, no organization, no gender-blind behaviour, and no singly purposed speech act in the *Decameron*, but because I believe that when we focus too much on the entertainment and on what is pleasing from a formal and organizational point of view, when we focus too much on homogenous unity, we may forget that this is also a book that encourages us to reflect on how to live well, a book that fosters debate about the roles men and women play in this process, and a book that asks us to consider how speech acts can achieve multiple objectives – and not always the ones we first expect.

In this chapter, I illustrate how moral and ethical concerns in the *Decameron* can pass unnoticed in our English-language translations. I will focus mainly on the *Decamerons* translated by G.H. McWilliam (Penguin Books), Mark Musa and Peter Bondanella (New American Library [Signet Classics]), and Guido Waldman (Oxford University Press) for the simple reason that these are the main translations currently in print.[5] My intention is not to denigrate these translators; if there is blame, there is no particular reason to lay it solely at their feet. We find similar blind spots and shifts of emphasis when we examine scholarly responses, whether in Italian or English, and this suggests that any issues with the English-language translators are but part and parcel of widespread tendencies in reading the *Decameron*.

Let us examine how translators represent the ten young Florentines who, having fled a plague-stricken city, construct a project of living together and telling stories together. This will allow us to see also how translators understand Boccaccio's goals in writing the *Decameron* and how they perceive meaning to be created in the *Decameron*.

I offer, as a key piece of evidence, the foundational exchange that takes place between Dioneo and Pampinea in the Introduction to Day 1.

Dioneo, who has been singled out for his wit and charm, is the first
man to speak in direct discourse to the women of the group,[6] and when
he does so, he attempts to put his own stamp on the group's activity.
In turn, Pampinea highlights her own role as founder of the group;
she then proposes the system of rotating leadership that will allow the
group to function over the time they spend together. Here is the Italian
text followed by my own translation:

E postisi nella prima giunta a sedere, disse Dioneo, il quale oltre a ogni
altro era piacevole giovane e pieno di motti: "Donne, il vostro senno,
più che il nostro avvedimento ci ha qui guidati; io non so quello che de'
vostri pensieri voi v'intendete di fare: li miei lasciai io dentro dalla porta
della città allora che io con voi poco fa me ne usci' fuori: e per ciò o voi a
sollazzare e a ridere e a cantare con meco insieme vi disponete (tanto, dico,
quanto alla vostra dignità s'appartiene), o voi mi licenziate che io per li
miei pensier mi ritorni e steami nella città tribolata."

A cui Pampinea, non d'altra maniera che se similmente tutti i suoi
avesse da sé cacciati, lieta rispose: "Dioneo, ottimamente parli: festevolmente viver si vuole, né altra cagione dalle tristizie ci ha fatte fuggire. Ma
per ciò che le cose che sono senza modo non possono lungamente durare,
io, che cominciatrice fui de' ragionamenti da' quali questa così bella compagnia è stata fatta, pensando al continuar della nostra letizia, estimo che
di necessità sia convenire esser tra noi alcuno principale, il quale noi e
onoriamo e ubidiamo come maggiore, nel quale ogni pensiero stea di
doverci a lietamente vivere disporre. E acciò che ciascun pruovi il peso
della sollecitudine insieme col piacere della maggioranza e, per conse-
guente da una parte e d'altra tratti, non possa chi nol pruova invidia avere
alcuna, dico che a ciascuno per un giorno s'attribuisca e il peso e l'onore;
e chi il primo di noi esser debba nella elezion di noi tutti sia: di quelli che
seguiranno, come l'ora del vespro s'avicinerà, quegli o quella che a colui
o a colei piacerà che quel giorno avrà avuta la signoria; e questo cotale,
secondo il suo arbitrio, del tempo che la sua signoria dee bastare, del luogo
e del modo nel quale a vivere abbiamo ordini e disponga." (1.Intro.92–5)

Just as soon as they had arrived and sat down, Dioneo, a young man
who surpassed everyone else with his charm and ready wit, said: "Ladies,
your wisdom and good judgment more than our foresight and planning
have guided all of us to this place. I don't know what you intend to do
with your thoughts; as for mine, I left them behind the city gates when I,
along with you, exited from there a short time ago. So either you prepare

yourselves to have fun and laugh and sing with me – as much, I'd say, as your dignity allows – or you give me leave to go back to my thoughts and remain in the troubled city."

To this Pampinea, precisely as if she had put aside all of hers too, responded on a bright and happy note: "Dioneo, you are supremely articulate. People have to live in joy, and that is the very reason that we women have fled a situation that is painful and overwhelming. But given that things that are extreme cannot last very long, I, who initiated the discussions that allowed this fine group to be formed, thinking about our happiness over the longer term, consider that it is really necessary for there to be a leader, whom we would both honour and obey as a superior, and whose every thought would be directed at preparing us to live happily and well. And in order for each one of us to experience the burden of caring along with the pleasure of pre-eminence, and thus to deal with both aspects, and to avoid having anyone feel envious at not having this experience, I say that each of us should get the burden and the honour for a day. As to who should be the first of us to be elected, let that be our joint decision. As for those who will follow, he or she who will have ruled that day can, as the hour of vespers approaches, select that man or that woman who is to his or her liking. And let this someone have, for the duration of time that said authority is in effect, the decision-making power to establish and arrange the place and the manner in which we are to live."

This passage shows us the rhetorical strategies that Dioneo and Pampinea use to pull the entire group in the direction each of them wants. Obviously, Dioneo is pulling towards fun and games. What is not so obvious in translations other than mine is that Pampinea is pulling towards living well – in the sense that philosophers and theologians would use the phrase, to describe a reflective and ordered practice that includes fun but does not have fun as its lone objective.

Boccaccio presents Dioneo so that we ask ourselves a crucial question: Is it right that the young man considered to be of matchless wit and charm should get to decide the direction of the company's activities, and is it right that he should encourage the company to engage in amusement activities? In fact, I would take my claim further. Boccaccio is recalling a crucial passage from the *Nicomachean Ethics*, Book 10, Chapter 6, where Aristotle discusses happiness, which he sees as the end goal of human activity. Boccaccio knew this passage as it appeared in Thomas Aquinas's commentary on the *Nicomachean Ethics* – a text that Boccaccio copied in his own hand.[7] I quote, however, from an English translation that more carefully tracks the medieval Latin version of Aristotle:

1. After the discussion of the various kinds of virtue, friendship, and pleasure, it remains for us to treat happiness in a general way, inasmuch as we consider this to be the end of human activity. But our discussion will be more concise if we reassert what has been stated already.

2. We have said that happiness is definitely not a habit. If it were it might be enjoyed by a person passing his whole life in sleep, living the life of a vegetable, or by someone suffering the greatest misfortune. If then this inconsistency is unacceptable, we must place happiness in the class of activity, as was indicated previously.

3. But some activities are necessary and desirable for the sake of something else while others are desirable in themselves.

4. Now it is clear that we must place happiness among the things desirable in themselves and not among those desirable for the sake of something else. For happiness lacks nothing and is self-sufficient. But those activities are desirable in themselves that are sought for no other reason than the activity itself.

5. Such actions are thought to be in conformity with virtue, for to do virtuous and honorable deeds is a thing desirable in itself. But agreeable amusements also seem to be desirable in themselves; they are not chosen for the sake of other things, since they are rather harmful than helpful, causing men to neglect their bodies and property.

6. Many apparently happy persons have recourse to such pastimes. This is why the ready-witted in conversation are favorites with tyrants; they show themselves agreeable in furnishing the desired amusement for which the tyrants want them. So these pleasures are thought to constitute happiness because people in high places spend their time in them.

7. But perhaps such persons prove nothing; for virtue and intelligence, the principles of good actions, do not depend on the possession of power. Nor should bodily pleasures be thought more desirable, if these persons without a taste for pure and liberal pleasure resort to physical pleasures. Children too think that objects highly prized by them are best. It is reasonable then that just as different things are valuable to a child and to a man, so also are they to good and bad men. Therefore, as we have often mentioned, those actions are worthy and pleasant that appear so to a good man. Now that activity is most desirable to everyone that is in accordance with his proper habit. But the activity most desirable to a good man is in accord with virtue. Consequently, his happiness does not consist in amusement.

8. Surely it would be strange that amusement should be our end – that we should transact business and undergo hardships all through life in order to amuse ourselves. For we choose nearly all things for the sake of something else, except happiness which is an end itself. Now it seems foolish and utterly childish to exert oneself and to labor for the sake of amusement. On the contrary, to play in order to work better is the correct rules according to Anacharsis. This is because amusement is a kind of relaxation that men need, since they are incapable of working continuously. Certainly relaxation is not an end, for it is taken as a means to further activity.

9. Moreover, a life lived in conformity with virtue is thought to be a happy one; it is accompanied by joy but not by the joy of amusement. Now we say that those things that are done in earnest are better than ludicrous things and things connected with amusement, and we say that the activity of the better part or the better man is more serious. But an activity that belongs to a superior faculty is itself superior and more productive of happiness. Surely anyone can enjoy the pleasure of the body, the bestial man no less than the best of men. However, we do not ascribe happiness to the bestial man, if we do not assign him a life properly human. Therefore happiness does not consist in pursuits of this sort but in virtuous activities, as has been stated already.[8]

What would Aristotle say if he were speaking directly to Dioneo? I venture he would say something like this: "Dioneo, to be supremely charming and witty, as the Author of the *Decameron* notes you are, is all very fine and good, but we have to remember that people like you are favoured by tyrants. That's because power-hungry people, who spend their leisure time having fun, like to have amusing people like you around. If we think about the matter of happiness, we will see that the fact that people like to have fun, and laugh, and sing doesn't mean these are worthy activities that bring people happiness. Happiness isn't about having fun. What a strange thought! Having fun isn't the final goal of people's lives – unless of course they're idiots or really childish."

This is also the answer to Dioneo that an educated male reader in the fourteenth century is likely to have offered, particularly if he was minimally versed in moral philosophy and if he did not hesitate to speak his mind.

I dare say I would welcome a Pampinea who would respond to Dioneo as thunderously as I imagine Aristotle would. Aristotle swiftly labels as despotic, stupid, or infantile anyone who thinks that life is about amusement. Fourteenth-century codes of conduct require that an upper-class woman respond more obliquely, and we should also keep in mind that Pampinea may be respectful of Dioneo's emotional ties to one or more women of the group. So even as Boccaccio gives an Aristotelian moral thrust to Pampinea's response, he has her adopt a rhetoric that is more restrained and accommodative than Aristotle's. Consequently, in my translation of Pampinea's response, I have sought to render her ethical vision while at the same time rendering her superbly nuanced rhetorical stance. In the section that follows, I seek to document this by comparing the published English translations of this passage to my own.

How we translate Pampinea's response to Dioneo's *captatio benevolentiae* is already crucial. And here the translators make their first misstep. They take her statement, "Dioneo, ottimamente parli," as a speech act indicating agreement. Musa and Bondanella have "Dioneo, what you say is very true," Waldman has "How right you are, Dioneo," and McWilliam offers a more attenuated "There is much sense in what you say, Dioneo." I translate "Dioneo, ottimamente parli" as "Dioneo, you are supremely articulate" because I want to highlight that Pampinea has said nothing yet about the legitimacy of Dioneo's proposal.[9] If one says "Dioneo, you are right," it is less likely that one could anticipate a move to disagree. If one focuses on the *quality* of Dioneo's speech, however, one still has room to question the validity of his plan.

The translators then risk taking the wrong road entirely as they render into English Pampinea's concession to Dioneo, "festevolmente viver si vuole, né altra cagione dalle tristizie ci ha fatte fuggire." McWilliam has "A merry life should be our aim, since it was for no other reason that we were prompted to run away from the sorrows of the city," Musa and Bondanella write "let us live happily, for after all it was unhappiness that made us flee the city," and for Waldman, "the thing is to have a good time, that's been the whole point of leaving all that misery behind us." With the exception of Musa and Bondanella, the translators emphasize amusement and good times, which I believe is a dreadful flattening of this line, although well in keeping with the notion of the *Decameron* as purely for entertainment.[10] I have chosen to translate "festevolmente viver si vuole" as "people have to live in joy," so as to leave open the possibility that Pampinea could be referring both to "joy" as Dioneo understands it and to "joy" as I believe Pampinea would understand it.

Likewise, I believe that the translators are putting too much emphasis on joviality and merriment when they translate Pampinea's declaration that their ruler's every thought would be "di doverci a lietamente vivere disporre." For Musa and Bondanella, this leader's "only thought shall be to keep us happily entertained." McWilliam has "whose sole concern will be that of devising the means whereby we may pass our time agreeably." According to Waldman, "that person's entire concern will have to be to assure us of happy days." I prefer "whose every thought would be directed at preparing us to live happily and well," because once again, I maintain that Pampinea's "lietamente vivere" is positioned so as to permit Dioneo to project his forms of happiness onto this formulation while at the same time allowing Pampinea to further her own understanding of what it means to find joy in life.

The translators might have had second thoughts about emphasizing good times if they had picked up on Pampinea's comment about gender difference. In response to Dioneo's statement that the women's wisdom has guided *all of them* – that is, men and women – out of the city ("il vostro senno ... ci ha qui *guidati*," emphasis mine), Pampinea makes it clear that the *women* have been made to flee ("ci ha *fatte* fuggire," emphasis mine). For Pampinea, given that the women are behind this project, the women's perspective needs to be acknowledged as the group decides its activities. I stand with Pampinea. Let us not render "ci ha fatte fuggire" as gender neutral.

Why would gender difference be a concern of Pampinea's at this very moment? I believe it is because men in festivity are one thing, but women in festivity are another. The translators may not be conscious of this, but in fact, their translations of the two other uses of "festevole" and "festevolmente" in the *Decameron* establish a clear gender difference. At the end of Day 1, when Dioneo is recognized as "sollazzevole uomo e festevole" (1.Concl.14), the translators call him "entertaining and jovial," "jovial and entertaining," "the life and soul of the party."[11] When Elissa is described just a bit earlier as being "tutta festevole" when she begins her novella, the translators call her "merry" or "joyous."[12] Can a woman who is "festevole" in the *Decameron* be "jovial," "entertaining," and the "life and soul of the party"? I suspect that would not be in keeping with her dignity.[13]

Regarding the main portion of Pampinea's response, I have to admit it strikes me as being just a bit bizarre. Dioneo proposes that everyone laugh and sing or else he will leave, and Pampinea says, in essence, "Very well, people need joy, and I think we need a leader chosen from among us who will have no thought other than to establish and arrange the manner in which we are to live." Pampinea's strategy strikes me as much like the strategy of certain quick-thinking people faced with a question to which they don't have an answer: They offer that the question is very, very interesting indeed, but in fact there is something else they believe is truly worthy of attention. But the translators, by anticipating Pampinea's attention to order and structure, are not allowing us to pick up on this logical disconnect. They take Pampinea's key counter-argument, "ma le cose che sono senza modo non possono lungamente durare," and translate it as "However, nothing will last for very long unless it possesses a definite form" (McWilliam), "But when things lack order they cannot long endure" (Musa/Bondanella), and "but anything that's going to last must have prescribed limits" (Waldman).[14] Order and structure are not Pampinea's primary concern in this moment, however. Here she seeks to label Dioneo's proposal as over-the-top while at the same time not appearing to criticize him. Thus, in keeping with other passages in the *Decameron* where excess is described as "senza modo," I translate "senza modo" as "extreme."[15]

Furthermore, in their translations of Pampinea's final sentence, McWilliam, Musa/Bondanella, and Waldman accentuate the question of governance by rendering "questo cotale" as "the person chosen to govern" (McWilliam), "the ruler" (Musa/Bondanella), and "the sovereign" (Waldman).[16] I maintain that "questo cotale" is best rendered as "this someone." This may seem a tiny point. But by choosing a term that remains indefinite, Pampinea can minimize the question of sovereignty, power, and rule at the same time she seeks to define the ruling responsibilities of the person who has been elected or chosen.

Pampinea expertly navigates the fine line between encouraging Dioneo to believe she agrees with his desire for entertainment and advancing a vision we could properly call philosophical. Crucial to this expert navigation is her oscillation between, on one hand, a masculine generic that could potentially shift into designating a person of the male sex and, on the other, a meticulous accounting of male and female players. By deploying phrases like "he or she" and "his or her," Pampinea insists that the women as much as the men will be involved in ruling and will be involved in the selection process. But in describing the leader, Pampinea also exploits a series of terms that are gendered masculine: "alcuno principale" ("a leader" masculine gender), "il primo" ("the first," masculine gender), and "questo cotale" ("this someone," masculine gender). Pampinea's careful denotation of gender parity is positioned in the middle; her offers of possible male pre-eminence are placed at the open and close. Her wording could encourage Dioneo to believe that he or one of the other men would be the first leader. Since the nuances of the terms gendered masculine are extraordinarily difficult to render in any language without grammatical gender, all of us translating the *Decameron* into English are limited in our ability to reveal this aspect of Pampinea's rhetoric.

Finally, there is the question of how we render the attention to a semantic group that has to do with thought, whether informed or troubled, overwrought or carefree. Dioneo's address to the women immediately calls attention to that key semantic cluster: "Donne, il vostro *senno*, più che il nostro *avvedimento* ci ha qui guidati; io non so quello che de' vostri *pensieri* voi v'intendete di fare: li miei lasciai io dentro dalla porta della città" ("Ladies, your *wisdom and good judgment* more than our *foresight and planning* have guided all of us to this place. I don't know what you intend to do with your *thoughts*; as for mine, I left them behind the city gates" [emphasis mine]). By speaking of the ladies' thoughts, Dioneo remains firmly within the semantic group he had established by talking about their wisdom and foresight. This temporarily masks the fact that he is trying to dictate the group's activities by going off on his own tangent. I would suggest that Dioneo's statement is an example of *clinamen*, a term Harold Bloom has used to describe a swerving away from a precursor (in this case, the women with their ethical bearing).[17] An audience would need a moment to figure out what Dioneo means when he asks what the women intend to do with their "pensieri" because he has left his behind. One could resolve this uncertainty by translating "pensieri" as "troubles" (McWilliam), or "troubled thoughts" (Musa/Bondanella), or "cares" (Waldman).[18] I am inclined to leave the content of these "thoughts" more vague, however.[19]

I might be willing to cede ground to the other translators on this point but for the fact that this is not the last place we have to worry about these thoughts. These thoughts swell in relevance when they get elided by the Author, who describes Pampinea's response to Dioneo: "A cui Pampinea, non d'altra maniera che se similmente tutti i suoi avesse da sé cacciati, lieta rispose" ("To this Pampinea, precisely as if she had put aside all of hers too, responded on a bright and happy note"). The translators have smoothed out the peculiarity of this phrasing by filling in the blank. Musa and Bondanella's translation is representative: "To this Pampinea, who had driven away her sad thoughts in the same way, replied happily."[20] The peculiarity of the original Italian text is crucial, however, because the peculiarity is the *Decameron*'s way of alerting us to gender difference. Consider how odd the sentence would sound if it read, "A cui, Pampinea, non d'altra maniera che se similmente tutti i suoi pensieri avesse da sé cacciati, lieta rispose" ("To this Pampinea, precisely as if she had put aside all of her thoughts too, responded on a bright and happy note"). Pampinea cannot afford to put aside *tutti i suoi pensieri*. She cannot afford to do so because the reader cannot be counted on to understand this to mean only that Pampinea has put aside all of her *troubled* thoughts. Her respectability as the founder of the group, and as a proper woman, is at risk. The Author's elliptical phrasing thus censors the troublesome content and marks two divides clearly: the hierarchical divide (between the reflective life and the fun-loving life) and the gender divide (between women and men).

Most importantly, we must highlight the word "thought" in Dioneo's address to the women if we care to understand why Pampinea maintains that the leader's every thought ("ogni pensiero") will be focused on preparing the group to live happily and well. Taking Dioneo's language about thoughts, worries, thoughtlessness, and carefreeness, Pampinea redirects it, reclaiming *clinamen* as her own rhetorical strategy. She reaffirms that there will be no taking time off from thought – at least not during one's period of authoritative rule.[21]

In summary, what happens in the currently published translations of this passage? The passage's moral vocabulary has been muted or excised; readers will have a more difficult time seeing how dividing tensions are both underscored and downplayed; readers will find it difficult or impossible to register the ambiguities of the original Italian text (especially if these have to do with gender).

What then should we do? As I made clear at the start, our main goal is not to take translators to task. Rather, it should be to understand better why translators might have made the choices they made, to understand how the text of the *Decameron* may seem to encourage the choices the translators have made, and to correct imbalances large and small. Clearly, the process will be dialectical: Our translations of the *Decameron* will not change until our reading of the text changes, and here scholars need to take the lead in weighing the effectiveness of the translated text. At the same time, in English-speaking countries, large numbers of readers will be unlikely to change their views unless our translators take the lead. If the collaboration follows a path such as the one I have suggested here, I believe the result will be a *Decameron* that better represents the moral and ethical reflection envisioned by Boccaccio.

2 He Said, She Said, We Read: An Ethical Reflection on a Confluence of Voices

In *A Rhetoric of the "Decameron,"* I argued that, given the ideological pre-scriptions regarding the kinds of language "proper" to men and women, a certain kind of figurative language about sexuality in the *Decameron* is marked as the prerogative of men.[1] In coming to this conclusion, I took into account factors that other readers had not considered, such as sex, gender, and class. I first examined how the narrators, both in their interactions with one another and in their novellas, use figurative language to speak about the act of sexual intercourse. I showed that the metaphorical language about sex that has become a hallmark of the *Decameron* is overwhelmingly the province of the three men, Dioneo, Filostrato, and Panfilo. (Think of putting the devil into hell, hearing the nightingale sing, and worshipping Saint Peter-Big-in-the-Valley.) I also showed that even where it appears women exercise control over metaphorical language, a story can ensure that figurative language remains the prerogative of men. As the analysis developed, I turned my attention to the very crucial role the *reader* plays in the *Decameron*'s sex wars. I found that the *Decameron* calls upon its readers to be participants – not just spectators – in the sex wars the *Decameron* stages at the site of figurative language. Unwittingly, the readers can end up doing service for a gender ideology they may not have signed up to defend. How can this happen? Characters, narrators, and the implied Author can make statements that readers grasp less precisely than they ought to. Often it seems we are encouraged to interpret these moments in a given way, but when one looks more closely, one often finds that readers have projected their own ideological (and gender) schemas onto these passages. The Author of the *Decameron* could well say to us: If you make my work say something it does not explicitly say, who is at fault?

To consider the role readers play in the reception and shaping of meanings is to acknowledge that the act of reading requires an ethical commitment. I believe that our task as readers is to evaluate the pervasiveness and persuasiveness of each particular rhetorical situation. This means attempting to understand the power – extensive or limited – that a rhetorical moment has had in shaping our own views of the world. However, it also means attempting to understand where, as an audience, we must take responsibility for our own views, because we have been excessively eager to privilege certain moments or too unresponsive to others.

In thinking about these issues here, I focus on *Decameron* 1.10, a story about the elderly Maestro Alberto from Bologna, who sees a beautiful young widow named Malgherida at a social gathering. He immediately falls in love with her and seeks, whenever possible, to pass by her house in order to lay eyes on her again. Soon Malgherida and her companions take notice of his frequent passings. They call him in to the courtyard and make fun of this seventy-year-old in love. He responds with a witty remark about women and vegetables, apparently intended to show this lady up. She and her lady friends back off, and Maestro Alberto leaves with a smile on his face.

Told by Pampinea, the person responsible for the group as well as its eldest member, this novella – like others she tells – appears designed to promote male authority. (Compare Pampinea's 2.3, 3.2, 6.2, 8.7, 9.7, and 10.7.) The authority depends on the efficacy of Maestro Alberto's witty retort, the key section of which is as follows:

> La speranza, la qual mi muove che io vecchio ami voi amata da molti giovani, è questa: io sono stato più volte già là dove io ho vedute merendarsi le donne e mangiare lupini e porri; e come che nel porro niuna cosa sia buona, pur men reo e più piacevole alla bocca è il capo di quello, il qual voi generalmente, da torto appetito tirate, il capo vi tenete in mano e manicate le frondi, le quali non solamente non sono da cosa alcuna ma son di malvagio sapore. E che so io, madonna, se nello elegger degli amanti voi vi faceste il simigliante? E se voi il faceste, io sarei colui che eletto sarei da voi, e gli altri cacciati via. (1.10.15–18)

> The hope that moves me, an old man, to love you, who are loved by many young men, is this: I have often been in places where I have observed ladies eating a light meal of lupini beans and leeks. While no part of the leek is good, its head is less objectionable and more pleasing to the palate.

But drawn by some perverse appetite, you ladies generally hold the head in your hand and eat the leaves, which are not only useless but taste terrible. And how do I know, my lady, if in choosing your lovers you will not make the same mistake? If that's the case, then I would be your chosen lover, and the others would be cast away.

Readers tend to normalize what Maestro Alberto is saying, undoing its logical contortions. For a long time, this was perhaps most notable in my undergraduate students, who, when I asked them to articulate for me the figural and literal correspondents of Maestro Alberto's analogy, would claim that he is saying that he is like the white part of the leek, which is better to eat, and the young lovers are like the green part, which he claims tastes bad.[2]

But it is not just the youngest and greenest readers who are giving Maestro Alberto a helping hand. More experienced readers rush to his defence as well.[3] Take, for example, Michelangelo Picone.[4] At first, he translates the encoded message more or less as I would: Maestro Alberto observes that women prefer not the head of the leek but the leafy green part, and then asks, "Who can say that they might not do the same thing with their lovers, choosing the less good (the elderly) over the others (the young)?" At that point Picone, noting that the Author of the *Decameron* uses the "same metaphor" in the Introduction to Day 4 in order to defend his love of younger women by saying that he has a "white head" but a "green tail," tells us – completely counter to the evidence provided by the text of *Decameron* 1.10 – that "Anche maestro Alberto (pure in questo *figura auctoris*) si vuole paragonare ad un porro, la cui testa è sì bianca, ma la cui 'coda' rimane sempre verde" ("Maestro Alberto – ever a figure of authorship and authority – also wishes to compare himself to a leek, whose head is white but whose 'tail' is still green").[5]

Aldo Busi, a contemporary Italian author responsible for, among other things, an original translation of the *Decameron* titled *Decamerone da un italiano all'altro*, contributes further to Maestro Alberto's success:

Sono stato spesso a fare merenda con le donne e le ho viste mangiare lupini e porri, e anche se il porro non è buono da nessuna parte, la capocchia è ancora il meno peggio da tenere in bocca. Ma siccome voi, sedotte e ingannate dall'appetito, tenete la capocchia in mano e mangiate il gambo, che non solo non vale niente ma ha anche un sapore perfido, cosa ne so io, signora, se lei non fa altrettanto scegliendosi gli amanti? E se lei lo facesse con discernimento, sarei io il prescelto e gli altri cacciati via. Tutto qua.[6]

I have often taken a light meal with women and I have seen them eating lupini beans and leeks. Although there is nothing good at all about the leek, its head is the less disagreeable part. But you women, seduced and deceived by your desire, hold the head in your hand and you eat the stalk, which not only is worthless but tastes really nasty. So who am I to say, madam, that you don't do the same as you choose your lovers? And if you were to do this judiciously, I would be the chosen one and the others would be sent away.

Busi not only smooths out the twists and turns of Maestro Alberto's logic but also renders the sexual innuendoes more prominent, both in the passage I have just cited and in a conclusion that makes it clear that the woman has gotten screwed over: "Così la signora, non sapendo chi aveva voluto prendere in giro, sicura di avere la meglio, fu invece messa sotto, seppure solo in senso figurato. Capito, furbette mie?" (And so this woman, not realizing who she had wanted to mock, convinced that she would succeed, got it stuck to her, even if only in a metaphorical sense. See that, my clever little friends?).[7]

Millicent Marcus also, by means of selective translation, recasts Maestro Alberto's metaphorical language. Early in her essay, as she provides an account of *Decameron* 1.10 for her readers, she states:

When asked how he dares compete with the lady's many young admirers, Alberto answers with a witticism about senior male sexuality. He points out the ladies' erroneous preference for the green leaves of the leek, whose flavour is decidedly inferior to that of the savoury white head. Chastened by Alberto's witty defence of sex with a septuagenarian, Malgherida accedes to his suit.[8]

Already here, Marcus is setting up the metaphor so that we misread its terms, taking senior sex to be equivalent to the "savoury white head." Later, when she cites the Italian text of Maestro Alberto's remark, she leads the reader to believe that the remark ends with, "Che so io, Madonna, se nello eleggere degli amanti, voi vi faceste il simigliante?," which Marcus translates as "How do I know, madam, if you do the same in choosing your lovers?"[9] By stopping one sentence short of the crucial punchline – in which Alberto points out that if Malgherida were to choose lovers as she chooses parts of the leek, she would choose him – Marcus eliminates the potentially problematic terms of the analogy.

At this point, let us consider how complicated a story this is and how complicated our response to it should be. I grant you that we might appropriately feel compassion for Maestro Alberto, and in keeping with that, we might not wish to side too soon with Madonna Malgherida. Does he really deserve harsh treatment? Was what he was doing so bad? She isn't married, so we can't compare Alberto to the king of France, who, four novellas earlier, becomes infatuated with a married woman. Maestro Alberto does not seem to be pestering Malgherida for sex – something that various men of the *Decameron* (particularly men of the clergy) are prone to do when they become infatuated with women in later stories. It seems all he hopes to do is gaze upon her. At the same time, we might not wish to condemn Madonna Malgherida as hastily as others have done. Isn't she getting a bad rap? Aren't Maestro Alberto and his supporters going too far? Was what she was doing so bad?

Let's read the words before us. Maestro Alberto is not saying that he is like the white part of the leek and therefore the ladies ought to choose him over younger (and greener) lovers. Rather, he is saying that he is like the green fronds of the leek; then he argues that since women tend to eat these greens out of some perverse desire, who knows that a woman might not make the same sort of mistake and select him? This man's remark is pushing at the bounds of logic. There is no reason for this woman to be put in her place, except for the fact that some professional readers have told us that Maestro Alberto is waving his vegetables apotropaically. Why do these professional readers see him as successful? For Luigi Russo and Mario Baratto, Maestro Alberto reaffirms a stilnovist cultural ethic.[10] For Michelangelo Picone, Maestro Alberto reaffirms both the stilnovist cultural ethic *and* a comic-realist ethic, since he sees love here as a force that even if exalted always reveals its sensual nature ("seppur mitizzato rivela sempre la sua natura sensuale").[11] Aldo Busi makes it clear that Maestro Alberto has dominated sexually, even if only metaphorically speaking. For Millicent Marcus, who grants that the novella does not clearly speak either the language of love we have inherited from the stilnovists or the language of love from other literary registers – where, as she notes, "sex organs masquerad[e] as vegetables" – Maestro Alberto still masterfully teaches these women, "through figurative language, that sexuality, like textuality, demands a superior understanding – one that goes beyond the letter to the hidden meaning of words, and one that goes beyond the obvious physical appeal of youth to the subtler attractions of older lovers."[12]

Something about this does not entirely convince me. First of all, in thinking about the treatment of Malgherida, I would point out that earlier on Day 1, witty remarks are used to curb hypocrisy (1.4 and 1.6), lust (1.5), avarice (1.7 and 1.8), and apathy (1.9). The crowning witty remark of the day is used to put a woman in her place for refusing a gift of amorous attention. What is going on here? Although Pampinea claims that Madonna Malgherida doesn't know how to speak well, it seems the real issue is that Malgherida has no right to say anything that would undermine a suitor's self-esteem or sense of male superiority.[13] Moreover, it seems that Malgherida has no right to refuse amorous attention. In this regard, Michelangelo Picone staunchly reaffirms Maestro Alberto's "right to love" and praises Madonna Malgherida as a "first exemplary model" of a woman willing to dedicate herself to the practice of love.[14] Here we are dangerously close to the logic of the infernal Francesca da Rimini, who in *Inferno* 5.103 proclaims the supremacy of "Amor, ch' a nullo amato amar perdona" ("Love that permits no one to say no to a lover"),[15] as well as to the logic of male stalkers who believe their right to "love" trumps a woman's right to say no.

We are not limited to the view of male–female power relations that emerges in this story. At least one other text provides us with an alternative perspective. As an astute and discerning reader of Dante, Boccaccio is recalling one of the most striking scenes from the *Vita Nuova*, the scene in chapter 18 where some well-spoken companions of Beatrice make fun of Dante, both for how he experiences his love and for how he expresses it.[16] It is worth our while to look closely at this passage:

Con ciò sia cosa che per la vista mia molte persone avessero compreso lo secreto del mio cuore, certe donne, le quali adunate s'erano dilettandosi l'una ne la compagnia de l'altra, sapeano bene lo mio cuore, però che ciascuna di loro era stata a molte mie sconfitte; e io passando appresso di loro, sì come da la fortuna menato, fui chiamato da una di queste gentili donne. La donna che m'avea chiamato era donna di molto leggiadro parlare; sì che quand'io fui giunto dinanzi da loro, e vidi bene che la mia gentilissima donna non era con esse, rassicurandomi le salutai, e domandai che piacesse loro. Le donne erano molte, tra le quali n'avea certe che si rideano tra loro. Altre v'erano che mi guardavano, aspettando che io dovessi dire. Altre v'erano che parlavano tra loro. De le quali una, volgendo li suoi occhi verso me e chiamandomi per nome, disse queste parole: "A che fine ami tu questa tua donna, poi che tu non puoi sostenere la sua presenza? Dilloci, ché certo lo fine di cotale amore conviene che sia novissimo." E poi che m'ebbe dette queste parole, non solamente ella, ma tutte l'altre cominciaro ad attendere in vista la mia risponsione. Allora dissi queste parole loro: "Madonne, lo fine del mio amore fue già lo saluto di questa donna, forse di cui voi intendete, e in quello dimorava la beatitudine, ché era fine di tutti li miei desiderii. Ma poi che le piacque di negarlo a me, lo mio segnore Amore, la sua merzede, ha posto tutta la mia beatitudine in quello che non mi puote venire meno." Allora queste donne cominciaro a parlare tra loro; e sì come talora vedemo cadere l'acqua mischiata di bella neve, così mi parea udire le loro parole uscire mischiate di sospiri. E poi che alquanto ebbero parlato tra loro, anche mi disse questa donna che m'avea prima parlato, queste parole: "Noi ti preghiamo che tu ne dichi ove sta questa tua beatitudine." Ed io, rispondendo lei, dissi cotanto: "In quelle parole che lodano la donna mia." Allora mi rispuose questa che mi parlava: "Se tu ne dicessi vero, quelle parole che tu n'hai dette in notificando la tua condizione avrestù operate con altro intendimento." Onde io, pensando a queste parole, quasi vergognoso mi partio da loro, e venia dicendo fra me medesimo: "Poi che è tanta beatitudine in quelle parole che lodano la mia donna, perché altro parlare è stato lo mio?" E però propuosi di prendere per matera de lo mio parlare sempre mai quello che fosse loda di questa gentilissima; e pensando molto a ciò, pareami avere impresa troppo alta matera quanto a me, sì che non ardia di cominciare; e così dimorai alquanti dì con desiderio di dire e con paura di cominciare. (*Vita Nuova*, 18.1–9)[17]

Because through my countenance many had known the secret of my heart, certain ladies, who had gathered to enjoy each other's company, knew my heart well, because each had been present at many of my defeats; and passing near them, as if guided by fortune, I was addressed by one of these gentle ladies. The lady who had called me was of a graceful way of speaking so that when I came before them and noted well that my most gentle lady was not with them, with assurance I greeted them and asked their pleasure. The ladies were many, among whom were some who laughed among themselves; there were others who watched me, awaiting what I would say; and there were others who spoke among themselves. One of them, turning her eyes toward me and calling me by name, said these words: "to what end do you love this lady of yours, since you cannot bear her presence? Tell us, for the end of such a love must be extraordinary." And after she had said to me these words, not only she but all the others began visibly to await my response. I then spoke these words to them: "Ladies, the end of my love was indeed the greeting of this lady, of whom you are perhaps thinking, and in that greeting lay my beatitude, for it was the end of all my desires. But because it pleased her to deny it to me, my Lord Love, in his mercy, has placed all my beatitude in that which cannot fail me." Then these ladies began conversing among themselves; and as when at times we see rain falling mixed with beautiful snow, so I seemed to hear their words come forth mixed with sighs. After they had spoken somewhat among themselves, the lady who had first spoken to me added these words: "We pray you, tell us where this your beatitude lies." And I, in reply, said so much: "In those words that praise my lady." And then replied the one who was speaking to me: "If you were speaking the truth to us, those words that you have said to us in making known your condition you would have used with another purpose." Hence I, thinking about these words, in shame departed from those ladies, saying within myself meanwhile: "Since so much beatitude lies in those words that praise my lady, why have other words been mine?" Therefore I resolved to take as the subject of my speaking always and ever what would be in praise of this most gentle one; and thinking much upon it, I seemed to have taken on a subject too lofty for me, so that I dared not begin; and thus I tarried for some days with the desire to speak and the fear of beginning.

In this very remarkable passage from the *Vita Nuova*, the excellence of the women is manifestly evident; theirs is the merit and theirs is the position of dominance. Already Dante's commitment to a poetry of praise is becoming clear. As for the women's power, at least part of it derives from the fact that they stand as a formidably mysterious group whose attitude towards Dante is not immediately clear. They have "gathered to enjoy each other's company." This might be innocuous enough. But then after one of the women addresses Dante, we are told that some of them are laughing among themselves. The tension ratchets up as we learn that some of the women have fixed their gaze upon Dante. Perhaps these are the women who have taken notice of him, and the others are laughing about their own affairs? Or are they laughing *at* him? The group further fragments as we find out that some of the women are talking among themselves. All this laughing, expectant waiting, and talking … Can this be a good sign? Are the women simply waiting for him to respond, or are they already judging him and even making fun of him?

Our attention then turns to the deliberate and paced questioning initiated by a singular woman of very graceful speech ("donna di molto leggiadro parlare"). She emerges from the group to ask a question; all the women look at Dante to await his answer; he answers all of them. The group reconstitutes itself, providing the occasion for the stunning simile that Dante uses to describe their language ("rain falling mixed with beautiful snow"); again the first woman emerges with a question; Dante answers. Now the pace picks up, for on the third round, the woman does not put forth questions or requests. Essentially, she tells Dante he is lying, although she does so with a hypothetical circumlocution: "If you were speaking the truth to us, those words that you have said to us in making known your condition you would have used with another purpose." With her pointed observation about the divergence between Dante's claimed intent and the actual results, she cuts our male protagonist down to size.

Chapter 18 of the *Vita Nuova*, which will be followed by the first of the *canzoni*, permits Dante to establish his absolute, unwavering commitment to a language in service of the *truth*. Consistent with this commitment to truthful reporting, Dante must document in direct discourse the woman's verbal contributions as well as his own, thus providing his audience with evidence they can use to judge these utterances for themselves. Consistent with his commitment to praise, and with a newly evolving experience of sexuality, Dante emphasizes his own defeats and his own smallness, allowing not only Beatrice but all gentle and well-spoken women to emerge victorious over him.

Obviously, the rhetorical purpose of this moment in the *Vita Nuova* is different from that of the novella of Maestro Alberto. Pampinea's stated objective is to show the women the defects in their speech, even though she criticizes a woman's speech without ever allowing us to evaluate that speech for ourselves. Pampinea wishes to reinforce our positive evaluation of Maestro Alberto's rhetoric and his sexuality, even though Maestro Alberto's perplexing mystifications and convoluted logic might not immediately draw our approbation. In the face of thin evidence and perhaps against our better judgment – and far from the only time in the *Decameron* – we are being asked to grant our approbation to the project of the novella.

Clearly, then, in the novella of Maestro Alberto there are lessons about how to speak and how to read. I would add that this novella is also the occasion for another lesson that is perhaps less obvious: a lesson about how discourses are constructed and, in particular, about how – as I said in the conclusion to *A Rhetoric of the "Decameron"* – it is not necessary to have a deliberate volitional program in order to allow for the foreclosure of possibilities available to women. Rather, it is enough, even if passively and unknowingly, to permit multiple voices to intersect, thus producing a particular rhetorical and/or political outcome.[18]

We see an astonishingly clear example of this when we look to Maestro Alberto, whose vegetable metaphors are past their sell-by date. I would like to know how it is that in the metaphor of the leek, with its various parts white and green, Maestro Alberto got to be:

(1) the green part of the leek (which tastes bad but who cares?),
(2) the white part of the leek (which tastes less bad so people think that's good),
(3) the whole leek (with a white part that is intellectually potent and a green part that is sexually potent, as long as we do not see this sexual potency as literal), and
(4) the whole leek (with a white part that is intellectually potent and a green part that is sexually potent, no questions asked).

Very curiously, the story of Maestro Alberto and Madonna Malgherida has been constructed – by Pampinea, by the author of the *Decameron*, and by most critics – so that, significant textual obstacles not withstanding, Maestro Alberto is always guaranteed a favourable outcome in the *Decameron*'s sex wars. That outcome could be summed up as "Heads I win, tails you lose."

Given this not terribly optimistic overview, which shows that various authorial parties seem to have stacked the cards so as to privilege what "he says" over what "she says," I would conclude as follows: If we are committed to understanding how rhetoric is a crucial element in the waging of sex wars – and indeed any and all political and ideological wars – we will have to return to instances like the ones I have identified here. I believe they are many and that the work still to be done is not trivial. We will have to examine in painstaking detail how reading publics respond to the language of a text, presenting it as clear where in many cases it is not. We will have to draw out the ideological implications of plot summaries, translations, critical analyses, and rewritings. We will have to think about the unstated, implicit discourses that are constructed as the result of a confluence of voices, not all of which need be in agreement to ensure the persistence of these discourses in our cultural thinking. Only when we do this sort of work will we have some chance of achieving a more accurate understanding of texts and of the role we play in shaping their meanings.

3 Can the Lower Classes Be Wise? (For the Answer, See Your Translation of the *Decameron*)

In asking "Can the lower classes be wise?", I invite us to consider our assumptions about who is prudent, judicious, and wise. Some readers might be tempted to think that the point of my question is to investigate the historical reality of fourteenth-century people who are not of the upper class. I would urge such readers to find comfort in histories of Florence written by proper historians. My own focus as a literary scholar remains on the filters affecting our perception of fourteenth-century class distinctions. I am interested less in what Giovanni Boccaccio or his ten fictional narrators in the *Decameron* might have thought and said about the lower classes (if indeed we can even say that fictional narrators "think") than I am in what twentieth- and twenty-first-century readers think Giovanni Boccaccio and his fictional narrators are thinking and saying. I am interested in how language, as both constitutive and reflective of culture, is a system for orienting experience; I am interested in how moral vocabularies, which change over time, do not translate as fluidly as we might imagine. Furthermore, as should already be clear from the preceding chapters, I hold that it is imperative for us to reflect critically our own ethical responsibilities in shaping meaning.

* * * * *

Decameron 3.2 is a story that efficiently allows us to see the consequences of the moral vocabulary we construct to speak about wisdom and intellective capacities. In this novella, told by Pampinea, a stablehand falls in love with queen Teudelinga, successfully manages to impersonate the king for a night so as to possess her carnally, and then manages to elude capture, thanks partly to his own quick thinking and partly to the prudence of the king.

As Pampinea introduces the three main characters, she makes it clear that each and every one of them is wise. King Agilulf's wisdom ("senno" [3.2.5]) brings the Longobards to prosperity; his wife Teude-linga is not only extremely beautiful but very wise and honourable ("savia e onesta molto" [3.2.4]); and the stablehand, his social condition notwithstanding, is wise too, although in a way that is necessarily invisible to those around him: "E per ciò che il suo basso stato non gli avea tolto che egli non conoscesse questo suo amore esser fuori d'ogni convenienza, sì come savio a niuna persona il palesava né eziandio a lei con gli occhi ardiva di scoprirlo" ("Given that his lowly condition had not kept him from understanding this love of his was inappropriate, he wisely told no one of his love, and he dared not reveal it to her through his glances" [3.2.6]).

The story allows us to ponder the subtle shadings of wisdom, especially as it fractures along the lines of perceptiveness, insight, cleverness, cunning, ingeniousness, quick thinking, discernment, and good judgment; it also permits us to consider the diverse manner and degree with which these qualities are apportioned among the main characters. To be more precise, the story places in focus the wisdom and intelligence of the two male protagonists, given that relatively little attention is dedicated to exploring what the queen sees and understands. This is, one might venture, an obligatory move, part and parcel of protecting her honour and chastity. Is she completely oblivious to the attention the stablehand pays to her as he tends to her horse? How can she not be aware that the man who enters her bed and has sex with her is not her husband? These are questions that the initial label of "very wise and honourable" can manage to keep at bay.

In a lengthy account of the stablehand's care for the queen, his distress at not being able to enjoy his love, and his plan for impersonating the king so as to be able to enter her room at night and enjoy her carnally, Pampinea tells how the stablehand attends to detail, how he takes in the features he himself must imitate successfully, how he anticipates and wards off things that might lead him to be recognized as an impostor, how he reluctantly leaves the queen after having lain with her because he realizes that remaining there too long could bring misery. All of these things require a certain perspicacity – the ability to see, to find out, to know, to exercise caution, to judge – and in her account, Pampinea relies heavily on verbs that communicate this. Since

Pampinea has already declared the stablehand "wise" for his ability to be aware of social norms and his ability to keep his love a secret, this focus on perspicacity is one way to reinforce the idea that he is "wise." (Granted, we have to be willing to suspend our judgment about how ethical it is to impersonate the king and to lie with the queen. But since Pampinea narrates the story without exposing this ethical quandary and without representing the stablehand's actions as base trickery, it is easy to find ourselves focusing on the stablehand's perceptiveness and his successful planning.)

The explicit mention of wisdom is made again only when the king reappears in the story, deciding wisely ("come savio" [3.2.18]) to remain silent after he discovers that someone other than him has lain with his wife. The king's silence, of course, is a double for the silence the stablehand was "wise" to maintain. Pampinea comments: "Il che molti sciocchi non avrebbon fatto ma avrebbon detto: '"Io non ci fui io: chi fu colui che ci fu? come andò? chi ci venne?'" ("Many idiots wouldn't have done this. Instead, they would have said, 'Me? Wasn't me! But who? Who was it? What went on? Who got in?'" [3.2.18]). The phrasing in Italian is startling. One gets the sense that the person pronouncing these words is so overwhelmed that he is reduced to blurting out a barely coherent response. The monosyllables are many, and many also are the accented syllables "uh!" and "ih!" and "oh!", combined with accents on hard and soft *c*. Why? Because this is completely at odds both with the king's character and with the style in which Pampinea narrates the rest of her novella. The reaction is marked as completely unlettered, unthinking, and therefore indiscreet.

Once Pampinea has secured the label of "wise" to the king and has articulated what unwise behaviour would sound like, she places into relief the king's ability to assess the situation and to identify the impostor; as with her description of the stablehand planning his moves, her account of the king's strategic moves is presented within a framework that encourages us to see him as keenly insightful. He *imagines* the culprit to be resident in the house and, whoever he is, to be still on the grounds; he *judges* that, whoever the culprit might be, his heartbeat would not have returned to normal; then he sets about to verify his hypothesis. All this he does quietly ("chetamente" [3.2.23], "tacitamente" [3.2.24]) and with diminutive and unobtrusive lights ("un picciolissimo lume in una lanternetta" [3.2.24]) made even more diminutive by the expansive space in which he moves ("se n'andò in una lunghissima casa" [3.2.24]). Feeling the breasts of each of his retinue for the telltale heartbeat, the king eventually identifies the guilty individual. The following passage tracks the king's crucial movements and decisions:

> Avendone adunque il re molti cerchi né alcun trovandone il quale giudicasse essere stato desso, pervenne a costui e trovandogli batter forte il cuore seco disse: "Questi è desso." Ma sì come colui che di ciò che fare intendeva niuna cosa voleva che si sentisse, niuna altra cosa gli fece se non che con un paio di forficette, le quali portate avea, gli tondè alquanto dall'una delle parti i capelli, li quali essi a quel tempo portavan lunghissimi, acciò che a quel segnale la mattina seguente il riconoscesse; e questo fatto, si dipartì e tornossi alla camera sua. (3.2.26–7)

> After having checked many of them without finding the one he judged to be him, the king came upon the man in question, found that the man's heart was beating fast, and said to himself: "This is him." But since he did not want anyone to be aware of what he intended to do, he limited himself to taking a small pair of scissors, which he had brought with him, and snipping off part of the man's hair on one side. (In those days, they wore their hair long.) This way, the next morning, he would be able to recognize him from that mark. Having done this, he left and went back to his room.[1]

Here, as previously, the king's diligent search is rendered with gerunds that terminate in a seeming dead end ("Avendone adunque il re molti cerchi né alcun trovandone il quale giudicasse essere stato desso"). Then suddenly the king finds the guilty man, and the pummelling accents on alternating syllables and a repeated pronoun "desso" ("him") now reinforce our awareness that the man has indeed been found: "*seco disse: 'Questi è desso.'*" The moment of triumph is immediately capped by a sentence that begins with an adversative: "But since he did not want anyone to be aware ..." Once again, we see that the game of "wisdom" being played depends on silence and on the careful guarding of information. That comes just before Pampinea tells of the king's understated response to his discovery and his foresight at having brought along a pair of little scissors, a fact she mentions here for the first time in a subordinate clause. This is a nice touch, for it is almost certain to surprise the reader, who is likely to marvel at the ability (or is it fortune?) of a man who just happens to have the right tool at the right time.

Thus far, the male protagonists are represented as evenly matched, interchangeable mentally as well as physically. Readers are invited to delight in this – in the idea that the clear distinction between the ruler and the ruled, between the prince and the pauper (to recall Mark Twain's terms), can be called into question. But then, in Pampinea's narration, the balance shifts slightly towards the king, at least if we accept the hierarchy of character attributes that sees wisdom as superior to cunning.

The crucial shift takes place when the stablehand realizes why the king has cut his hair: "Costui, che tutto ciò sentito avea, sì come colui che malizioso era, chiaramente s'avisò per che così segnato era stato" ("The man in question, who was a cunning fellow, noticed all this and clearly understood why he had been marked in this way" [3.2.28]). The adjective *malizioso* ("cunning," "clever," "shrewd," "crafty") underscores a quality that fourteenth-century readers, if they were following the reasoning of Thomas Aquinas in his *Commentary on Aristotle's Nicomachean Ethics*, would have perceived as less admirable than "prudence" and "practical wisdom" (*prudentia*).[2] Also important is the use of the verb "sentire" to describe how the stablehand "sees" (or as I have translated the verb above, "notices") what is going on. Since "sentire" typically involves a range of sense perception that was long considered to be less privileged than sight – it means "to hear," "to feel," and generally "to sense" – some readers have understood that Pampinea may be setting qualifications on the stablehand's capacity "to see." Thus the 1620 translation attributed to John Florio offers that the stablehand is someone "who partly saw, but felt what was done to him."[3] John Payne has it that "the culprit [...] had felt all this."[4] G.H. McWilliam says he "had witnessed the whole episode," Aldo Busi says he followed the king's every move ("aveva seguito ogni sua mossa"), and Guido Waldman opts for the negative form that seems to dominate in English translations of the stablehand's behaviour ("had missed none of this").[5]

Although with this nuanced move, Pampinea circumscribes and delimits the stablehand's ability even as she describes actions that parallel those of the king, she also tells of a king willing to acknowledge his rival's wisdom. Not his cleverness, his wit, or his shrewdness, but his *wisdom*. It seems, however, that we are reluctant to grant this stablehand more than partial recognition for his merits. To himself, the king says, "Costui, il quale io vo cercando, quantunque di bassa condizion sia, assai ben mostra d'essere d'alto senno" ("The man I am looking for, though he is of low status, clearly shows that he possesses lofty wisdom" [3.2.29]). I translate *senno* as *wisdom*. And that is, I believe, how many other people might translate this word were the stablehand's social station not what it is. Consider, for example, Dante, the sixth among "cotanto senno" ("such great wisdom") in the circle of poets in Canto 4 of the *Inferno*.[6] Would a translator think to place Dante sixth among "such wit"? Unlikely. But in thinking about the stablehand's *senno*, not a single translator calls this "wisdom" or "understanding" or any of the things we might think comparable. Here is how other translators render the sentences that communicate the King's thought:

> Of a surety this fellow, whom I go about to detect, evinces, for all his base condition, a high degree of sense. (Rigg)[7]

> He whom I seek, for all he may be of mean estate, showeth right well he is of no mean wit. (Payne)[8]

> This man, the one I am looking for, may be of low station, but he evidently has his wits about him! (Musa/Bondanella)[9]

> "This fellow I'm looking for may be low-born," he said to himself, "but he clearly has all his wits about him." (McWilliam)[10]

> The man I'm looking for may be the basest varlet, but clearly he's no simpleton. (Waldman)[11]

> The man I am looking for may be a poor wretch but he's got brains for sale. (Busi)[12]

> The man whom I seeke for, though he be but of meane and base condition, yet it plainely appeareth, that he is of no deject or common understanding. (Florio [?])[13]

In sum, previous translators have focused on wits, brains, sense, and occasionally understanding. They are willing to accept that the stablehand is not stupid. But they studiously avoid the king's active tribute to his rival.

Based on the cues Pampinea gave us earlier when she labelled the stablehand as *malizioso* ("shrewd," "cunning," "crafty"), we might think that she too would balk at any characterization of the stablehand as "wise." Not so. In the concluding sentence of her story, Pampinea tells us that the stablehand "*sì come savio*, mai, vivente il re, non la scoperse, né più la sua vita in sì fatto atto commise alla fortuna" ("*wisely* never, during the king's lifetime, let this incident be known nor did he ever risk his life in a similar venture" [3.2.31]). While early-twentieth-century translators see the way in which the adjective "savio" is used to acknowledge the stablehand's wisdom or at least his discretion,[14] the most recent translators of the *Decameron* decline to do so. In defence of Waldman's translation, which reads "And as long as the king lived, the groom had the sense never to explain the utterance – and never again to stake his life in such a venture,"[15] one could argue that the kind of sense involved here is indeed the "good sense" that is prudential wisdom.[16] The same argument cannot be made to justify the translation choices made by McWilliam, Musa and Bondanella, and Busi, all of whom cast the stablehand in a light we ourselves might see as positive but that would have been seen quite differently in the fourteenth century:

[…] and he was far too shrewd ever to throw any light on the subject while the King was still alive, nor did he ever risk his life again in performing any deed of a similar nature. (McWilliam)[17]

And he, clever man that he was, never revealed their meaning as long as the King lived, nor did he ever again entrust his life to the hands of Fortune by performing a similar deed. (Musa/Bondanella)[18]

The groom, being shrewd, never spoke a word about the incident as long as the king lived, nor did he ever dare even once more to risk his life with a similar stunt. (Busi)[19]

Having examined how wisdom, intelligence, and shrewdness are portrayed in the story of the stablehand and king Agilulf, we must return to the words with which Pampinea introduces the story. There it becomes clear that readers, in the grip of erroneous assumptions about the story's meaning, have distorted a deviously difficult passage. Here is the Italian text of Pampinea's words and my own translation of them:

Sono alcuni sì poco discreti nel voler pur mostrare di conoscere e di sentire quello che per loro non fa di sapere, che alcuna volta per questo, riprendendo i disaveduti difetti in altrui, si credono la lor vergogna scemare là dove essi l'acrescono in infinito: e che ciò sia vero nel suo contrario, mostrandovi l'astuzia d'un forse di minor valore tenuto che Masetto, nel senno d'un valoroso re, vaghe donne, intendo che per me vi sia dimostrato. (3.2.3)

Some people are so lacking in discretion that they insist on showing that they know things that it would be better for them not to know. At times, they believe that by criticizing other people's hidden faults, they will minimize their own shame, whereas in fact, they add to it beyond measure. I intend, dear ladies, to show you how this is true by focusing on its opposite. In recounting the cleverness of someone who might be considered of lesser worth than Masetto, I shall show you this contrary example in the wisdom of a worthy king.

One thing is quite clear: Pampinea is being contrary. Nevertheless, while readers have understood correctly that Pampinea will demonstrate her point by contrary means, they have misunderstood the complex grammatical structure of her statement, and therefore they have gotten her point wrong.

My reading of these very challenging lines requires us to reject the readings found in Vittore Branca's edition and in all of the translations that follow his lead. Readers have missed the fact that this story is really about wisdom and discretion, and especially about the king's wisdom and discretion. They have made this error because they have fallen into the trap of seeing the story as about the stablehand's cleverness.

As we review what previous translators have done, let us begin with Pampinea's concluding words, "nel senno d'un valoroso re ... intendo che per me vi sia dimostrato," which I have translated as "I shall show you this [contrary example] in the wisdom of a worthy king."

Earlier translators understood the prepositional phrase "nel senno d'un valoroso re" to mean "according to a worthy king who thought himself wise" or "in the view of a wise and worthy king," and they have therefore focused on the way the king assesses his own worth and social rank in contrast to the (perhaps lesser) worth and social rank of his shrewd antagonist. The 1620 translation attributed to John Florio reads, "For proofe whereof, faire company, in a contrary kinde I will shew you the subtill cunning of one, who (perhaps) may bee reputed of lesse reckning then Massetto; and yet he went beyond a King, that thought himselfe to be a much wiser man."[20] Following this lead perhaps, J.M. Rigg focuses on "the astuteness of one that held, perhaps, an even lower place than would have been Masetto's in the esteem of a doughty king."[21] Likewise, John Payne writes "that this is so I purpose, lovesome ladies, to prove to you by the contrary thereof, showing you the astuteness of one who, in the judgment of a king of worth and valour, was held belike of less account than Masetto himself."[22]

In the second part of the twentieth century, translators take a different tack. The stablehand and the king are now portrayed as pitted one against the other. McWilliam says that "the wisdom of a mighty monarch was matched by the guile of a man whose social standing was possibly inferior to that of Masetto."[23] Musa and Bondanella would have us see "how the cleverness of a man of even lower station than Masetto matched the wisdom of a valiant king."[24] Waldman presents "this story of a fellow (maybe not quite on par with Masetto) who pitted his wits against those of a noble king."[25] A French translation of the *Decameron* emphasizes the "triumph" of shrewdness over wise discretion: "c'est de cela, chères amies, que j'entends vous fair la preuve en vous exposant le cas inverse, c'est-à-dire celui d'un homme sans doute réputé moins intelligent que Masetto qui, grâce à son astuce, triompha de la sage précaution d'un roi valeureux" ("this is what, dear ladies, I intend to prove to you by setting out the contrary instance, that is, the case of a man, undoubtedly considered less intelligent than Masetto, who, thanks to his shrewdness, triumphed over the wise discretion of a worthy king" [my translation]).[26] The origin of these more recent translations appears to be Vittore Branca, since he provides the following paraphrase of these lines in his critical edition of the *Decameron*: "Cioè; intendo che da me vi sia dimostrato che questo è vero mostrandovi in senso opposto l'astuzia usata, per vincere l'assennato accorgimento di un valente re, da un uomo ritenuto anche inferiore a Masetto" ("That is: I intend to demonstrate to you that this is true by showing via contrary means the cunning that a man considered inferior to Masetto used in order to triumph over a valiant king's wisdom and discernment ").[27]

According to my own reading of the passage, Pampinea opposes the foolhardiness of people who think that advertising other people's faults will ease their own shame; she then offers as an antidote her own praise of *the king's wisdom and discernment*. "Nel senno d'un valoroso re" ("in the wisdom of a worthy king") must be taken as an appositional phrase, parallel to the earlier "nel suo contrario" ("by contrary means," or more literally "in its contrary"). In contrast to previous readers, editors, and translators who establish the principal opposition as between the foolhardiness of blabbermouths and the shrewdness of a lowly person who pits himself against a worthy king, I hold that the principal opposition is between the stupidity of blabbermouths and the wisdom of the king, an opposition that emerges in the course of a story about a cunning person of relatively low rank.[28]

At least two structural aspects of the *Decameron* may encourage readers to misconstrue the evidence. It is true that, in accord with the prescribed topic for Day 3, Pampinea must show how, through ingenuity, someone achieves a thing desired or a thing that had been lost. Unmindful of the way that some Decameronian narrators (and especially Pampinea) can manipulate the prescribed topic to their own ends, readers may assume that this desiring subject can only be the stablehand who longs to possess the queen carnally. Equally compelling as a desiring subject, however, would be the king, who seeks to regain his lost honour. The Author of the *Decameron* further encourages us to focus on the stablehand when he provides a rubric that – by its grammar and rhetoric – preserves the stablehand's primacy: "Un palafreniere giace con la moglie d'Agilulf re, di che Agilulf tacitamente s'accorge; truovalo e tondalo; il tonduto tutti gli altri tonde, e così campa della mala ventura" ("A stablehand lies with the wife of king Agilulf, who secretly becomes aware of this; the king finds him and clips his hair; the clipped man clips everyone else and in this way saves his hide" [3.2.1]).[29] This rubric never mentions the issues of intelligence, wisdom, and honour that are so central to Pampinea's narration.

Our own unconscious schemas are at work in the translations and readings of *Decameron* 3.2. Virginia Valian has studied how unconscious gender schemas affect our expectations and evaluations of men and women, and I would contend that unconscious schemas shape our expectations and evaluations of people who hail from different classes as well.[30] One of the most eloquent participants in the debate about gender inequities and what can be done to counter them, Valian sets out a persuasive argument for improving our social perceptions:

> Only by recognizing how our perceptions are skewed by nonconscious beliefs can we learn to see others, and ourselves, accurately. Fairness requires a more sophisticated understanding of social perception than most of us acquire in the ordinary course of life. To be really fair, we need to know what perceptual distortions are likely and what steps we can take to perceive others more accurately.[31]

The case I have brought before us reveals perceptual distortions about class status, intellect, and judgment that need to be rectified if we are to read texts and situations more accurately. Readers have erred at both extremes. First of all, by emphasizing the prudence of the king and the shrewdness of the groom, readers have made a class distinction that is more marked than the one represented in the text. Readers working within this schema are assuming that social standing is essential to how intelligence manifests itself. Second, readers have produced a system of values inconsistent with the text's when, by putting the stablehand on par with the king or even *above* the king, they level all class distinctions. Readers working within this schema are assuming that social standing is utterly irrelevant to how intelligence manifests itself.

The first unconscious schema, which derives from Aristotelian and Thomistic conceptions of prudential wisdom, has long-standing currency in the Western philosophical tradition, so it is not surprising that we might reproduce it unconsciously. Consider, for example, Thomas Aquinas's *Summa Theologica*, II–II, Q. 47, A. 12, where he asks "whether prudence is in subjects, or only in their rulers?"[32] After setting out a series of possible Objections, which he has abstracted from Aristotle's *Politics* and *Ethics* – statements that would seem to suggest that prudence is found only in rulers and never in subjects and slaves – he clarifies how we are to understand Aristotle's views on prudence:

> I answer that, Prudence is in the reason. Now ruling and governing belong properly to the reason; and therefore it is proper to a man to reason and be prudent in so far as he has a share in ruling and governing. But it is evident that the subject as subject, and the slave as slave, are not competent to rule and govern, but rather to be ruled and governed. Therefore prudence is not the virtue of a slave as slave, nor of a subject as subject.

Still, Aquinas had to clarify, both here, in the passage from the *Summa Theologica*, and elsewhere, in his *Commentary on the "Nicomachean Ethics."* He distinguished between "prudence" (defined as "the right plan of things to be done in the light of what is good or bad for one man, that is, oneself") and "civic prudence" (which deals with "things good or bad for the whole civic multitude").[33] Did Aquinas believe it was possible for the lower classes to be prudent and wise? He certainly did. But he understood the area in which they could exercise this wisdom to be delimited. He would have underwritten Aristotle's assertion in the *Nicomachean Ethics* that "political wisdom and practical wisdom are the same state of mind, but their essence is not the same" (Book 6, Chapter 8).[34]

The second unconscious schema arises from a conception of "intelligence" that moves it far from prudential wisdom. One salient example of this conception of intelligence can be found in Lino Pertile's essay on "Dante, Boccaccio, e l'intelligenza."[35] Against the background of Dante's harsh moral criticism of the "intelligence" of Guido da Montefeltro in *Inferno* 26, Pertile draws our attention to "l'esaltazione dell'intelligenza pura, libera da remore morali, emergente da tante novelle del *Decameron*" ("the exaltation of a pure intelligence, free of moral hesitations, that emerges in so many of the *Decameron*'s novellas").[36] In this scheme of things, the *Decameron*'s answer to Guido da Montefeltro turns out to be ser Cepparello, and "è proprio la spregiudicata intelligenza di Cepparello che ne redime e riscatta l'amoralità, rendendola degna di diventare materia di novella agli occhi nostri, del Boccaccio e della sua brigata" ("it is precisely ser Cepparello's unscrupulous intelligence that redeems and ransoms his amorality, making it worthy matter for storytelling for us, for Boccaccio, and for the narrators of the *Decameron*").[37]

Pertile works hard to obtain our assent. The judicious reader will be mindful of the kinds of strategies he adopts, however. Pertile writes about intelligence without differentiating among the word's possible connotations, whether positive (prudence, wisdom) or negative (astuteness, craftiness, guile). He draws the vast majority of his examples of intelligence from Days 3 and 7, where instances of cunning and trickery abound; and he refrains from pointing this out as a feature of the *Decameron*'s organization. Since Pertile defines intelligence as either a character's ability to get out of a tough situation thanks to a use of intelligence that completely disregards moral rules or religious faith[38] (a category to which he assigns *Decameron* 1.1, 1.3, 6.10, 7.2, 7.3, 7.4, 7.6, and 7.8) or a character's ability to fulfil uncontainable natural instincts without openly transgressing social rules[39] (a category in which he would place *Decameron* 3.3, 3.4, 3.7, 3.8, 7.5, and 7.9), he excises stories in which intelligence is used to deflect illicit and/or unwanted sexual contact, to speak out against vice, to promote virtue (especially generosity), or to re-establish the moral, social, and political order.[40] At key moments, Pertile staves off reservations about his claims by telling us we should not doubt. But when we read that "there is no doubt" that readers, whether in the fourteenth century or now, willingly recognize themselves in the ruthless characters of the *Decameron*,[41] I believe we should not grant our assent so willingly. Pertile tells us that we admire the intelligence of characters whose moral records are questionable.[42] I would say that if we admire such characters, we should consider what strategies have been used to undermine our better judgment. Pertile tells us that our sympathies lie with weaker human beings who use their intelligence in order to express their individuality, to give free reign to their appetites, and to triumph over the more powerful.

I would ask what is to be gained by advancing a vision of freedom, individualism, and democracy that is based on exaltation of less than admirable human traits.

Pertile grants *Decameron* 3.2 singular status when he assigns this story to both of his categories: On one hand, the stablehand manages to fulfil his sexual desire without transgressing the rules; on the other, the stablehand finds an ingenious way to get himself out of a tough situation. The categorization proves unstable, however. That instability should clue us in that the story is even more complex than Pertile had judged it to be. The extra level of complexity is added by king Agilulf, who decides not to use extraordinary means in order to discover the man who had sex with queen Teudelinga. Pertile concludes that this safeguarding of personal honour depends on a distinction, unquestioned throughout the *Decameron*, between a public and a private morality. He is indeed correct that this distinction between public and private is one of the most significant features of the *Decameron*. More is in play here, however. Although in no other case does he identify more than a single character as intelligent, Pertile now shifts suddenly from a discussion of the stablehand and his intelligence, labelled "ingegno," to a discussion of king Agilulf and his intelligence, labelled "intelligenza."[43] Pertile speaks of the "poor but clever stablehand" ("povero ma ingegnoso palafreniere") whose clever intelligence ("ingegno") teaches him how to lie with the queen without being recognized; as for Agilulf, his "intelligence" ("intelligenza") persuades him not to pursue torture and interrogation as means of discovering the traitor. This subtle shift tells us that Pertile does not view the king and the stablehand to be intelligent in the same way.

If the focus of Pertile's essay is *intelligenza*, as his title "Dante, Boccaccio, e l'intelligenza" announces, what is the place of *ingegno*? *Ingegno* would appear to be classified as secondary. In keeping with this, Pertile speaks about *intelligenza* when he offers his more generalizing statements about the *Decameron*.[44] It is not immediately obvious, of course, that "intelligenza" is the overarching term we should use. For corroborating evidence of this, we can look to Valerio Ferme's "*Ingegno* and Morality in the New Social Order: The Role of the *Beffa* in Boccaccio's *Decameron*," where *ingegno* is put forth as the *Decameron*'s operative principle.[45] Not surprisingly, readers are not one hundred per cent in agreement about which form of intelligence the *Decameron* celebrates.

Moreover, in examining the specific instances in which Pertile sees *intelligenza* and *ingegno*, we find that he uses the term *intelligenza* to describe a faculty possessed by male characters who display outstanding rhetorical ability. Pertile establishes such a link between intelligence and rhetorical ability very early in his essay when he names as his first examples ser Cepparello, who possesses a "spregiudicata intelligenza" ("unscrupulous intelligence" [64]), and Frate Cipolla of 6.10, who is characterized by "lo scatto dell'intelligenza e l'abilità retorica che l'accompagna" ("the expression of intelligence and the rhetorical ability that accompanies it").[46] *Ingegno*, on the other hand, appears relegated to an earlier stage of planning out a ruse. This may explain why Pertile uses *ingegno* when he speaks of Melchisedech the Jew (1.3), who needs to "sharpen his wits" ("aguzzare l'ingegno") when he is confronted with the trap the Sultan sets for him but who shows an "intelligente indifferenza in materia di fede" ("intelligent indifference with regard to faith") when he narrates his parable of the three rings.[47] The gendered articulation between *ingegno* and *intelligenza* starts to peek through as Pertile speaks about Madonna Ermellina and Tedaldo degli Elisei in 3.7. When he seems still to be speaking about Madonna Ermellina, he comments that "*l'ingegno* interviene utilmente nella vita umana quando asseconda la natura" ("*ingegno* appears as a useful force in human life when it goes along with nature"); and when he speaks about Tedaldo, Pertile notes that he operates with "*intelligenza*" (emphasis mine).[48] A pattern materializes: Pertile uses the term *intelligenza* to talk about men – and especially men with rhetorical ability – but he uses the term *ingegno* to talk about women and the lower classes.

Many of us would claim that intelligence is a democratic arm that could help level the playing field, and many of us would claim that gender and social class are ultimately irrelevant to measures of intelligence. Based on what he says in his essay about the *Decameron*'s contagious ideological beliefs and our own sympathy for them, Pertile could be counted on to assert that these things are true for the fictional world of the *Decameron*. But his rhetoric is telling a different story, a story at odds with his ideological claim. His rhetoric is telling us that, at least in the *Decameron*, social class and gender remain constitutive of intelligence. Isn't this a striking example of how powerful unconscious schemas about class are? Even as Pertile makes arguments designed to counter the Aristotelian–Thomistic view of human decision making and action, he reproduces the social distinctions that are part and parcel of that Aristotelian–Thomistic view. If we want to be really fair, however, we need to ask ourselves if this characterization of intelligence along gender and class lines is valid, where it comes from, and how it is that such subtle biases can coexist even with overt promises to extinguish these very biases.

So can the lower classes be wise? The answer, based on the evidence I have examined here, suggests that indeed they can – but their success in this arena depends not only on them. It depends also on our own willingness to shed the perceptual distortions that continue to deny them wisdom.

4 Some Restrictions Apply: Testing the Reader in *Decameron* 3.8

Thus far, I have encouraged us to restore to the *Decameron* the fine ethical texturing that might get lost in reading and translation, and I have asked us to acknowledge our ethical obligation to examine the role we play, even unwittingly, in propagating discourses about gender, sexuality, and class. In this chapter, I invite us to reflect on the language we use to describe and assess human conduct. My focus will be *Decameron* 3.8, narrated by Lauretta. This story tells of Ferondo, a stupid and jealous man, who finds himself dispatched to a make-believe Purgatory by a Benedictine abbot who has designs on Ferondo's spouse. While Ferondo is in Purgatory being cleansed of his jealousy – though apparently not of his stupidity – the abbot has a fine time with the wife. An ensuing pregnancy requires that Ferondo be returned to his earthly state, where he praises God for reforming him and giving him a son, whom he names Benedetto Ferondi.

What does this novella do? Encourage us to admire the cleverness of someone like the abbot and entertain us with the stupidity and jealousy of someone like Ferondo? Show us Boccaccio's techniques for writing comedy? Alert us about the claims of religious leaders to speak with the voice of God? Bring us to reflect on the historical context the novella evokes as it imagines the afterlife or as it highlights mathematical calculations? These are the lessons that readers have emphasized thus far.[1] But while these lessons are nestled within the novella, another important area of reflection remains unnoticed.

As I see it, the novella highlights how difficult it is to disentangle truth from non-truth as we read representations of human conduct.[2] Putting us to the test, it brings us to ask: How accurate are our evaluations and our judgments? How do we determine what the generalizable rules are, what the exceptions are, and which exceptions will or won't nullify the rules? How do we deduce a person's motivation for behaving in a particular way? How do we process and characterize evidence? All of these questions, I would have us note, regard *our own abilities of discernment*, not the qualities or abilities of the characters in the story or the connections between the text and extratextual historical developments. Once we shift our focus to ourselves as readers, once we see the story as the source of questions about how truthfully and accurately we evaluate evidence, we may have a chance to learn how to be wiser judges of people, events, and evidence.

A Theory of the Way Things Are (Some Restrictions Apply)

Decameron 3.8 repeatedly calls into question any totalizing evaluations. Time and time again, we get told, in essence: "Here is an assertion for you." That assertion could be a description, an explanation, a promise of future action. Then we find out that "by the way, there's another (exceptional) factor you might need to take into account." We could call that the fine print. What is most intriguing about *Decameron* 3.8 is that it shows us how advertisements for wonderful things (in this case sanctity, virtue, morality, and character improvement) work when they contain the fine-print disclaimer that "some restrictions apply."

When we first see this fine print, it doesn't look all that subtle. The narrator tells us, in introducing her first character, an abbot, that he is "santissimo fuori che nell'opera delle femine" ("most saintly except in the matter of women" [3.8.4]). Having been introduced to the world of holiness in the first novella of the *Decameron*, we are unlikely to find this to be news. The narrator then adds: "sapeva sì cautamente fare, che quasi niuno, non che il sapesse, ma né suspicava; per che santissimo e giusto era tenuto in ogni cosa" ("he knew how to work things so carefully that almost no one really ever suspected, let alone knew, and as a result he was held to be most saintly and ethical in all things" [3.8.4]). Almost no one ("quasi niuno") really ever suspected, let alone knew. How many people are the exception to the rule here? Looking at several translations of this passage, we find that the potential exception must be causing cognitive dissonance for some translators, so it gets excised. Aldo Busi renders this passage into modern Italian as "non solo nessuno ne sapeva niente ma neppure avrebbe mai lontanamente sospettato" ("not only did no one know anything, but they would not even have ever faintly suspected"). In his use of negatives and dense alliterations,

Busi brilliantly grasps the opacity of this man's workings, but he leaves out that crucial "almost."[3] That "almost" is also elided by Mark Musa and Peter Bondanella, who translate "no one knew about it or even suspected him of it."[4] More subtle is Guido Waldman: "practically no one ever found out or even suspected him."[5] Using "practically" as a springboard, I tried out a couple of other translations. How about "virtually no one" knew? Basically no one? Approximately no one? (Evidently, it doesn't take much to expose the peculiarity in sentences that teeter between the absolute and the fuzzy.)[6]

Before we see evidence of the weakness for women that mars the abbot's saintliness, however, we get to see the abbot with a man. Even there, weakness is evident. When Ferondo, "uomo materiale e grosso senza modo" ("a man who was exceedingly dense and boorish" [3.8.5]), decides to cultivate the abbot, we discover some fine print in a parenthetical observation: "né per altro la sua dimestichezza piaceva all'abate, se non per alcune recreazioni le quali talvolta pigliava delle sue simplicità" ("the abbot didn't like his company except for the entertainment that on occasion he derived from Ferondo's dim-wittedness" [3.8.5]). Remember that the abbot was said to be saintly in all matters except those regarding women. What sort of saint finds someone else's lack of sense entertaining, even if just occasionally? The narrator skims over this disruption, however, to make our perceptions fall into place consistent with what the audience is likely to expect of the abbot: "in questa dimestichezza s'accorse l'abate Ferondo avere una bellissima donna per moglie, della quale esso sì ferventemente s'innamorò, che a altro non pensava né dì né notte" ("in the course of keeping company with him the abbot noticed that Ferondo was married to a very beautiful woman, with whom he so ardently fell in love that he thought of nothing else day or night" [3.8.5]).

In this novella, where chiastic oppositions will abound, if we have a man whose saintliness is untroubled by a few grazing deficiencies, we must have a fool who remains foolish despite evidence that could speak to the contrary. Indeed. Ferondo is foolish, but the abbot hears tell that "in amare questa sua moglie e guardarla bene era savissimo" ("in loving this wife of his and in keeping a close eye on her he was very wise" [3.8.6]). At first the reader might be inclined to reverse her opinion of Ferondo. After all, wisely loving one's wife seems quite uncontroversial, so perhaps the earlier move to tag Ferondo as a complete fool was excessive. Ferondo's wisdom gets relegated to the fine print, however, when we learn that he wisely keeps a close watch on his wife. The word "jealous" is not used here, and we have relatively little experience with jealous spouses at this point in the *Decameron*, restricted mainly to Catella in 3.6. So we are less likely to associate Ferondo's watchfulness with stupidity than if we had already read the whole of Day 7 with its accumulation of stupid, jealous husbands. Still, the information about Ferondo's watchfulness allows our moment of generosity to dissolve, as we might ask, "How wise can a husband be if he is keeping an exceedingly close watch on his wife?" Once the perception of Ferondo as stupid has crystallized, assertions to the contrary will tend to get set aside.

The central portion of the novella offers us two segments in which we are invited to explore the relationship between our assumptions about "what is" and the exceptions we make to these without ever revising our assertions of "what is." First, the narrator provides us with the conversation between the abbot and Ferondo's wife, a conversation divided into two parts (one concerning the solution to Ferondo's jealousy and one concerning the nature of the reward the abbot should receive for curing Ferondo of his jealousy). The narrator then turns to Ferondo, whose character is again explored on two fronts: in the statements he makes about Purgatory and in the statements he makes about his wife while he is in Purgatory.

Throughout, we find that characters accept and affirm ideas and situations that are quite atypical; they do so even when evidence is severely lacking or there exists arresting evidence to the contrary. Ferondo's wife accepts that Ferondo could be shipped off to Purgatory to be cured of his jealousy, despite the fact that nothing in her lived experience would suggest this could be possible. Although she balks initially at the notion of a holy man asking a woman for sexual favours – after all, the commonly accepted view of well-behaved clergy is that they hold to their vows of chastity – she is eventually willing not only to have sex with him but even to reaffirm his sanctity when she speaks about him to her companions. Ferondo accepts that he is dead and that he is in Purgatory despite the fact that his ideas about being dead and being in Purgatory could be contradicted by his lived experiences. Perhaps most curiously, Ferondo provides vigorous declarations that he could have changed and would change – declarations that in themselves also provide vigorous evidence to the contrary.

Let us look at the last example I have cited, especially since it involves passages that readers of this novella have tended to discount. Readers have been drawn mainly towards the comical exchange that Ferondo and his Purgatorial guardian (a Bolognese monk) have about how far Purgatory is from our earth. In fact, readers delight in quoting this dialogue, which highlights Ferondo's silliness and his less than masterful control of language. I would like instead to look at Ferondo's assertions of goodwill towards his wife, which, as we shall see, include some extraordinary exclusions.

Ferondo first speaks about his wife after his Purgatorial guardian communicates that the wife has sent food and has arranged for masses to be said in his name. The narrator seems poised to make us sympathize with Ferondo, who has just been beaten soundly and who has also lost a wife for whom he appears to feel genuine affection. But the narrator thwarts our compassion and opts for irony instead: She shows Ferondo turning on a dime, first blessing his wife and remembering his moments of physical intimacy with her, then focusing on his own individual appetite and repealing his blessing:

> "Domine, dalle il buono anno! Io le voleva ben gran bene anzi che io morissi, tanto che io me la teneva tutta notte in braccio e non faceva altro che basciarla e anche faceva altro quando voglia me ne veniva" e poi, gran voglia avendone, cominciò a mangiare e a bere, e non parendogli il vino troppo buono, disse: "Domine falla trista! Ché ella non diede al prete del vino della botte di lungo il muro." (3.8.45)

> "God bless her always! I really loved her a real lot before I died, so much that I used to hold her all night in my arms and I did nothing but kiss her and I also did other stuff when I got hungry for it," and then, feeling really hungry, he started to eat and drink, and since the wine didn't seem very good to him, he said, "Goddamn her! She didn't give the priest the wine from the barrel along the wall."

This is a brilliantly hilarious passage. Ferondo's speech (which gets a stylistic upgrade in translations other than my own) produces clumsy repetitions like "le voleva ben gran bene" ("I really loved her a real lot") and "e non faceva altro che basciarla e anche faceva altro" ("I did nothing but kiss her and I did other things"). Lauretta adds to the comedy by anticipating Ferondo's reversal of "God bless her" into "Goddamn her" with her own representation of Ferondo's criss-crossing desire: "'anche faceva altro *quando voglia me ne veniva*' e poi, *gran voglia avendone*, cominciò a mangiare e a bere" ("'and I also did other stuff *when I got hungry for it' and then, feeling really hungry,* he started to eat and drink" [emphasis mine]).[7]

Nor does this prove to be the last case where Ferondo finds cause for exception. After a second beating, Ferondo again affirms his wife's excellent qualities as "the best wife in the area" and "the sweetest" (3.8.50–51). He even admits his own jealousy and indicates that he would have been open to change had he known: "ma io non sapeva che Domenedio avesse per male che l'uomo fosse geloso, ché io non sarei stato" ("but I didn't know that God considered a man's jealousy to be a bad thing, otherwise I wouldn't have been jealous" [3.8.51]). Hearing this, we might be inclined to sympathize with Ferondo. Is it really necessary to beat him to get him to reform? Wouldn't a simple reprimand, or an invocation of God's authority in this matter, have sufficed? The narrator then undercuts our sympathy in short order. At the very moment when Ferondo promises change, should he ever manage to return to earth, he recalls wifely transgressions that would obviate change:

"Oh!" disse Ferondo "se io vi torno mai, io sarò il migliore marito del mondo; mai non la batterò, mai non le dirò villania, se non del vino che ella ci ha mandato stamane; e anche non ci ha mandato candela niuna, e èmmi convenuto mangiare al buio."

Disse il monaco: "Sì fece bene, ma elle arsero alle messe."

"Oh!" disse Ferondo "tu dirai vero: e per certo, se io vi torno, io le lascerò fare ciò che ella vorrà. Ma dimmi, chi se' tu che questo mi fai?" (3.8.55–7)

"Oh!" said Ferondo, "if I ever go back, I'll be the best husband in the world. I won't ever beat her, I won't ever cuss at her, except about the wine that she sent this morning; and she didn't send any candles, either, and I ended up having to eat in the dark."

"Actually, she did," said the monk, "but they got used during mass."

"Oh!" said Ferondo, "you must be right. And certainly, if I go back, I'll let her do whatever she wants. But tell me, who are you that you treat me like this?"

Just beneath the surface of Ferondo's lovey-doveyness, there are fractures in his promised conversion. Note the quick U-turns from praise to blame, from tolerance to intolerance, and from generosity to self-absorption. Almost nobody seems to have noticed that Ferondo seems to suffer from entrenched frustration, which apparently manifests itself in physical and verbal abuse that can be triggered by quotidian infractions on the wife's part, such as her lack of foresight about the candles. Why would Ferondo promise not to beat his wife and not to swear at her in the future if he weren't already abusing her? Moreover, as is evident from the final question, "So who are you?", it doesn't take much to divert Ferondo's attention from his promises of reform to whatever happens to be of greater immediate concern (in this case, his own existence and well-being).[8]

The final sentences of the novella are the crowning achievement of a narration that has shown us how a narrator can proceed with moral assertions unperturbed by the very provisions that ought to render them null and void:

> La tornata di Ferondo e le sue parole, credendo quasi ogn'uom che risuscitato fosse, acrebbero senza fine la fama della santità dell'abate; e Ferondo, che per la sua gelosia molte battiture ricevute avea, sì come di quella guerito, secondo la promessa dell'abate fatta alla donna, più geloso non fu per innanzi: di che la donna contenta, onestamente, come soleva, con lui si visse, sì veramente che, quando acconciamente poteva, volentieri col santo abate si ritrovava, il quale bene e diligentemente ne' suoi maggior bisogni servita l'avea. (3.8.76)

The reappearance of Ferondo and his portrayal of events added infinitely to the abbot's reputation for saintliness, as almost everyone believed that he had been resurrected. Ferondo, who had received many beatings for being jealous, was cured of that, in keeping with the promise that the abbot had made to his wife, and he was jealous no longer. His wife, pleased about this, lived an honorable life with him as before, provided that when she could coordinate it, she willingly met with the holy abbot, who had served her diligently and well in her greatest needs.

Since the preoccupation with fine print restrictions has been constant throughout the novella, we might ask why it should have to be repeated here. I think it is because the conclusion doesn't simply restate the problem; it offers a new twist on it.

Throughout, perceptions of the abbot have remained unblemished despite his irregular adherence to sanctity. Now his sanctity is taken to the next level by means of a logical fallacy known as "post hoc ergo propter hoc," or coincidental correlation. People conclude that because the abbot and others are said to have prayed for Ferondo and then Ferondo has returned to life, then the abbot must have special saintly powers. No matter that the abbot didn't pray, that he wasn't the only one who was said to have prayed (even though virtually no one may have prayed), and that the ultimate source of the "resurrection" would be God. Likewise, because the abbot told Ferondo's wife that Ferondo would be cured of his jealousy and then Ferondo stopped being jealous, people conclude that Ferondo's transformation is proof that the abbot's promises are reliable.

And as for virtuous behaviour where "some restrictions apply," this is now definitively transferred to Ferondo's wife in the final line, as she lives an honourable life that still allows for encounters with the holy abbot.

Ferondo's Wife: A Test for the Reader

In her final words in the novella, Lauretta states that the wife continued to meet with the holy abbot, "who had served her diligently and well in her greatest needs" ("il quale bene e diligentemente ne' suoi maggior bisogni servita l'avea" [3.8.76]). This line tips us off that Ferondo's wife stands as a supreme test for the *Decameron*'s reader. Why? Because everything turns on how we understand what the woman's "greatest needs" are. We might think that the answer is quite clear. In fact, the more anxious we are to praise the woman or condemn her, the more likely we are to want her needs and her motivations to be clear-cut. Here the *Decameron* resists us, and in doing so, it tries to show us that it functions less as a chronicle of good and bad behaviour and more as a mirror for our own processes of discernment and judgment.

Let us look again at the final lines of the novella. In my own translation of them, I try to reproduce the wariness I perceive in the original:

> La tornata di Ferondo e le sue parole, credendo quasi ogn'uom che risuscitato fosse, acrebbero senza fine la fama della santità dell'abate; e Ferondo, che per la sua gelosia molte battiture ricevute avea, sì come di quella guerito, secondo la promessa dell'abate fatta alla donna, più geloso non fu per innanzi: di che la donna contenta, onestamente, come soleva, con lui si visse, sì veramente che, quando acconciamente poteva, volentieri col santo abate si ritrovava, il quale bene e diligentemente ne' suoi maggior bisogni servita l'avea. (3.8.76)

The reappearance of Ferondo and his portrayal of events added infinitely to the abbot's reputation for saintliness, as almost everyone believed that he had been resurrected. Ferondo, who had received many beatings for being jealous, was cured of that, in keeping with the promise that the abbot had made to his wife, and he was jealous no longer. His wife, pleased about this, lived an honorable life with him as before, provided that when she could coordinate it, she willingly met with the holy abbot, who had served her diligently and well in her greatest needs.

Most other translations draw Ferondo's wife into a circle of Decameronian women who seek their own erotic fulfilment.[9] They emphasize erotic context, and they give the woman an extra dose of chastity and virtue, if only to be ironic about her chastity and virtue. Thus, they make it more likely that we will see the woman's "greatest needs" as sexual needs. Aldo Busi uses fascinating figurative language that tempts us to give these needs a predominantly erotic stamp:

> la donna perciò, tutta contenta, continuò a dividere col marito lo stesso focolare, onesta e premurosa come prima, ma in maniera tale che adesso, appena le circostanze erano acconce, si incontrava col suo santo abate, che era stato così bravo a tapparle tutte quelle falle coniugali.[10]

> [A]s a result, the woman very gladly continued to share the same hearth with her husband, and she was as honest and caring as before, but in such a way that now, as soon as circumstances allowed, she met with her holy abbot, who had been so good at filling in all of those spousal gaps.

McWilliam allows for a "renewal of intimacy" that is nowhere in the original:

> Of this [the lady] was very glad, and thereafter she lived no less chastely with her husband than she had in the past, except that, whenever the occasion arose, she gladly renewed her intimacy with the Abbot, who had ministered to her greatest needs with such unfailing skill and diligence.[11]

Musa and Bondanella are more careful in their portrayal of the meetings between the woman and the abbot, but they still stipulate them as an exception to her chastity:

> [T]he lady was most pleased about this, and from then on she lived with Ferondo just as chastely as she had in the past, except that whenever she

could, she was always happy to find herself with the holy Abbot, who had so skillfully and most diligently attended to her most pressing needs.[12]

In a more subtle move, Waldman has the wife "consorting willingly" with the abbot, and he chooses to render "sì veramente che" more as an addition than as an exception or a proviso:

> [His wife] was happy enough to live with him virtuously as before – and indeed, when the occasion offered, she would willingly consort with the holy abbot, who had served her so faithfully and well in her greatest need.[13]

Because the story of motivation this novella tells is an extremely complex one, it would be worth our while to review other key passages that pertain to the issue of motive.

A subtext for *Decameron* 3.8, a French fabliau titled "Du Vilain de Bailluel," offers an enlightening comparison."[14] In this very short fabliau of 116 verses, the wife, who does not care for her husband at all, is in love with a priest, whom she is preparing to meet when her husband suddenly appears at home, famished. The wife first convinces her husband that he is dead; subsequently, she and the priest engage in sexual activity in full view of her husband.[15] Her motive – to deceive in order to engage in sexual activity she has already planned – is indisputable.

In contrast to the wife of the fabliau, Ferondo's wife is not clearly an adulteress or an agent of fraud. She is not already engaged in adultery when the story begins, she does not participate in convincing Ferondo that he is dead, and it is not clear that she ever knowingly betrays her husband, for if she genuinely believes Ferondo to be dearly departed (a possibility the text leaves unresolved), she presumably is not guilty of adultery.

I suspect that readers attribute sexual desire to Ferondo's wife because to do so dispatches a number of thorny passages in the novella. If we look closely at the passages that highlight her perceptions, her motivation, and her responses, we find that Ferondo's wife turns out to be a curious character who disrupts any attempts to label definitively her motives and her desires.[16]

My first piece of evidence is drawn from the moment when Ferondo's wife and the abbot first meet, in circumstances that appear alternately quite innocent and just a tad suspicious. The abbot, who we know is enamoured of the woman, has managed to get Ferondo to come to the abbey garden and to bring his wife as well. A garden can be a risky place, particularly when the abbot is described as a person who knows how to manipulate Ferondo to do his bidding. Our guard goes up. But then we discover that the abbot is speaking with Ferondo and his wife about the joys of the afterlife and the works of saintly men and women of old. Our guard goes down. The abbot "discusses [these matters] most unassumingly" ("ragionava modestissimamente" [3.8.6]). Now our guard is even lower. When, in this context, the narrator tells us that "alla donna venne disidero di confessarsi da lui" ("it occurred to the woman that she would be interested in going to him for confession" [3.8.6]), we face our first challenge in interpreting the woman's motivation. We might think Ferondo's wife entirely innocent, or we might think (as was certainly the case in 3.3) that a woman who seeks out a confessor must have sex on her mind. If the latter, we might be uncertain whether this is a desire for a sexual encounter with another man (as in 3.3) or with the abbot himself (who, we might imagine, could be sending signals even as he is speaking unassumingly about paradisiacal joys and the works of holy people). Likewise, we might puzzle over whether Ferondo's wife is conscious or unconscious of her own motive. These are the issues with which translators of the *Decameron* struggle. Most twentieth-century translators seek to emphasize a desire that overtakes the woman or happens without her full agency. Thus John Payne translates "the lady was taken with a desire to confess herself to him,"[17] McWilliam has her "seized with the desire of going to him for confession,"[18] and Waldman writes that "the wife conceived the wish to go to the abbot for confession."[19] Musa and Bondanella, by contrast, remove the sexual charge entirely with "she wished to go to him as her confessor."[20] I read Lauretta's statement as hovering between these two poles. In support of my choice, I would urge readers to remember that not every use of the word "desire" has as strong a charge as translators like Payne and McWilliam would want. (Think of the moment when you are sitting at a table in an Italian bar and a waiter approaches you with the question, "Desidera?" ["What would you like to order?"]. Only in the most unusual of situations would the Italian waiter be asking whether you have desires.) At the same time, Lauretta's statement is not quite as pale as Musa and Bondanella would have it. Lauretta is indeed communicating something about the wife's interest, which is why I have translated the phrase as "it occurred to the woman that she would be interested in going to him for confession."

My second piece of evidence comes from the dialogue that takes place after Ferondo's wife approaches the abbot to confess. The narrator only rarely comments on the emotions felt by the two parties as the dialogue progresses, yet the exchange is fascinating for its highly emotional texture. Although the wife has appeared presumably to confess, she begins with a complaint about what she is to do given that she has a husband so stupid and so controlling. What is it she wants? Is she complaining because she lacks sexual satisfaction? As the abbot proposes his solution – namely, that Ferondo will go to Purgatory, that Ferondo will have to leave her a widow for a short time, and that Ferondo will be able to return – the woman can seem angling as well as innocent because she is the one who asks all of the probing questions: How can Ferondo be cured? Will he be able to go to Purgatory while he is still alive? So, given that's not feasible, will she remain a widow? But there is no solid evidence that she is approaching the abbot in order to fulfil a physical desire. In fact, she appears genuinely to care about Ferondo's well-being. More than anything else, she seems to want to cure him of his defects and make it possible for her to live with him. Consistent with this, she refers to his problematic behaviour as a "mala ventura" ("an unfortunate thing"), a defect of fortune rather than of nature, and therefore something that might be remedied, as indeed the abbot has told her it could be.

Throughout this dialogue, the narrator gives us no indication of what the woman perceives or how she responds emotionally. All we have are her words. On the basis of those words, we can venture that Ferondo's wife is trustworthy (she promises to keep silent), that she is cautious (she wants to know exactly how this will go, and she wants to be able to foresee the moves), that she is worried about the prospect of loss (whether it is occasioned by Ferondo's death, or her being a widow, or Ferondo being forever in prison). Her words may also tell another story, however. She has been thinking about what it would be like to have a husband other than Ferondo, so she may not be completely above suspicion. Furthermore, even though she begins with a double complaint about Ferondo's stupidity *and* his supreme watchfulness, by the end, her ultimate concern appears to be only that Ferondo stop being so controlling. This too may suggest that she has mischief on her mind.

Following the abbot's sexual proposition to her, Ferondo's wife does not always act like someone whose primary motivation is sex. The narrator states that the wife is "sbigottita" ("bewildered") at the abbot's first clear proposition and later says that the wife agrees "vergognosamente" ("with shame and embarrassment") when the post-death-of-Ferondo meeting of the wife and abbot is finalized. She never realizes that Ferondo's stay in Purgatory is a hoax: She seems genuinely to believe that Ferondo is dead, she shows all the signs of mourning his loss and of requiring consolation, and she is – like other people in the district – terrified by his reappearance after his ten-month stay in Purgatory, as if he is indeed a ghost. True, the narrator tells us that when the abbot dressed in Ferondo's clothes was believed to be Ferondo's ghost, wandering the countryside, Ferondo's wife was quite aware of what the reality was – but this does not mean that Ferondo's wife is motivated by a desire for sex.

In a novella where the narrator tends not to tell us much about the wife's state of mind, it seems telling that the emotional indicators turn bright only after the abbot, announcing that Ferondo should be sent to Purgatory as soon as possible, surreptitiously places an exquisite ring in the woman's hand. The narrator states: "La donna, lieta del dono e attendendo d'aver degli altri, alle compagne tornata maravigliose cose cominciò a raccontare della santità dell'abate e con loro a casa se ne tornò" ("The woman, delighted with the gift and anticipating other such gifts, went back to her women friends, and began to tell them amazing things about the abbot's holiness; then in the company of these friends she returned home" [3.8.29]).

There emerges a new possibility: that Ferondo's wife could be motivated by desire for material things, which may be the reason she tolerates Ferondo, who is quite wealthy. Indeed, upon hearing of Ferondo's death, the wife immediately retreats to their house, where she sets about administering his fortune; and following Ferondo's demise, when the abbot appears to console the woman and reminds her of the promise made to him, the narrator focuses again on the woman's eye for material gain: "La donna, veggendosi libera e senza lo 'mpaccio di Ferondo o d'altrui, avendogli veduto in dito un altro bello anello, disse che era apparecchiata, e con lui compose che la seguente notte v'andasse" ("The woman, now seeing herself free and unimpeded by Ferondo or anyone else, and having caught sight of another fine ring on the Abbot's finger, told him that she was ready, and in concert with him, she arranged a meeting the following night" [3.8.36]). Although the narrator Lauretta tells us of the great pleasure the abbot has in his nocturnal visits to the woman, she holds silent about the woman's emotional response. Although we may like to think that Ferondo's wife, like some other women in the *Decameron*, is glad to engage in extramarital relations, we might also imagine that she is motivated more by a material gain that threatens to be interrupted when Ferondo is brought back from the dead, returns home to his wife, and takes possession of his property (3.8.75). If we see things from this perspective, we should hesitate to assume that the woman's "most pressing needs" are sexual.

How we read any particular moment in which Ferondo's wife is portrayed very much depends on whether we postulate that she is any of the following or any combination of the following: Mischievous. Angling. Innocent. Well-meaning. Morally upstanding. Easily swayed, especially by an authority figure. Gullible. Uncomprehending. Puzzled. Bewildered. Dim-witted. A shrewd pursuer of things that could be turned to her advantage. In trying to evaluate a character who remains a cipher, readers are continually put off balance. We risk revealing more about our own intellectual and emotional investments than about the text of the *Decameron* – unless we use this challenge from the *Decameron* to learn about our own preconceived notions of motivation and psychological coherence.

Competing Summaries, Competing Subjects

The more I read this novella and summaries of this novella, the less I feel I understand what its subject matter is and how its subject matter fits into the overall picture of things on Day 3 of the *Decameron*, which is dedicated to stories about "people who obtain, through their hard work, something they greatly desire or recover something they have lost" ("di chi alcuna cosa molto disiderata con industria acquistasse o la perduta ricuperasse" [2.Concl.9]).

Let me begin with the Author's rubric for *Decameron* 3.8, which is positioned to shape the reader's perception of the novella:

> Ferondo, mangiata certa polvere, è sotterrato per morto; e dall'abate, che la moglie di lui si gode, tratto della sepoltura è messo in prigione e fattogli credere che egli è in Purgatoro; e poi risuscitato, per suo nutrica un figliuol dell'abate nella moglie di lui generato. (3.8.10)

> Ferondo, upon consuming a particular powder, is buried for dead. He is taken out of the tomb by the Abbot, who is having a fine time with Ferondo's wife. He is put into prison and made to believe that he is in Purgatory. Then, brought back to life, he raises as his own a son that the Abbot has begotten on his wife.

A reader has to work hard to make this story fit the topic for Day 3. Every previous story on this day bears an Author's rubric that highlights an industrious protagonist: Masetto (3.1), the stablehand (3.2), the woman in love with a young man (3.3), Dom Felice (3.4), Zima (3.5), Ricciardo Minutolo (3.6), and Tedaldo degli Elisei (3.7). The Author's rubric to *Decameron* 3.8, while focusing on Ferondo, never gives us much sense of how Ferondo might be acting with effort and industriousness. The rubric for 3.8, by contrast, highlights Ferondo's position as a passive subject who is buried, is taken out of the tomb, is put into prison, is made to believe that he is in Purgatory, and is brought back to life. Whatever effort there is could only belong to the abbot. (Of course, if the story is not about an effort to attain something greatly desired but rather about the recovery of something lost, one could conclude that Ferondo "loses his life" and then "regains" it.)

Lauretta's introduction to her story will prove even more puzzling:

> Carissime donne, a me si para davanti a doversi far raccontare una verità che ha, troppo più che di quello che ella fu, di menzogna sembianza; e quella nella mente m'ha ritornata l'avere udito un per un altro essere stato pianto e sepellito. Dirò adunque come un vivo per morto sepellito fosse, e come poi per risuscitato, e non per vivo, egli stesso e molti altri lui credesser essere della sepoltura uscito, colui di ciò essendo per santo adorato che come colpevole ne dovea più tosto essere condannato. (3.8.3)

> Dearest ladies, I am confronted with having to tell of a true thing that has, much more than it actually was, the appearance of a falsehood. I was reminded of this when I heard about someone who was mourned and buried for someone else. I will therefore recount how a living man could be buried for dead, and how he himself and many others could believe that he had emerged from the tomb not as a living man but as someone who was resurrected, and for that he was venerated as a saint who should instead have been condemned as culpable.

With considerable ingenuity, of course, we could cram this summary within the confines of Neifile's theme. It would be more illuminating, however, to examine the force required to make summary and story and Neifile's topic come into alignment.

If we think about Lauretta's summary from the point of view of anyone who has already read either the story or the Author's rubric, we will notice that Lauretta speaks in a roundabout way that allows her to refer to Ferondo, the living person who will be buried for dead and then brought back to life. But if we think about Lauretta's summary from the point of view of her companions (who have no idea what kind of story she will deliver), we are struck by just how murky her summary is. Oppositions crop up left and right: truth and the appearance of falsehood, one man and someone else, a live man and a dead man, a resurrected man and a live man, a venerated man and a condemned man, a saint and a culpable soul. And early in the passage, just about the time the audience arrives at the "true thing," the summary begins to sprout one indistinct patch after another.

So murky is Lauretta's summary, in fact, that translators come to opposite conclusions about whether the last clause refers to Ferondo at all. In my own translation, I have sought to maintain the lack of clarity that I see in the original Italian:

> Dirò adunque come un vivo per morto sepellito fosse, e come poi per risuscitato, e non per vivo, egli stesso e molti altri lui credessero essere della sepoltura uscito, colui di ciò essendo per santo adorato che come colpevole ne dovea più tosto essere condannato. (3.8.3)

> I will therefore recount how a living man could be buried for dead, and how he himself and many others could believe that he had emerged from the tomb not as a living man but as someone who was resurrected, and for that he was venerated as a saint who should instead have been condemned as culpable.

Musa and Bondanella and McWilliam make Ferondo out to be worshipped as a saint when he should have been condemned. In order to do this, they introduce a reason for the condemnation (viz. Ferondo's stupidity and foolishness), despite the fact that the Italian original never says anything of the sort:

> I shall tell you, then, how a living man was buried for dead, how he was later resurrected, and how he himself, as well as any other people, thought he was actually dead rather than alive when he rose from his tomb, and how, as a result of this, he was worshiped as a saint instead of being condemned for stupidity. (trans. Musa/Bondanella)[21]

> My story, then is about a living man who was buried for dead, and who later on emerging from his tomb, was convinced that he had truly died

and been resurrected – a belief that was shared by many other people, who consequently venerated him as a Saint when they should have been condemning him as a fool. (trans. McWilliam)[22]

Waldman, on the other hand, sees the abbot as the one who is worshipped as a saint. In order to do this, he produces the "man who wrought this wonder," despite the fact that the Italian original includes no such periphrasis:

This [story] is about a living man who was buried for dead and then resurrected; many people, himself included, took him for a man back from the dead – and the man who wrought this wonder, far from getting any blame, was worshipped thereafter as a saint.[23]

The impulse to clarify Lauretta's meaning appears to be a late-twentieth-century phenomenon. Earlier English translations tend to respect the lack of clarity. Thus, the 1620 translation attributed to John Florio tells us that "[they] adored him as a Saint, who was the occasion thereof, and who (as a bad man) deserved justly to be condemned."[24] J.M. Rigg, in his 1903 translation, offers "whereby he was venerated as a saint who ought rather to have been condemned as a criminal."[25] When a translator like John Payne gives in to the urge to specify, he tries to refrain from doing so in the text of his English translation. Instead, Payne inserts an asterisk after the ambiguous "he":

I purpose then, to tell you how a live man was entombed for dead and how after he and many other folk believed himself to have come forth of the sepulcher as one raised from the dead, by reason whereof he* was adored as a saint who should rather have been condemned as a criminal."[26]

That asterisk sends the reader to a note at the bottom of the page, where Payne writes:

* *i.e.*, the abbot who played the trick upon Ferondo. See post.[27]

These recent translators of the *Decameron* are anxious to pin down matters with greater certainty than the original text would authorize. If we wish to respect the complex configuration of the evidence, however, we must strive to render it in all of its intricacies.

Conclusion

Although it is common to think of the *Decameron* as a text that entertains and teaches, the evidence I present here tells another story. Rather than thinking about the *Decameron* as "teaching" readers, we should think about it as "testing" them. Remember, however, that this is no usual test. Rather, this is a test where we don't know what the instructions are when we start reading, and we have to try to figure out how the test works as we go along.

And what kinds of learning outcomes are being assessed in the *Decameron*? I believe that even in some of its most unassuming novellas, such as this one, the *Decameron*:

- offers the reader an opportunity to reflect on the relation between rule and exception, or in other words, it offers the reader an opportunity to think about how we construct propositions about our world and how we consider alternate propositions that could lead us to modify or reject those propositions.
- disrupts attempts to assign labels or neat categories.
- disrupts two-valued logic (true/false) and tries to get readers to recognize gradations of truth (multivalued logic, fuzzy logic).

In testing the reader in this fashion, the *Decameron* does work that is absolutely vital, because it brings us (assuming we are at all willing) to see how complex human behaviour and motivation is, and it constantly reminds us that our conceptualizations of the world, if they are to be true and accurate, must be as finely tuned as humanly possible.

5 Rushing to Judge? Read the Story of Tofano and Ghita (*Decameron* 7.4)

From early on in the *Decameron*, many a story is promptly followed by a peremptory judgment. Praise abounds. A story is praised by all the women (1.1) or praised by everybody (1.2); a particular action or a particular character trait is praised by the women or by everybody (1.5; 1.6; 2.2). A story can be pronounced "beautiful" (2.9). The truth of what a narrator says can be affirmed (as happens, curiously enough for the first time, when the group responds to Dioneo's story of Bartolomea and Paganino [2.10]). And whether or not the word "blame" is used, certain characters or traits or actions can be marked as disagreeable (as happens – again, curiously enough for the first time – with the response to 2.10, when the women pronounce Bernabò to be an ass).

One of the peremptory judgments that most interests me, given what I see as people's penchant for labelling, is the one where the good and the bad are prominently put on display. At the end of Lauretta's story about Tofano and Ghita (7.4), for example, each member of the *brigata* praises Ghita, saying "that she had done the right thing, and what that creep [her husband] deserved" ("che ella bene avesse fatto e come a quel cattivo si conveniva" [7.5.2]).

So what is it that Ghita does? She marries Tofano, she finds out he is jealous even though he has no reason to be, she decides she will give him a reason, so she finds herself a lover. To be with that lover, she plays on her husband's penchant for drink, encouraging him to drink himself into a stupor so that she can be with her lover while her husband sleeps. When Tofano starts to figure this out and comes up with a plan to catch her, by only pretending to be drunk, she almost gets caught. As she returns from her lover's house one night, Tofano locks her out of the house. When her pleas do not work, she threatens to commit suicide by throwing herself into a well and assures Tofano that the blame for her death will rest squarely on him. Then she picks up a stone and throws it into the well. Hearing the noise, Tofano comes running to save her, whereupon she slips into the house and locks him out. In the ensuing argument, witnessed by neighbours male and female, Ghita convinces the bystanders that Tofano is at fault and that he, a drunkard, has tried to besmirch her name by throwing a stone into the well and claiming to have committed suicide. Now, she says, she is teaching him a lesson by locking him out of the house. The woman's relatives arrive, beat Tofano to a pulp, and take Ghita and her things home with them. Tofano, who really does want to be with his wife, resorts to intermediaries to get her back, and the story ends with his promise to allow her to do as she pleases as long as he doesn't become aware of it.

If these are the "facts," one could have a variety of opinions about where fault lies and who the victim is. As I know from discussions of this story, particularly with first-year students at the university, not everyone agrees that Ghita "does the right thing," and not everyone agrees that her husband "got what he deserved." Nevertheless, even among scholars, it is still possible to find peremptory judgments that reaffirm the *brigata's* response to Lauretta's story. For example: "Ghita, while not especially virtuous, is clearly the victim. Tofano has two fatal flaws: he is abnormally jealous and he drinks heavily. These two flaws get him into trouble and bring his ruin; the reader has little sympathy for him at the end."[1] In fact, many contemporary scholars of the *Decameron* seem to have definitively put aside any negative assessments of the "not especially virtuous" Ghita, preferring to see her as victim of an overbearing husband and champion of a new ideal of Love and personal fulfilment.[2]

Faced with stories of women throwing a stone in a well to fake their deaths and triumph over their less lucky husbands, medieval and Renaissance texts did not side with these women or see them as victims, even when the jealous husband locked the woman in the house. Medieval texts offered mistrust of women, at least as an initial response. Thus, after the teacher in the *Disciplina clericalis* tells a version of this story as Exemplum 14, "The Well," his young student announces that the story is clearly an exhortation not to get married.[3] (His teacher offers an alternative point of view, pointing out that he shouldn't believe all women are like that; as proof, he cites Solomon's praise of a woman in Proverbs.)[4] In the *Libro dei sette savi*, the Philosopher who relates a version of this story to the emperor concludes by saying "Onde vedete, messer l'imperatore, quali sono l'opere delle femine; e non credete alle mai parole di vostra mogliere" ("So you see, lord emperor, what women's deeds are like. Don't believe your wife's wicked words").[5] In the sixteenth century, the Giolito edition of the *Decameron* encourages the reader to see both Tofano and Ghita as flawed; the editor, Francesco Sansovino, introduces this story with the rubric "Nel che si riprende la semplicità de' mariti, & dimostransi le fraudi delle mogli" ("In which the foolishness of husbands is criticized, and the fraud of wives is shown").[6]

I am not interested in arguing that we should return to a medieval or Renaissance reading of this story by focusing less on Tofano, or focusing more on Ghita, or spreading the blame more evenly. True, I am mildly curious about how the finger pointing has changed over time. Premodern readers were predisposed to notice female imperfection, particularly if falsehood and fraudulence were involved. Many contemporary readers, believing that the right to sexual freedom is inviolable and that control of one's personal circumstances is supremely desirable, prefer seeing women like Ghita as "victims" or "heroes" and men like Tofano as "villains." Moreover, many people now seem predisposed to side with a winner even when that winner is a clever manipulator of appearances.[7] Whatever the reasons, we should not be so curious about the finger pointing or the cheerleading as to engage in these pursuits. It is not primarily the business of literary scholarship to pass judgments on moral character. We can do that without reading a text closely. Once we go beyond reading for pleasure (which, I would add, is a perfectly legitimate activity), the point of reading is to understand better how texts may encourage certain kinds of judgments and how readers process textual information in order to arrive at their conclusions.

What path would one have to travel in order to arrive at the conclusion that Ghita has done the right thing and that Tofano deserves what happens to him? As I will show, to come to such a conclusion, one would have to

(1) ignore the force of parodical statements,
(2) accept misrepresentations and partial representations as true, and
(3) ignore contradictions.

In order to produce the conclusion that Ghita is right and Tofano is blameworthy, the story, like any successful ideology, must absorb and neutralize opposing views.

In what follows, I offer a step-by-step reading of *Decameron* 7.4 that includes my own translation of the novella. While this mode of presentation will not be as compact as a summary argument, it has the advantage of revealing the elaborate path the narrator Lauretta takes to obtain her audience's ringing endorsement of Ghita. At many a turn on that elaborate path, the reader gets signals that something could be amiss: the rhetoric seems rambling and disjointed; the praise seems excessive; the evidence isn't reliably in Ghita's favour; there are signs of a rush to judgment. There where the narration is tangled and untidy, there where we should be most wary of summary judgment, the narrator presses the audience to relinquish doubt.

The Author's rubric prepares us for a judgment potentially at odds with the one the narrator of the story wants. In summarizing the story, the Author presents a more balanced view, one in which both protagonists do things that could merit blame:

Tofano chiude una notte fuor di casa la moglie, la quale, non potendo per prieghi rientrare, fa vista di gittarsi in un pozzo e gittavi una gran pietra; Tofano esce di casa e corre là, e ella in casa se n'entra e serra lui di fuori e sgridandolo il vitupera. (7.4.1)

One night Tofano locks his wife out of the house, and she, unable to talk and plead her way back in, makes it look as if she is going to throw herself into a well and then throws in a large stone. Tofano comes out of the house and runs there, and she goes into the house, locks him out, and shouts insults at him.

Initially, since locking the wife out of the house seems unmotivated, and since the wife resorts to deception only after her pleas prove useless, we may be more inclined to look askance on Tofano. But about halfway through the rubric, when Tofano runs out of the house, our perception of him may well change: For whatever reason, it appears that he isn't such a lout as to let his wife die in the well. When he gets locked out of the house and his wife shouts insults at him, we may even feel that he is the victim of unmerited ill treatment – unless we have so firmly sided with the wife that we think he now deserves anything she does to him. Based on the Author's rubric, we might judge that the situation results in a tie.

Granted, the Author's rubric is the introduction to *readers* of the *Decameron*. Lauretta, the narrator who addresses her Florentine companions, chooses a different tack. Her introduction opens with a paean to Love and slants things in favour of an as yet unnamed woman:

> O Amore, chenti e quali sono le tue forze, chenti i consigli e chenti gli avvedimenti! Qual filosofo, quale artista mai avrebbe potuto o potrebbe mostrare quegli accorgimenti, quegli avvedimenti, quegli dimostramenti che fai tu subitamente a chi seguita le tue orme? Certo la dottrina di qualunque altro è tarda a rispetto della tua, sì come assai bene comprender si può nelle cose davanti mostrate; alle quali, amorose donne, io una n'agiugnerò d'una semplicetta donna adoperata, tale che io non so chi altri se l'avesse potuta mostrare che Amore. (7.4.3–4)

> O Love, of what sort, of what quality are your powers, of what sort your counsel, of what sort your insights! What philosopher, what artist could ever in the past or in the future put forth those assessments, those insightful discernments, those logical arguments the way you do instantly for those who follow in your footsteps? Certainly anyone else's learning is far behind compared to yours, as one can understand very well from the things that have been shown previously. And to these things, loving ladies, I will add one employed by a rather simple woman, and given what it was like, I don't know who other than Love could have shown it to her.

Scholars have noted the ironic force of this passage, the heightened rhetoric of which seems incongruent in a tale focused on comic trickery.[8] David Wallace, for example, writes that "such rhetoric seemed appropriate as part of the great love narratives of the fourth and fifth days" but sees "it as oddly out of place here in introducing the short urban farce of this fourth novella."[9] But I am not convinced that this particular rhetoric would prove appropriate even on the fourth and fifth days of the *Decameron*. Granted, the first sentence, with its anaphora on the overly elaborate *chenti* (which I render with "of what sort," the closest I can get in English to the preciousness of the Italian), could probably function in a great love narrative. Immediately thereafter, we see, even if we do not know what the tale will be about, that the narrator is straining unduly to make her point. Lauretta wants to make sure she covers all the bases in the second sentence: by comparing both philosophers and artists to Love, then by including both past and future, and finally by using a rhetorical device called homeoteleuton, in which she rhymes the endings of three words (*accorgimenti / avvedimenti / dimostramenti,* which I translate as *assessments / insightful discernments / logical arguments*). Especially by the time we link up the verb of this sentence with its third direct object ("mostrare ... dimostramenti"), we have to realize that Lauretta is stumbling over her words. To render the awkwardness of this, I would have to translate "mostrare dimostramenti" not as "to put forth logical proofs" but as "to demonstrate demonstrations" or "to reveal revelations" or "to prove proofs." Unfortunately, once I opt to include the homeoteleuton with a rhyme on "-ments," I lose the possibility of showing how silly "mostrare dimostramenti" sounds.

Furthermore, the logic of Lauretta's praise of Love is questionable because her cited evidence is inexact. To what can she be referring when she says that the things shown previously are evidence of Love's power? It is not at all clear. The statement seems designed to have the audience fill in the blank with whatever evidence from previous stories the audience finds valid. And why on earth would the woman's relative simplicity be proof that only Love could have shown her what to do? In the end, it appears that Lauretta may be relying on her characterization of the women in her audience as "loving" in order to get them to agree with her characterization of Love.

Having set up the expectations, Lauretta introduces her characters, opting to focus first not on the simple little woman but on a rich man named Tofano:

> Fu adunque già in Arezzo un ricco uomo, il qual fu Tofano nominato. A costui fu data per moglie una bellissima donna, il cui nome fu monna Ghita, della quale egli senza saper perché prestamente divenne geloso, di che la donna avvedendosi prese sdegno; e più volte avendolo della cagione della sua gelosia addomandato né egli alcuna avendone saputa assegnare se non cotali generali e cattive, cadde nell'animo alla donna di farlo morire del male del quale senza cagione aveva paura. (7.4.5)

> So in Arezzo there was once a rich man known as Tofano. He received in marriage a really beautiful woman named Ghita, of whom he, without explanation, immediately became jealous. Upon noticing this, the woman became scornful; and after she asked him a number of times why he was jealous and after he was unable to cite any grounds but faulty general ones, it occurred to the woman to make him die of the ill that he had no grounds to fear.

The introduction is curious for the way it brings the reader to look at Tofano and Ghita with ever shifting emotional responses. Ghita, who had been classified as a "rather simple woman" (*una semplicetta donna*), rises in our estimation when she gets introduced here as "a really beautiful woman" (*una bellissima donna*). Shortly thereafter, Ghita gains our sympathy as we discover that her husband has become jealous of her for a reason that cannot be identified. And how much is the husband descending in our estimation? Part of this will depend on how we understand the phrase "senza saper perché." Do we take this to mean "without any reason" or "without any known reason," as it can legitimately be interpreted (and is by McWilliam and Musa/Bondanella)? Or, like Rigg and Payne, do we take this to mean "without knowing why" so that it tells us about the husband's lack of self-awareness?[10] Or might we allow for both possibilities, as the translation attributed to John Florio does, saying that Tofano became exceedingly jealous "without any occasion given, or reason knowne to himselfe,"[11] and as I try to do when I translate "senza saper perché" as "without explanation"? Not long after, we are presented with a new dilemma, this time involving Ghita, to whom it occurs to "make him [Tofano] die of the ill that he had no grounds to fear." Some wife, we might exclaim! Would she really think of making him die? A footnote in the recent Einaudi edition hastens to reassure us that *morire* is meant not literally but in its psychological sense.[12] But the quadrifold appearance of the verb *fu* in the first lines of the novella proper, which locates the characters as *having been* and *having existed* in a delimited past, flirts with the suggestion that Tofano and Ghita existed in the past but may not be alive any more.

Having painted a picture of complex attributes and motivations, Lauretta then encourages identification with the woman by describing the state of things from the woman's point of view:

E essendosi avveduta che un giovane, secondo il suo giudicio molto da bene, la vagheggiava, discretamente con lui s'incominciò a intendere; e essendo già tra lui e lei tanto le cose innanzi, che altro che dare effetto con opera alle parole non vi mancava, pensò la donna di trovare similmente modo a questo. E avendo già tra' costumi cattivi del suo marito conosciuto lui dilettarsi di bere, non solamente gliele cominciò a commendare ma artatamente a sollicitarlo a ciò molto spesso. E tanto ciò prese per uso, che quasi ogni volta che a grado l'era infino allo inebriarsi bevendo il conducea; e quando bene ebbro il vedea, messolo a dormire, primieramente col suo amante si ritrovò, e poi sicuramente più volte di ritrovarsi con lui continuò, e tanto di fidanza nella costui ebbrezza prese, che non solamente avea preso ardire di menarsi il suo amante in casa, ma ella talvolta gran parte della notte s'andava con lui a dimorare alla sua, la qual di quivi non era guari lontana. (7.4.6–8)

Having noticed that a young man, who was in her estimation very respectable, was interested in her, she discreetly began to frequent his company; and as things between him and her went so far along that there remained nothing to do but to put words into deeds, the woman thought about how to find a way to do this. Once she had realized that among her husband's bad habits was his fondness for drink, not only did she begin to praise this in him but very often she artfully encouraged it. And so much did she get accustomed to doing this, that almost every time he was so inclined she got him to drink until he was drunk, and when she saw that he was really drunk, she put him to bed and went off to meet with her lover, and then without fear she continued to meet with him repeatedly. So confident did she become in this guy's drunkenness, that not only did she dare to bring her lover into the house, but sometimes she even would go to spend a good part of the night at his house, which was not very far from there.

In this passage, Lauretta draws attention to the woman's cognitive and reasoning processes: her perception, her realizations, her discretion, her judgment, and her thinking about a way to proceed. When Lauretta turns back to Tofano, she has Ghita identify his fondness for drink as "among his bad habits" ("tra' costumi cattivi"), leaving the audience to fill in for themselves how many other bad habits there might be and just how grave those bad habits might be. Thus far, Lauretta has given far more detail about the wife's cognitive and reasoning processes than she has about the husband's (and in any case, his reasoning is being called into question); she has also invited the audience to consider his bad character.

At this point, the audience is challenged for the first time to consider what is praiseworthy and what is blameworthy. Where is there more fault? With the husband who has "bad habits" (*costumi cattivi*) and likes to drink? With the wife who not only praises his fondness for drink but artfully promotes his habit? With the man who gets himself drunk or the wife who, at whim, manages to get him to drink himself into a stupor? Once again, our understanding of a single word – in this case *artatamente*, which I have translated as *artfully* – may reveal where we stand. How charged with moral judgment is this word? Are we more inclined to see Ghita's cleverness and her skilfulness in a positive light or a negative one, as a mark of intelligence to be cultivated, on one hand, or as a mark of wily underhandedness that begs for reproach? Let's say that the audience remains on the fence, choosing not to cast judgment on either party. Just as Lauretta attempts to force the audience's hand, by recalling that the woman is in love (*innamorata*), the narrative takes a crucial turn, marked by the ominous "it happened that" (*avvenne che*):

> E in questa maniera la innamorata donna continuando, avvenne che il doloroso marito si venne accorgendo che ella, nel confortare lui a bere, non beveva per ciò essa mai: di che egli prese sospetto non così fosse come era, cioè che la donna lui inebriasse per poter poi fare il piacer suo mentre egli adormentato fosse. (7.4.9)

> As the enamored woman continued in this way, it happened that the pitiful husband started to notice that while she was encouraging him to drink, she never drank at all. This made him suspect that things might be as they were, namely that the woman might be getting him drunk so that she could do as she pleased while he was asleep.

For the first time, we see things from the husband's point of view. And almost as if our perspective, meshed with his, gives him new powers, the husband, who has not fared well when he had to respond with reason and logic, begins to develop insight. He distinguishes himself as the first husband on Day 7 to notice that something is amiss. His wife, who is encouraging him to drink, is not drinking at all herself; this leads him to a suspicion, beautifully articulated in imperfect subjunctives and a pleonastic negative, that things may be other than they initially appear. Suddenly, the husband inhabits a world that is considerably more complex (at least in Italian, of course, since those subjunctives and the pleonastic negative are harder to render in English).

> E volendo di questo, se così fosse, far pruova, senza avere il dì bevuto, una sera mostrandosi il più ebbro uomo e nel parlare e nei modi, che fosse mai, il che la donna credendo né estimando che più bere gli bisognasse a ben dormire il mise prestamente. E fatto ciò, secondo che alcuna volta era usata di fare, uscita di casa, alla casa del suo amante se n'andò e quivi infino alla mezzanotte dimorò. (7.4.10–11)

Wishing to verify if this were indeed the case, one evening, without having drunk anything during the day, he made himself look, both in word and deed, like the drunkest man there ever was. The woman, believing this and judging that he didn't need anything more to drink, quickly put him right to sleep. Once she had done this, as she had on other occasions been inclined to do, she left the house, went to her lover's house, and there she stayed up until midnight.

The positive representation of the husband's abilities continues: The husband has a plan, he sets up an experiment to test his hypothesis (rendered again with the imperfect subjunctive), he pretends to be terribly drunk, and he gets the wife to believe he needs no more to drink. The husband remains the grammatical subject of this sentence. Curiously, however, the minute she puts him to bed in the final subordinate clause of 7.4.10, "a ben dormire il mise prestamente" ("quickly put him right to sleep"), it is as if she snaps back into being in control, becoming the grammatical subject of the next sentence. As she returns to a customary way of doing things, the accented syllables ("fatto ciò … se n'andò … dimorò"), particularly on the indicative verbs in the past, grant her actions a firm finality – at least until midnight.

But it is too early for such conclusiveness. Predictably, Tofano regains the narrative point of view and the command of events, which includes the first instance of direct discourse in the novella:

Tofano, come la donna non vi sentì, così si levò e andatosene alla sua porta quella serrò dentro e posesi alle finestre, acciò che tornare vedesse la donna e le facesse manifesto che egli si fosse accorto delle maniere sue; e tanto stette che la donna tornò, la quale, tornando a casa e trovandosi serrata di fuori, fu oltre modo dolente e cominciò a tentare se per forza potesse l'uscio aprire. Il che poi che Tofano alquanto ebbe sofferto, disse: "Donna, tu ti fatichi invano, per ciò che qua entro non potrai tu tornare. Va tornati là dove infino a ora se' stata: e abbi per certo che tu non ci tornerai mai infino a tanto che io di questa cosa, in presenza de' parenti tuoi e de' vicini, te n'avrò fatto quello onore che ti si conviene." (7.4.11–12)

When Tofano did not hear the woman, he got up and went to the door, which he shut from the inside, and stationed himself at the windows, so that he would be able to see the woman return and would be able to make clear to her that he was aware of what she was up to. He remained there long enough that the woman returned, and she, returning home and finding herself locked out, became extremely upset and began to try to force the door open. After Tofano had put up with this for a while, he said, "Woman, your efforts are in vain, because you will never be able to set foot here again. Go back to where you were up until now, and rest assured that you won't ever come back again until I, in the presence of your relatives and the neighbors, have done you that honor that you deserve."

Given that the above passage begins by focusing on Tofano – what he hears, how he moves to the door and then to the windows, his wish to see the woman returning, and his wish to communicate his awareness to her – we might well expect that when she returns, he would actually *see* her, which would be the first step to making it evident that he *had seen* what she was up to. Nevertheless, when the woman returns, even though the narrator uses the verb *return* twice, the narrator deftly avoids mentioning anything about Tofano *seeing* the woman. This is in marked contrast to the version of the tale in the *Disciplina clericalis*, where the husband sees his wife coming back half-naked ("in camisia sua mulierem suam nudam revertentem vidit") and where the husband can see and hear his wife when he questions her ("Vir mulierem suam audiens et videns ac si nesciret interrogavit quis esset").[13] Unbeknownst to Tofano, the die is now cast, and not in his favour. As we shall see in a subsequent moment, Tofano, who wanted to see what was happening, isn't seeing as well as he should. In the *Decameron*, this is never a good subject position to occupy.

What follows, again predictably, is a "he said/she said" moment:

La donna lo 'ncominciò a pregar per l'amor di Dio che piacer gli dovesse d'aprirle, per ciò che ella non veniva donde s'avvisava ma da vegghiare con una sua vicina, per ciò che le notti eran grandi e ella nolle poteva dormir tutte né sola in casa vegghiare. Li prieghi non giovavano alcuna cosa, per ciò che quella bestia era pur disposto a volere che tutti gli aretin sapessero la lor vergogna, là dove niun la sapeva.

La donna, veggendo che il pregar non le valeva, ricorse al minacciare e disse: "Se tu non m'apri, io ti farò il più tristo uom che viva."

A cui Tofano rispose: "E che mi puoi tu fare?"

La donna, alla quale Amore aveva già aguzzato co' suoi consigli lo 'ngegno, rispose: "Innanzi che io voglia sofferire la vergogna che tu mi vuoi fare ricevere a torto, io mi gitterò in questo pozzo che qui è vicino: nel quale poi essendo trovata morta, niuna persona sarà che creda che altri che tu per ebrezza mi v'abbia gittata; e così o ti converrà fuggire e perder ciò che tu hai e essere in bando, o converrà che ti sia tagliata la testa sí come a micidial di me che tu veramente sarai stato."

Per queste parole niente si mosse Tofano dalla sua sciocca opinione; per la qual cosa la donna disse: "Or ecco, io non posso più sofferire questo tuo fastidio: Dio il ti perdoni! farai riporre questa mia rocca che io lascio qui"; e questo detto, essendo la notte tanto obscura, che appena si sarebbe potuto veder l'un l'altro per la via, se n'andò la donna verso il pozzo; e presa una grandissima pietra che a piè del pozzo era, gridando "Idio, perdonami!" la lasciò cadere entro nel pozzo. (7.4.13–18)

The woman began to plead with him that for the love of God he please open the door for her, because she was not coming from where he thought but rather from sitting up with one of her neighbor ladies, on account of the fact that the nights were long and the neighbor couldn't sleep all night nor be awake alone in the house. Her pleadings came to naught, because that idiot was determined to have all of the population of Arezzo know their shame, there where nobody knew about it.

The woman, seeing that pleading was of no use to her, resorted to threats and said, "If you don't open the door for me, I'll make you the most miserable man alive."

To which Tofano responded, "And what can you do to me?"

The woman, whose wits had already been sharpened by Love's counsel, responded: "Before I allow myself to bear the shame that you unjustly want me to receive, I will throw myself into this well right here. And when they find me dead, nobody will believe that I was thrown in by anybody other than you when you were drunk. So either you will have to flee and lose everything you have and be in exile, or you'll end up with your head cut off as the murderer of me that you really will have been."

Hearing these words, Tofano didn't budge one bit from his silly views, so the woman said, "Look, I can't stand how aggravating you are – God forgive you for it! You'll have to put away my rock for spinning that I'll leave here." And having said this, in the night that was so dark that it would have been really difficult for people to see each other on the street, the woman went to the well, picked up a big stone that was near the well's base, shouted "God, forgive me!," and let it fall into the well.

Although this sort of "he said, she said" could easily have been portrayed as a draw, Lauretta nudges the audience to accept the woman's dominance, first by calling Tofano an idiot, then by reminding the audience of the role Love plays in sharpening the woman's wits, and finally by labelling Tofano's views as silly. Those "silly views" even get presented as the cause of the woman's decision to respond as she does.

The passage also includes two details that do not appear in the subtexts, details that are used to reinforce the woman's dominance in a far subtler way. The first original detail involves visibility. Remember how earlier, we never get any indication that Tofano sees his wife as she returns? Here, we find out why. Lauretta observes that the night is so dark that even people in fairly close proximity wouldn't be able to see each other. Shortly before Lauretta mentions this, however, she associates the verb "to see" (*vedere*) with the woman, who *sees* that pleading is of no use. Even if the woman's sight is mental and not physical, Lauretta gives the woman an edge on Tofano, thanks to her ability to see in the dark. The second original detail involves the distaff (*rocca*), which the woman puts down just before she pretends to throw herself into the well. That distaff, for which I have used the equivalent "rock for spinning," functions as an imaginary object shoring up the woman's claim that she has come back from keeping vigil with a neighbour. But it also may be included here because of the association between *pietra* and *rocca*, between the word for what the woman throws into the well (*pietra*) and a word that can mean both "a rock for spinning" and "a large rock or stone." The woman tips her hand by providing an auditory clue about what one would see if there were more light.[14] So the woman has an ability to see that Tofano does not have, and she is telling him what he could see if he could listen carefully.

Questions about what one hears and what one sees continue to emerge in what follows:

La pietra giugnendo nell'acqua fece un grandissimo romore, il quale come Tofano udì credette fermamente che essa gittata vi si fosse; per che, presa la secchia colla fune, subitamente si gittò di casa per aiutarla e corse al pozzo. La donna, che presso all'uscio della sua casa nascosa s'era, come vide correre al pozzo, così ricoverò in casa e serrossi dentro e andossene alle finestre e cominciò a dire: "Egli si vuole inacquare quando altri il bee, non poscia la notte."

Tofano, udendo costei, si tenne scornato e tornossi all'uscio; e non potendovi entrare le cominciò a dire che gli aprisse.

Ella, lasciato stare il parlar piano come infino allora aveva fatto, quasi gridando cominciò a dire: "Alla croce di Dio, ubriaco fastidioso, tu non

c'enterai stanotte; io non posso più sofferire questi tuoi modi: egli convien
che io faccia vedere a ogn'uomo chi tu se' e a che ora tu torni la notte a casa."
    Tofano d'altra parte crucciato le 'ncominciò a dir villania e a gridare; di
che i vicini sentendo il romore si levarono, e uomini e donne, e fecersi alle
finestre e domandarono che ciò fosse. (7.4.20–3)

As it hit the water, the stone made a really loud noise, and when Tofano
heard this, he truly believed that she had thrown herself in. So taking the
bucket with a rope, he immediately hurled himself out of the house to
help her and ran to the well. The woman, who had hidden near the door
to the house, saw him run to the well and in that moment she slipped into
the house, locked herself in, went to the windows and began to say, "It's
a good thing to water your wine down when you're drinking it, not later
on during the night."

Hearing her, Tofano realized he had been bamboozled and he went
back to the door. Since he couldn't get in, he began to tell her to open up
the door for him.

Leaving aside the way she had been speaking softly until then, almost
screaming, she began: "By God, you aggravating drunk, you won't come
in tonight. I can't stand your behavior any more – I'll have everybody see
who you are and what hour you come home at night."

Tofano, who was infuriated, started to curse at her and to scream. Hearing
the noise, the neighbors, both men and women, got up, went to the windows,
and asked what was happening.

Tofano reacts only to sounds: He hears the noise that he believes to be his
wife hitting the water, and he hears her speak from the house. Tofano is
not described as seeing anything, a fact we can justify because we have
already been told it is very dark and because the woman would not be
visible as she hides near the door. But the situation is oddly asymmetri-
cal; the wife is privileged to do more than hear. She *sees* Tofano run to
the well; moreover, presumably because she can "see," she can threaten
to let everybody "see who [he] is and what time he comes home at
night." But presumably, if we were there looking out at the scene, we
would see very little; we would only hear. The question is whether we
would be in the position of Tofano, who hears sounds and is unable to
see, or in the position of the wife, who captures the position of she-who-
sees. It remains to be seen, of course, whether the other observers, the
neighbours at the windows, will manage to see. For the moment, we
know only that Lauretta tries to set up this internal audience as fair and

balanced, since the audience is composed of both men and women and since they ask for information before judging.

> La donna cominciò piagnendo a dire: "Egli è questo reo uomo, il quale mi torna ebbro la sera a casa o s'adormenta per le taverne e poscia torna a questa otta; di che io avendo lungamente sofferto e non giovandomi, non potendo più sofferire, ne gli ho voluta fare questa vergogna di serrarlo fuor di casa per vedere se egli se ne ammenderà."
>
> Tofano bestia, d'altra parte, diceva come il fatto era stato e minacciavala forte.
>
> La donna co' suoi vicini diceva: "Or vedete che uomo egli è! Che direste voi se io fossi nella via come è egli, e egli fosse in casa come sono io? In fé di Dio che io dubito che voi non credeste che egli dicesse il vero: ben potete a questo conoscere il senno suo! Egli dice a punto che io ho fatto ciò che io credo che egli abbia fatto egli. Egli mi credette spaventare col gittare non so che nel pozzo, ma or volesse Iddio che egli vi si fosse gittato da dovero e affogato, sì che egli il vino, il quale egli di soperchio ha bevuto, si fosse molto bene inacquato." (7.4.24–7)

In tears, the woman started out saying: "He's this wicked man, who comes back home to me drunk or he falls asleep in the taverns and then he comes home at this hour. I've put up with this for a long time without this doing any good, and since I'm not able to stand this any more, I decided to shame him by locking him out of the house to see if he'll mend his ways."

On the other hand, Tofano, the fool, said what had happened and threatened her loudly.

The woman, speaking with her neighbors, said: "Now you see what kind of man he is! What would you say if I were on the street like he is, and he were in the house as I am? By God, I wouldn't doubt that you could believe that he could be telling the truth. From this you can sure tell how intelligent he is! He says that I have done exactly what I believe he has done. He thought he could frighten me by throwing who knows what into the well, but now I wish to God that he had thrown himself in and drowned so that he could do a good job of watering down that wine that he drank too much of!"

Since Lauretta gives the woman ample space to communicate in direct discourse, we are able to see how expertly the woman controls her manifest lie. The verb *vedere* appears again, both as the woman claims to want to *see* the effects of her turning the tables on Tofano and as she invites the neighbours to *see* what sort of man he is. And before she tells her lie, she asks her neighbours what they "would say"; she tells them she does not doubt they could believe the husband's version to be true, and in doing so, she drops God's name. Her strategy is to convince them that she is not jumping to conclusions; rather, she (ever cognizant of a God that requires truth) is allowing her audience to consider all the information, including the possibility that she could be at fault, and reach a conclusion independently. Since hers is the language of possibility channelled towards a conclusion, her address to the neighbours contains multiple subjunctives (particularly in hypothetical clauses) and multiple instances of the verb "to believe" (*credere*).

If we are inclined to be impressed by this sort of skill and subtlety, we will side with the woman. In contrast, Tofano, who simply tells "what happened," is again labelled a fool. Since Tofano is given no direct discourse at this moment and we have no way of judging his version of events for ourselves, there is no way to tell whether the narrator is simply reiterating what she has already said or whether the narrator wants us to believe that Tofano is a fool for believing that a simple rendition of "what happened" will exonerate him.

One of the most peculiar features about this passage is the line "La donna co' suoi vicini diceva," which I have translated as "The woman, speaking with her neighbors, said."[15] All the translators normalize the phrase *co' suoi vicini diceva* by having the woman speak "to her neighbors." In my translation, I want to preserve something of the peculiarity created by the Italian preposition *con*, which most frequently means *with*, so I would want us to imagine the woman *amid* her neighbours. Thus, as the woman introduces her argument, her solidaristic tie with her neighbours is highlighted. Tofano is edged out even more, given that we never see "Tofano co' suoi vicini."

Now Lauretta brings her story to an end:

I vicini, e gli uomini e le donne, cominciaro a riprendere tututti Tofano e a dar la colpa a lui e a dirgli villania di ciò che contro alla donna diceva: e in brieve tanto andò il romore di vicino in vicino, che egli pervenne infino a' parenti della donna. Li quali venuti là, e udendo la cosa e da un vicino e da altro, presero Tofano e diedergli tante busse, che tutto il ruppono; poi, andati in casa, presero le cose della donna e con lei si ritornarono a casa loro minacciando Tofano di peggio. Tofano, veggendosi mal parato e che la sua gelosia l'aveva mal condotto, sì come quegli che tutto 'l suo bene voleva alla donna, ebbe alcuni amici mezzani; e tanto procacciò, che egli con buona pace riebbe la donna a casa sua, alla quale promise di mai più non esser geloso: e oltre a ciò le diè licenzia che ogni suo piacer facesse, ma sì saviamente, che egli non se ne avvedesse. E così, a modo del villan matto, dopo danno fé patto. E viva amore, e muoia soldo, e tutta la brigata. (7.4.28–31)

The neighbors, men and women alike, all started to criticize Tofano and to blame him and to curse him for what he said against the woman. In short, word traveled from neighbor to neighbor until it got to the woman's relatives. They came there, and hearing of this thing from one neighbor and then from another, they took hold of Tofano and gave him such a thrashing that they reduced him to a pulp. Then they went into the house, got the woman's things, and, with her, returned to their home, threatening Tofano with worse. Tofano, seeing himself in bad shape, and seeing that his jealousy had led him astray, got some friends who were go-betweens, for he was someone who loved that woman with all his being. He managed to get the woman back to his house, in peace, promising her that he would never be jealous again. And what's more, he gave her license to do as she pleased, but so judiciously that he would never notice. So like a dolt, he waited til the harm was done and then he made amends. Long live love, and down with money! And ditto the whole group!

Once the neighbours have entered the scene, there is a speedy, almost breathless, resolution and denouement. To ensure the virulence of the response against Tofano, Lauretta again reminds her audience that these neighbours, who all take issue with Tofano in a crescendo of verbal abuse, are a group of both men and women. Words, seeming to take on a life of their own, travel to those people whom Tofano had wanted to enlist in his cause, namely the woman's relatives, and the message is firmly aligned with the woman. When the relatives hear about this *thing*, again from more than one neighbour, there is no room for disagreement about what it is. Even though there are multiple reporters, there is no room for multiple versions of the thing that has happened.

Given that the woman's version of events has prevailed, Lauretta can allow Tofano to *see*: He *sees* that he is in bad shape, he *sees* that his jealousy has led him astray. At the same time, Lauretta masks the fact that Tofano fails to see the bigger picture, since he does not see what his wife has done to him, and he does not see how the blame for what has happened might be placed on something other than his own jealousy. Lauretta even tells us that Tofano will permit his wife to do as she pleases on the condition that he "not notice," *che non se ne avvedesse*. The choice of the verb *avvedersene* (to notice, to catch sight of, to realize), semantically related to the verb *vedere* ("to see"), draws attention to the fact that for Tofano, *seeing* means *not seeing*.

As I point out what Tofano doesn't notice, let me add that there are also things the *reader* might not notice. In fact, editors and translators, even though they mean well, may be helping the reader not to notice these things. The starkest example appears in Lauretta's parting line, "E viva amore, e muoia soldo, e tutta la brigata" (7.4.31). Here is how some of the translators have rendered this line into English:

So long live Love and death to war and all its company! (Payne)[16]

Now long live Love, and perish war, and all that wage it! (Rigg)[17]

Long life to love, and death to jealousy and all cuckolds! (Aldington)[18]

Hurrah for Love, then, and death to discord and the rest of its clan! (Winwar)[19]

So long live love, and down with greed, and good luck to all the company! (Ó Cuilleanáin)[20]

So long live Love and all our company and death to every tightwad! (Musa/Bondanella)[21]

Long live love, therefore, and a plague on all skinflints! (McWilliam)[22]

So three cheers for Love, and down with churls, skinflints, curmudgeons – and that goes for us too! (Waldman)[23]

One critic has called this a slip-up or blunder (*uno sproposito*) on Lauretta's part.[24] In a somewhat more positive vein, another critic has classified it as among the *Decameron*'s "snappy" conclusions that are loosely gnomic and disquieting ("le 'belle' conclusioni ambiguamente gnomiche e stranianti").[25] Possibly because it seems so baffling, the line was omitted from some early editions of the *Decameron*.[26]

All of the translators agree that Lauretta is cheering for Love to be long lived; but if one did not have access to the original Italian, it would be difficult indeed to figure out who or what is the target of her death curse. War and warriors (or discord more generally)? Jealousy? Greediness and stinginess, with some churls and curmudgeons thrown in for good measure? The trigger for trouble is the Italian word *soldo*, which appears in the phrase *muoia soldo*, "let *soldo* die!" Earlier translators, probably taking their cue from the single other use of *soldo* in the *Decameron*, focus on war and discord because "al soldo" is a term that designates mercenary soldiers.[27] More recently, translators have tended to understand *soldo* as avarice, greed, or stinginess, and they may extend this to mean people who are avaricious, greedy, or stingy.[28]

We find the next puzzle generated by the syntax of "Viva Amore, muoia soldo, e tutta la brigata." If we are translating word for word, we end up with something like "Long live love, let *soldo* die, and all the *brigata*!" Let all the *brigata* die? Could Lauretta be wishing death upon her own group, the honourable company of ten Florentines frequently referred to as the *onesta brigata*? The most prominent editor of the *Decameron* argues against such a grim thought; he offers that "naturalmente anche a *tutta la brigata* si riferisce l'iniziale *viva*" ("naturally, the initial *long live* refers also to *the whole group*").[29] Consistent with this view, Musa and Bondanella and Ó Cuilleanáin modify the syntax of the phrase so as to get the *brigata* away from the most proximate verb, *morire* (*to die*), and link it clearly to the first verb, *vivere* (*to live*). Some translators interpret the line to mean that Lauretta wishes ill not upon her fellow members of the *brigata* but rather upon anyone who keeps company with *soldo*, understood as discord, or jealousy, or stinginess. McWilliam chooses to avoid the problem by eliminating any reference to the *brigata*. Only Waldman accepts the ambiguity, felicitously rendered in his "So three cheers for Love, and down with churls, skinflints, curmudgeons – and that goes for us too!"

Waldman's solution strikes me as right. As a general rule, we should not assume that textual peculiarities should be normalized to conform to readers' expectations. And in this specific case, there is evidence that Lauretta is a narrator capable of committing such a gaffe. Martin Marafioti has argued that Lauretta functions as the "*brigata*'s bearer of bad news."[30] She is, according to Marafioti, the lone member of the group to disobey Pampinea's injunction against mentioning contemporary tragic events, when she introduces Monna Nonna de' Pulci as a Florentine woman whose life was taken by "questa pistolenzia presente" ("this current plague" [6.3.8]). Moreover, based on a review of selected stories by Lauretta, Marafioti sees her as "the voice of reality, no matter how bleak that may be in a context such as the plague of 1348," and as a voice that "anchors the *brigata* to the truth."[31]

This full translation of the novella brings us back to the retrospective look on Lauretta's contribution, which appears in the opening lines of the following novella:

> Posto aveva fine la Lauretta al suo ragionamento; e avendo già ciascun commendata la donna che ella bene avesse fatto e come a quel cattivo si conveniva, il re, per non perder tempo, verso la Fiammetta voltatosi, piacevolmente il carico le 'mpose del novellare. (7.5.2)

> Lauretta had brought her account to an end, and when everybody had praised the woman that she had done the right thing, and what that creep deserved, the king, so as not to waste time, turned to Fiammetta, and pleasantly imposed upon her the burden of storytelling.

Now that the novella is over, the Author of the *Decameron* uses a subtle recall of Dante to let us judge what Lauretta has done. As several scholars have pointed out, the phrasing of "Posto aveva fine la Lauretta al suo ragionamento" ("Lauretta had brought her account to an end") brings to mind the opening verses of *Purgatorio* 18:[32]

> Posto avea fine al suo ragionamento
> L'alto dottore, e attento guardava
> Ne la mia vista s'io parea contento
> > > (*Purgatorio* 18.1–3)[33]

> The eminent teacher had brought his account to an end, and he attended carefully to my eyes to see if I looked satisfied ...

As Francesco Tateo has shown, Boccaccio echoes Dante in order to show how Lauretta's views are diametrically opposed to Dante's ethically committed view of Love.[34] At the beginning of *Purgatorio* 18, Virgil, the eminent teacher, has just finished giving an account of the omnipresence and omnipotence of Love, and he has just finished explaining how Love, without error as a natural force, "puote errar per malo obietto o per troppo o per poco di vigore" ("can err owing to a bad object, or a drive that is either excessive or deficient" [*Purg.* 17.95–6]). And when

Virgil sees that Dante still has concerns, he goes on, in *Purgatorio* 18, to demonstrate both the ethical neutrality of the first impulses of love and our ethical responsibility to subject erotic instincts to the control of reason. Boccaccio, by recalling the first verses of *Purgatorio* 18, is suggesting that we think about the relation between Lauretta's and Dante's views of Love.

And we may be able to take this argument even a bit further, by looking not only at Lauretta but also at Dioneo, who turns to Fiammetta "per non perder tempo" ("so as not to waste time"). Why does Dioneo not wish to waste time? Wouldn't Dioneo, champion of leisure activities, be the single member of the group who might be in favour of wasting time?

The issue of wasting time takes us again to *Purgatorio* 17 and 18. These are the cantos of the Slothful, those who, on account of insufficient love, did not move as fast as they should have. Now, as a penance, the spirits are so anxious to advance that they are unable to halt. Perhaps Boccaccio is also recalling the Terrace of Sloth so that we think about the relation between Dioneo's and Dante's views of apathy and sluggishness?

I suppose this is possible, but given that I see the novella as raising questions about how hastily or meticulously we judge, I am inclined to ask instead whether "not wasting time" unfortunately means also "not stopping to reflect" and, conversely, whether a critical investigation into assertions like Lauretta's would be labelled a "waste" by those who did not wish to spend time on such intellectual and philosophical reflection.

On this point, a "maverick philosopher" named Bill Vallicella has had some very interesting things to say in his blog titled "On Wasting Time With Philosophy (And a Jab at Pascal)":

> People talk glibly about wasting time on this, that, and the other thing – but without reflecting on what it is to waste time. People think they know which activities are time-wasters, philosophy for example. But to know what wastes time, one would have to know what is a good, a non-wasteful, use of time. And one would presumably also have to know that one ought to use one's time well. One uses one's time well when one uses it in pursuit of worthy ends. But which ends are worthy? Does this question have an answer? Does it even make sense? And if it does, what sense does it make? And what is the answer? Now these are all philosophical questions.

Someone who holds that philosophy is a waste of time must therefore hold that these questions are a waste of time. He must simply and dogmatically assume answers to them. He must assume that the question about choice-worthy ends makes sense and has an answer. And he must assume that he has the answer. He must assume that he knows, for example, that piling up consumer goods, or chasing after name and fame, is the purpose of human existence. Or he must assume that getting to heaven, or bringing down capitalism, or "helping other people," is the purpose of human existence.[35]

Dante would appear to agree entirely, for on the Terrace of the Slothful, he does not have Virgil and Dante rushing along with the penitents; rather, he has them pause on their journey upward and take time to enter into a philosophical and ethical exchange about Love and free will. From Virgil, the pilgrim learns that the impulse to respond to pleasurable things is natural but must be controlled by the faculty of reason; objects of desire must be judged carefully to determine whether they are worthy.

Perhaps Dioneo is interested in having the group use their time well, but it is also conceivable that he considers any critical investigation of Lauretta's novella to be a waste of time, since such a critical investigation could lead the group to question Lauretta's black-and-white portrayal of Tofano and Ghita. Boccaccio's recall of the beginning of *Purgatorio* 18 is his way of sounding an alert: Yes, those who stop to question and to judge carefully could be accused of wasting time, but we should recognize that the accusation is unfounded.

What, then, does a story like *Decameron* 7.4 achieve as it both encourages a rush to judgment and reveals the precarious framework on which the hurried judgment is based? It tells us that if we are readers who want to rush to judge and want to learn those techniques by which we can avoid wasting time in ethical reflection, we should by all means read the story of Tofano and Ghita. The story will not stop us from rushing to judge; quite the contrary, it can offer lessons in how to distort information. If, on the other hand, we are readers who want to learn to think carefully before judging, the story of Tofano and Ghita is, once again, a story for us. In its subtler rhetorical moves, the story can point towards what gets glossed over in a rush to judgment.

As a result, we have to decide *before we begin reading the story* what our objective in reading is. Since each of the story's lessons could be described as "useful," everything turns on how we understand this "usefulness." Do we want to pursue utility by clever and self-serving means, or is our ultimate goal the pursuit of wisdom? The story will provide us with the answer we seek. The narrators of the *Decameron* are able to portray shrewdness and ingeniousness in appealing colours, but in the end, it falls to us to decide whether or not shrewdness and ingeniousness have been mobilized in the interest of the good we most desire.

6 New Lessons in Criticism and Blame from the *Decameron*

When we hear an opinion touted as gospel truth or rejected as utterly loathsome, when we get a report of something done well or something done badly, how careful are we to take measured account of the manner in which the information has been delivered to us? Are we confident we have enough information to pronounce praise or to blame?

The *Decameron* offers us a spectacular opportunity to witness how information can be expertly controlled. The narrators and the Author function as "filtering mechanisms." To the extent that any fictional construct can be said to choose, they make choices about what to report in direct discourse or indirect discourse. They represent thoughts that could belong to a given character, could belong to alternative publics, or could be some combination thereof. Such reporting happens with the greatest frequency when frametale narrators re-present a scene that has been imagined, heard about, read about, or actually witnessed. It also happens as the Author conveys the frametale narrators' reactions or tells us what the stories are about (as for example, in the Author's rubrics). There are plenty of other medieval literary texts that expertly control information – the French fabliaux provide some outstanding examples of this – but on account of its length and complexity, the *Decameron* provides an especially sustained reflection on the ethics of reporting.

I would like to draw our attention to a specific kind of reported event in the *Decameron*, namely, moments where a wife – most especially a wronged, virtuous wife – criticizes her husband for behaviour that a reader could objectively find blameworthy. Since the *Decameron*'s Author offers that women in love will be able to take useful advice and pleasure from his book, we are led to pause, almost inevitably, over instances where the woman reader could reasonably expect to find "advice about how to speak," most especially when a woman addresses a man whom she knows intimately and to whom she is joined by legal and perhaps emotional bonds. As I intend to show here, multiple voices from the *Decameron* come together in order to tell a story about how "good women" (which is to say women who are both virtuous and of elevated social standing) should speak when they have been aggrieved. The situation I describe has broader implications. It raises questions such as these: Can the less powerful ever really speak truth to power? Can they ever really name blameworthy behaviour as such? Finally, I shall ask us to reconsider how we, as critical readers of the *Decameron*, assign praise and blame, and I shall propose some strategies for "new lessons in criticism."

Among the wronged wives of the *Decameron*, perhaps none is more striking than Madonna Zinevra (2.9), whose denunciation of the injustices done to her emerges as the model against which all subsequent criticisms of husbands will be judged. Looking to Madonna Zinevra, we will gain a more accurate understanding of how a narrator can handle a situation in which a woman reprimands her husband. This in turn will shape our perceptions of how admirable or blameworthy she may be.

In the moment that interests us, Madonna Zinevra, disguised as Sicurano da Finale, stands in the presence of three other men: (1) the Sultan; (2) Ambrogiuolo, who has falsely claimed to have taken his pleasure with Zinevra, winning a bet against Zinevra's husband, Bernabò; and (3) Bernabò himself, who had ordered Zinevra killed and believes she is dead. Sicurano has already managed to have Ambrogiuolo tell his entertaining version of the story to the Sultan, and then to arrange a situation in which the Sultan forces Ambrogiuolo to tell the truth of the matter in the presence of Bernabò. Exactly what that truth is, we are not fully certain at first, since we learn only that Ambrogiuolo told all ("narrò ogni cosa" [2.9.60]). When Sicurano asks Bernabò, "E tu che facesti per questa bugia alla tua donna?" ("And what did you do to your wife on account of this lie?" [2.9.61]), we learn what the summary statement had stopped short of saying, namely, that Ambrogiuolo lied.

In exposing the lies about her, Zinevra demonstrates superb rhetorical control. It no doubt serves her well that she had begun speaking as Sicurano (i.e., as a man), in a public setting, and to a figure of authority.

In a single, skilfully crafted sentence, she labels each of the personages in the dramatic situation she has constructed: First she acknowledges the Sultan as her lord, then she identifies herself, then she identifies the perpetrator of the wrong done to her and the nature of the injury, and finally, she indicates the man who must be her husband, Bernabò, and the wrong he had committed against her:

> Signor mio, io sono la misera sventurata Zinevra, sei anni andata tapinando in forma d'uom per lo mondo, da questo traditor d'Ambrogiuol falsamente e reamente vituperata, e da questo crudele e iniquo uomo data a uccidere ad un suo fante e a mangiare a' lupi. (2.9.69)

> My lord, I am the poor unfortunate Zinevra, who spent six years wandering the world as a man, who was by this traitor Ambrogiuolo wrongly and maliciously dishonored, and who was by this cruel and unjust man given over to one of his servants to be killed and then eaten by wolves.

Throughout her eloquent condemnation of lies,[1] Madonna Zinevra refrains from identifying her husband by name or calling him a "murderer," though she does call him "cruel and unjust" ("crudele e iniquo"). This may indicate an unwillingness to assign to Bernabò the kind of blame that has been placed squarely on Ambrogiuolo, whose name appears prominently along with the designation of "traitor." This moment asks us to reflect on how we assign gradations of culpability. Is attempted murder a lesser offence than fraud and treachery? How does ordering someone's murder compare to providing false testimony that could lead to the ordering of someone's murder?

Thus far, Madonna Zinevra's speech is directed at the Sultan, so we have not yet seen anything like a direct reprimand of a guilty party. This changes when, with dramatic flair, Madonna Zinevra seals her statement with visual proof of her identity. Having proved that she is indeed a woman, she can now prove that Ambrogiuolo is the traitor she has claimed him to be:

> E stracciando i panni dinanzi e mostrando il petto, sé esser femina e al soldano e a ciascuno altro fece palese, rivolgendosi poi ad Ambrogiuolo, ingiuriosamente domandandolo quando mai, secondo che egli avanti si vantava, con lei giaciuto fosse; il quale, già riconoscendola e per vergogna quasi mutolo divenuto, niente dicea. (2.9.69)

[...] and ripping her clothes and baring her breast, she made it manifestly clear both to the sultan and to everyone else that she was a woman; turning then to Ambrogiuolo, with great indignation she asked him when, as he claimed previously, he had ever lain with her. Recognizing her and falling just about mute with shame, Ambrogiuolo said nothing.

Let us pause over the information that the narrator, Filomena, offers in indirect discourse: "ingiuriosamente domandandolo quando mai, secondo che egli avanti si vantava, con lei giaciuto fosse" ("with great indignation she asked him when, as he claimed previously, he had ever lain with her"). How might Madonna Zinevra have formulated her question to Ambrogiuolo? One possibility slips out of the indirect discourse. It is a shimmeringly elegant question, consisting of two septenaries cloaking a hendecasyllable: "Ambrogiuolo, quando mai, secondo che tu avanti ti vantavi, sei tu giaciuto con me?" (As for the shamed Ambrogiuolo's silence, we might reproduce it, as would Elsa Morante, with "! . . .") This, of course, assumes that we translate "ingiuriosamente" as "with great indignation" (as I have) or "scathingly" (as Guido Waldman translates it).[2] What if we render the word, as G.H. McWilliam does, as "haughtily"?[3] I could imagine Zinevra being haughty here – after all, she certainly has the right to be haughty, seeing how her virtuous behaviour gives her the upper hand. But what if we translate "ingiuriosamente," along with Mark Musa and Peter Bondanella, as "abusively"?[4] What if we understand "ingiuriosamente" to mean, as Fanfani does, "mescolando alla domanda parole d'ingiuria" ("mixing in with her question words of insult and injury")?[5] I admit that I would not like to think of Madonna Zinevra as "abusive." And I am not sure how much insult and injury we can imagine in her speech before she stops being Zinevra and becomes instead Bartolomea (2.10), or Catella (3.6), or Tessa, the wife of Calandrino (9.5).

The indirect discourse asks us not to think about Madonna Zinevra's language. Or rather, it asks us to believe what we may already be too willing to believe, namely, that whatever we imagine her to say is what she might actually have said. Indirect discourse can serve as a protective mechanism. It can allow for the possibility of insult and injury without ever tarnishing Madonna Zinevra's reputation with any undignified words.

In a later passage, Filomena again uses indirect discourse to describe a moment that some readers will have long awaited: the reconciliation of Madonna Zinevra and her husband. The Sultan orders that dresses and women's companions – both markers of femininity that must be present for the situation to right itself – be brought for Madonna Zinevra. Furthermore, Bernabò gets pardoned. Exactly what that pardon looks like should be of great interest to us:

> E, fattile venire onorevolissimi vestimenti femminili e donne che compagnia le tenessero, secondo la dimanda fatta da lei a Bernabò perdonò la meritata morte; il quale, riconosciutala, a' piedi di lei si gittò piagnendo e domandando perdonanza, la quale ella, quantunque egli mal degno ne fosse, benignamente gli diede, e in piede il fece levare, teneramente sì come suo marito abbracciandolo. (2.9.71)

> Having ordered fine dresses and women that could keep her company, in response to her request he pardoned Bernabò the death that he deserved. Bernabò, having recognized her, threw himself at her feet, weeping and asking forgiveness, which she kindly granted him, though he was not deserving of it; and she had him rise to his feet, where she tenderly embraced him as her husband.[6]

What precisely does Madonna Zinevra say when she advances her request? Could it be "Vi prego di perdonare mio marito" ("I beseech you to pardon my husband")? In that case, the comment about a death well deserved would be attributed to the narrator. Or might Madonna Zinevra herself recognize the gravity of Bernabò's crime, with a request such as "Vi prego di perdonare a mio marito la meritata morte?" ("I beseech you to pardon my husband the death that he deserves")?

Even more pressing would be the questions that arise when Zinevra forgives Bernabò "even though he didn't deserve it" ("quantunque egli maldegno ne fosse"). Is it conceivable that Zinevra would say to him "I forgive you even though you do not deserve it?" To whom should we attribute this comment? To Madonna Zinevra? To Bernabò? To the Sultan? To the narrator Filomena? Here, editorial interventions are telling. Although the original autograph text reveals no punctuation that would allow us to decide where to assign responsibility for this comment, editors in the sixteenth century intervene with punctuation in order to set the comment off as a parenthetical interpolation, thus encouraging us to read the comment as belonging to the narrator rather than to Zinevra. Representative is the following from a 1522 edition of the *Decameron*:

> secondo la domanda fatta dallei a Bernabo perdono la meritata morte. Il quale riconosciutala a piedi di lei si gitto piagnendo; & domando

perdonanza: la quale ella (quantunque egli mal degno ne fusse) benignamente gli diede.[7]

in response to her request he pardoned Bernabò the death that he deserved.
Bernabò, having recognized her, threw himself at her feet, weeping and
asking forgiveness, which (though he was not deserving of it) she tenderly
granted him.

Only by reflecting on the use of indirect discourse can we realize that
we never have to come to terms with what a Zinevra openly critical of
her husband would sound like. Would we agree with her particular
combination of disapproval and forgiveness? Would we find that she
strikes the right balance? The indirect discourse draws a veil over this,
simply reassuring us with its elegant formulations that a resolution has
been achieved.

Now let us look at another approach to criticism and blame, one from
which we are invited to distance ourselves. I am thinking of Catella
(3.6), who, believing that she has successfully substituted herself for
her husband's presumed lover, has sex in the dark with the man she
believes to be her husband and then proceeds to reveal her true identity
and to rail against him. (Unfortunately for Catella, the man she is rail-
ing against is Ricciardo, who has tricked her into this sexual encounter.)
Here is what Catella says:

Ahi quanto è misera la fortuna delle donne e come è male impiegato
l'amor di molte ne' mariti! Io, misera me, già sono otto anni, t'ho più che
la mia vita amato, e tu, come io sentito ho, tutto ardi e consumiti nello
amore d'una donna strana, reo e malvagio uom che tu se'. Or con cui ti
credi tu essere stato? Tu se' stato con colei la qual con false lusinghe tu hai,
già è assai, ingannata mostrandole amore ed essendo altrove innamorato.
Io son Catella, non son la moglie di Ricciardo, traditor disleale che tu se':
ascolta se tu riconosci la voce mia, io son ben dessa; e parmi mille anni che
noi siamo al lume, ché io ti possa svergognare come tu se' degno, sozzo
cane vituperato che tu se'. Oimè, misera me! a cui ho io cotanti anni por-
tato cotanto amore? A questo can disleale che, credendosi in braccio avere
una donna strana, m'ha più di carezze e d'amorevolezze fatte in questo
poco di tempo che qui stata son con lui, che in tutto l'altro rimanente che
stata son sua. Tu se' bene oggi, can rinnegato, stato gagliardo, che a casa
ti suogli mostrare così debole e vinto e senza possa! Ma, lodato sia Idio,

che il tuo campo, non l'altrui, hai lavorato, come tu ti credevi. Non mara-
viglia che stanotte tu non mi ti appressasti: tu aspettavi di scaricar le some
altrove e volevi giugnere molto fresco cavaliere alla battaglia: ma lodato sia
Idio e il mio avvedimento, l'acqua è pur corsa all'ingiù come ella doveva.
Ché non rispondi, reo uomo? ché non di' qualche cosa? Se' tu divenuto
mutolo udendomi? In fè di Dio io non so a che io mi tengo che io non ti
ficco le mani negli occhi e traggogliti! Credesti molto celatamente saper
fare questo tradimento? Par Dio! tanto sa altri quanto altri; non t'è venuto
fatto, io t'ho avuti miglior bracchi alla coda che tu non credevi. (3.6.33–8)

Oh, how wretched is women's lot! How thankless is the love that many of
them have for their husbands! Me – wretched me! – for eight years now
I have loved you more than my life itself, and you, as I've heard, are completely consumed with passion for another woman, evil and wicked man
that you are! Now who do you think you've been with? You've been with
the woman you have been deceiving with bogus flattery for quite some
time, exhibiting love for her when all the time you were enamored elsewhere. I am Catella, I am not Ricciardo's wife, you dishonest traitor that
you are. Listen – do you recognize my voice? It really is me. I can't wait
until we're out of here so that I can shame you the way you deserve, dirty
shameful dog that you are. Oh, wretched me! Who have I loved for all these
years? This dishonest dog who, thinking he had another woman in his
arms, offered me more caresses and affection in this little bit of time that I've
been here with him than in all the rest of the time that I was his. Today, you
two-timing dog, you were daring and bold, while at home you prove feeble
and defeated and lifeless. But praise be to God that it was your own field,
not someone's else's, that you were plowing, contrary to what you thought!
It's no surprise that you didn't come near me last night! You were waiting
to unload yourself elsewhere, and you wanted to be a fully rested knight
entering the battlefield. But praise be to God and to my keen foresight, the
water ended up running down the way it was supposed to! How come you
don't answer, you wicked man? How come you aren't saying anything?
Have you become mute as you've been listening to me? By God, I don't
know what's keeping me back from sticking my fingers into your eyes and
tearing them out! You thought you would know how to keep this affair
secret? By God, other people know how things work too. It didn't turn out
as you expected – I had better hounds on your tail than you thought.

While the first words out of Catella's mouth could have been spoken by Madonna Zinevra, the resemblance between these "virtuous

wives" soon starts to look shaky. That double repetition of "misera" ("quanto è misera la fortuna delle donne ...! ... Io, misera me! ...") forecasts the excess that will soon be evident. The attack turns exceedingly vicious and vulgar. Catella relies on pounding repetitions and frequent jabbing monosyllables (with a particular emphasis on the pronoun "tu" with which she addresses him). Harsh dental consonants *t* and *d* reinforce the sense of attack. She moves from calling him "evil and wicked man that you are" to "dishonest traitor that you are" to "dirty shameful dog that you are" to "dishonest dog," "two-timing dog," and "wicked man" ("reo e malvagio uom che tu se'," "traditor disleale che tu se'," "sozzo cane vituperato che tu se'," "questo can disleale," "can rinnegato," "reo uomo"). This moment is presumably about self-revelation and intended to shame a wayward husband by making him see that he has had sex with his own wife while believing he was having sex with another woman. But Catella goes beyond naming him a wrongdoer (as does Zinevra with her husband in 2.9 and as the wife of Guglielmo Rossiglione will do with her husband in 4.9); she descends into name-calling. This attempt to define Filippello soon proves to be her greatest blunder. As Catella attacks Filippello for his sexual shortcomings over the eight years she has been with him – shortcomings redressed in the encounter she has just had – she reveals her own sexual frustration and gives Ricciardo hope he can indeed win her over.

Nor does Catella's self-revelation stop here. After a brief interlude in which Fiammetta represents Ricciardo's pleasure at hearing this ("in se medesimo godeva di queste parole" [3.6.39]) and in which she calls attention to Ricciardo's pleasuring of Catella ("e senza rispondere alcuna cosa l'abbracciava e basciava, e più che mai le facea le carezze grandi" [3.6.39]), Catella is given yet another long speech, in which she continues the name-calling, in which she repeats that Filippello has performed sexually beyond what is usually the case for him, in which she threatens Filippello with public shaming, and in which she concludes by saying that perhaps it would not be so bad after all if she were to take up with Ricciardo, who has always loved her. This speech reinforces our perception that (1) Catella has a few notes that she sounds insistently, and (2) the more she rants, the more she will reveal information that will undermine her authority.

This is the first time in the story that we hear Catella speak at any length, so we might assume that this is the only register available to her. Yet in her final speech, delivered after she is stunned to discover the identity of the man she has been with, she strikes a different tone:

> Ricciardo, io non so come Domenedio mi si concederà che io possa comportare la 'ngiuria e lo 'nganno che fatto m'hai. Non voglio gridar qui, dove la mia simplicità e soperchia gelosia mi condusse, ma di questo vivi sicuro, che io non sarò mai lieta se in un modo o in un altro io non mi veggio vendica di ciò che fatto m'hai; e per ciò lasciami, non mi tener più: tu hai avuto ciò che disiderato hai e ha'mi straziata quanto t'è piaciuto. Tempo hai di lasciarmi; lasciami, io te ne priego. (3.6.47–8)

> Ricciardo, I do not know how the lord God will grant me the ability to withstand the injury and the deception you have perpetrated on me. I do not wish to scream here, where my foolishness and excessive jealousy have brought me, but be certain of this: that I shall never be content if, in one way or another, I do not see myself avenged of what you have done to me. And so leave me, let me go. You have gotten what you longed for and you have tormented me as much as you liked. It is time for you to leave me; leave me, I beg of you.

Now we have evidence that Catella is capable of delivering a composed and deliberate speech. The string of septenaries and hendecasyllables at the conclusion of this speech renders it elegant and memorable. Even more stunning is the mournful lamenting sound "ai" that sounds repeatedly, particularly at the end of sentences. Catella is saying "hai" (i.e., "you have" done this or that), but the effect on the listener is also to register "ahi!", an exclamation that in Italian would be pronounced the same way. What if Catella had begun her earlier speech with a phrase like, "Filippello, io non so come Domenedio mi si concederà che io possa comportare la 'ngiuria che fatto m'hai" ("Filippello, I do not know how the lord God will grant me the ability to withstand the injury and the deception you have perpetrated on me")? Would she have descended as easily into name-calling? I suspect not. Rather, an exordium like this would more likely have led into an elegant hendecasyllable like "ha'mi straziata quanto t'è piaciuto" ("you have tormented me as much as you liked") and, in closing, to polished double septenaries, marked by a poignant chiasmus: "Tempo hai di lasciarmi: lasciami io te ne priego" ("It is time for you to leave me; leave me, I beg of you" [3.6.48]).

And what do we make of the fact that, when Catella actually has her chance to call Ricciardo a fraudulent rapist, she does not do so? It is as if

Catella has used up all her rhetorical weaponry and is no longer able to apply to Ricciardo all the epithets she hurled at him when she thought he was Filippello. This affects the reader's perception of him. If Catella doesn't find it within herself to call him a dirty dog, can we?

But Catella may not be the only person protecting Ricciardo from criticism. The narrator of the story, Fiammetta, by means of her selective use of direct and indirect discourse, can also shape our reaction.

When Ricciardo reveals himself to Catella, Fiammetta gives us the entire text of his speech. Already from the opening lines, we see his rhetorical power: "Anima mia dolce, non vi turbate: quello che io semplicemente amando aver non potei, Amor con inganno m'ha insegnato avere, e sono il vostro Ricciardo" ("Sweet darling, don't be upset. What I could not have simply by loving, Love taught me to have by deception, and I am your Ricciardo" [3.6.42]). From the opening phrased as a hendecasyllable ("Anima mia dolce, non vi turbate") to the closing septenary ("sono il vostro Ricciardo"), this statement is remarkable for its mellifluous sophistication. As Ricciardo proceeds to demonstrate that what has happened cannot be otherwise, and as he asserts that Catella has no recourse to justice, he reveals a full arsenal of literary, historical, and judicial weaponry. Multiple footnotes alert us to the sources for his argumentation: Livy, Valerius Maximus, and a range of passages in Boccaccio's earlier works.[8] The direct discourse asks us to consider the basis for his authority.

But when Ricciardo responds to Catella's threat of retaliation, Fiammetta opts for indirect discourse:

> Ricciardo, che conoscea l'animo suo ancora troppo turbato, s'avea posto in cuore di non lasciarla mai se la sua pace non riavesse: per che, cominciando con dolcissime parole a raumiliarla, tanto disse e tanto pregò e tanto scongiurò, che ella, vinta, con lui si pacificò ... (3.6.49)

> Ricciardo, who saw that she was still very agitated, had made up his mind not ever to leave her until he reconciled with her. So, beginning by placating her with sweet words, he spoke at length and pleaded at length and appealed at length, with the result that she, defeated, made peace with him.

Ricciardo has already exerted control over Catella by putting his hand over her mouth, and he has already stated that she has no recourse other than to accept him as a lover. What could he possibly say to pacify her? Why is his speech not rendered with direct discourse? I think it is because, no matter what Ricciardo says – and it clearly was quite a bit – we would not look kindly upon his arguments. If, in reading "tanto disse e tanto pregò e tanto scongiurò" ("he spoke at length and pleaded at length and appealed at length" [3.6.49]), we imagine the progression that could be required if Catella were to mount resistance, it would have to look something like "tanto disse e tanto pregò e tanto scongiurò e tanto implorò e tanto esortò e tanto invocò e tanto impetrò e tanto sollecitò e tanto supplicò" ("he spoke at length and pleaded at length and appealed at length and implored at length and exhorted at length and invoked at length and importuned at length and solicited at length and beseeched at length"). In the final accounting it is better – better for Ricciardo, that is – to leave his exact words cloaked in mystery.

The story of Catella and Ricciardo, along with the story of Madonna Zinevra, shows that if we wish to position ourselves to make informed judgments, we must be aware of how the information we receive – and the form in which we receive it – will affect our judgment. Direct and indirect discourse can be used selectively to solicit approval (even if tacit) or blame. We would do well to remember these lessons from literature every time we ourselves report events to others and every time we listen to the accounts others offer us.

I have long maintained that we must attend not only to single exemplary moments that invite praise or blame but also to the dialogue among the narrators that emerges as they are drawn to certain narrative moments, pause over them, draw out the narrative possibilities, contest the conclusions that others draw, and use the stories as means of exploring ways of being in the world.[9] Many are the questions that the stories of Zinevra and Catella pose, so I cannot in good faith claim that the story I am about to tell you is the lone one. I urge readers to consider what other stories there may be. As for myself, when I begin with the story of a virtuous wife who responds to the husband who has wronged her, and when I begin to examine other wives who respond to husbands who are blameworthy, this is what I hear:

Against the bet of a man like Ambrogiuolo and in a certain sense against all odds, Madonna Zinevra upholds ideals of loyalty, resourcefulness, prudence, foresight, and commitment to the truth. When she defends herself and exposes the wrongdoing of others, she does so in a language that is presented as above reproach. With Zinevra, the narrators will begin in earnest a series of reflections about marital fidelity, about women's abilities, about their right to self-assertion, about their use of deception, and about the strategies a wife might use to criticize blameworthy behaviour in her husband. How legitimate is the kind of deception that Zinevra uses to unearth Ambrogiuolo's deceptions? How realistic is it to expect women to respond to adversity as she does? (Just for starters, how many women can go about for six years dressed as men? What if you don't happen to have collegial relations with a wealthy ruler outside the Western legal system? And how deep do the wells of forgiveness run if your husband has ordered you killed and left as repast for the wolves?)

Upon hearing the story of Bernabò and Zinevra, Dioneo attacks Bernabò for his foolishness; Dioneo then tells of Bartolomea of Pisa, who advocates rights to sexual fulfilment that her husband Ricciardo Chinzica has denied her. Extraordinarily important, as Mario Baratto has shown, is the moment when Bartolomea quite unexpectedly becomes the arbiter of the situation. She vituperates against her husband for his pitiful sexual performance. Dioneo's story turns on the question of male sexuality: If you're a real man, unlike Ricciardo, you'll remember that women need to be satisfied, and you won't try to advertise your abilities beyond what they are. The narrators – all of them – laugh. They approve of Dioneo's story and agree with Dioneo that Bernabò was a fool. As for what they now think of Zinevra, we are not told. The question arises, however: Was Zinevra also a fool? Should she have acted and spoken like Bartolomea?

Catella (3.6) is the next woman to assert herself as a wronged wife. She does so by bringing to light her husband's failings. In fact, we have every reason to believe that Catella will triumph, since she has the scales of the literary tradition tipped in her favour. In the sources and analogues for *Decameron* 3.6, when a woman sets out to expose her husband's infidelities and seeks to do so by trapping him with a bed trick, she is generally guaranteed success.[10] In some stories, even when she is an equally guilty partner, she substitutes herself for the woman with whom her husband believes he is having sex, and when she angrily confronts him, the shamed husband learns his lesson. In "Le Meunier d'Arleux" ("The Miller of Arleux"), the fabliau often considered to be Boccaccio's direct source, the wife successfully substitutes herself for the other woman, and her husband ends up acting as his own pimp when he allows another man to have sex with her too. Boccaccio has Fiammetta, the narrator of Catella's story, turn all this on its head. The literary tradition might say one thing, but *Decameron* 3.6 shows us that things don't always work out for the wife who wishes to expose her husband's infidelities, no more than things work out for a man like Ambrogiuolo who wishes at all cost to broadcast that women are unfaithful. When Catella finds herself in the darkened room, all the literary and historical narratives that put the wife in control get lost. What is foregrounded is Catella's excess in her attack on her husband. And superimposed on the narratives of faithful wives who seek to teach their wayward husbands a lesson is a narrative of a faithful wife who maintains her own (and her husband's) honour: Lucretia. Lucretia takes the sword to herself. Now Catella is in a bind. The literary tradition predicts success; the narrative about Lucretia tells us that a suicide could be in the making. As it turns out, in the *Decameron*, the result is neither self-assertion nor suicide, but making do. For Catella, that means accepting failure and humiliation, accepting her own excesses, and accepting that hers is a society that will not recognize the wrong done to her.

In the wake of *Decameron* 3.6, the narrators work off two possibilities: the wronged wife as played by Madonna Zinevra (who is a difficult exemplar to criticize, even though her kindness towards a husband who tried to kill her does strike some of us as inexplicable) and the wronged wife as played by Catella (who displays a kind of excess that we are invited to condemn, even if we know she has been duped by Ricciardo). These are not the only two possibilities the world offers us, of course, but the fact is that the narrators of the *Decameron* – like people in general – tend to work off binaries like this.

Neifile, the Queen of Day 3, is the first to take up the challenge presented by Zinevra and Catella. In *Decameron* 3.9, her female protagonist Giletta di Narbona appears as a redeemed blend of those earlier wives. Not to be deterred by a husband (Beltramo) who sets her aside, Giletta successfully conceals her identity, substitutes herself for a woman with whom Beltramo intends to have sex, and succeeds in fulfilling the ostensibly impossible conditions he himself has established: She acquires Beltramo's ring and bears his offspring.

At pains to render Giletta a wronged virtuous wife, Neifile describes the sexual encounter between Giletta and Beltramo in a most summary fashion. Once another woman arranges for Giletta to lie with the count, this is what we are told:

Ne' quali primi congiugnimenti affettuosissimamente dal conte cercati, come fu piacer di Dio, la donna ingravidò in due figliuoli maschi, come il parto al suo tempo venuto fece manifesto. Né solamente d'una volta contentò la gentil donna la contessa degli abbracciamenti del marito ma molte, sì segretamente operando che mai parola non se ne seppe, credendosi sempre il conte non con la moglie ma con colei la quale egli amava essere stato; a cui, quando a partire si venia la mattina, avea parecchi belle e care gioie donate, le quali tutte diligentemente la contessa guardava. (3.9.49)

In these first embraces most affectionately sought out by the count, as it pleased God, the woman conceived two sons, as their birth later made evident. The noblewoman arranged for the countess to enjoy the embraces of her husband not only once, but many times. The whole matter was managed so secretly that no word was ever known about it, and the count believed unwaveringly that he was not with his wife but with the woman he loved. When he had to leave her in the morning, he presented her with a number of beautiful and precious jewels, all of which the countess preserved most carefully.

We might not find this exercise of discretion strange but for the fact that, up until now in the novella, Giletta has been doing quite a bit of talking in direct discourse, mainly to other women who will provide her with necessary support for her plan to win back her husband. By drawing a veil over Giletta and Beltramo's sexual encounters, Neifile neatly circumvents the problem of what they might be saying to each other. There is no risk that Giletta could sound like a woman of whom an audience could disapprove.[11]

Our lasting memory of Giletta, then, comes near the very end of the story when, dressed as a pilgrim and carrying her two children, she re-enacts a version of a plea to authority that readers will recognize as Zinevra's:

E sentendo le donne e' cavalieri nel palagio del conte adunati per dovere andare a tavola, senza mutare abito, con questi suoi figlioletti in braccio salita in su la sala, tra uomo e uomo là se n'andò dove il conte vide, e gittataglisi a' piedi disse piagnendo: "Signor mio, io sono la tua sventurata sposa, la quale, per lasciar te tornare e stare in casa tua, lungamente andata son tapinando. Io ti richeggio per Dio che le condizioni postemi per li due cavalieri che io ti mandai, tu le mi osservi: e ecco nelle mie braccia non un sol figliuol di te, ma due, ed ecco qui il tuo anello. Tempo è adunque che io debba da te sì come moglie esser ricevuta secondo la tua promessa." (3.9.57–8)

Hearing that the ladies and knights had gathered in the count's palace and were ready to dine, she went forward – in the clothes she was wearing and with these children of hers in her arms – to the head of the room when she saw the count. Then, crying, she threw herself at his feet and said, "My lord, I am your unfortunate bride, who has long gone wandering through the world in order to allow you to return and remain in your home. I ask, by God, that you respect the conditions placed on me by the two knights I sent to you. Behold here in my arms not one but two children by you, and behold here your ring. The time has come therefore that I should be received as your wife, as you promised."

In passages preceding and following this one, Neifile refers insistently to Giletta as the "countess" ("contessa" [3.9.60]), reminding us that Giletta is Beltramo's legitimate spouse. Giletta reaffirms her own parity with Beltramo when she addresses him with the informal second-person singular even as she calls him her "lord." Like Zinevra, whose words she echoes, Giletta remains humble supplicant, and like Zinevra, she receives new clothes and a sumptuous celebratory feast. Giletta, also like Zinevra, mutes her criticism of a husband who has not acted very admirably. As for the aspects of Zinevra's behaviour that could raise eyebrows, Neifile deftly transforms them. There is no cross-dressing, no ripping open a bodice to reveal breasts. Rather, "proof" of Giletta's femininity is displaced onto the twins she holds in her arms even as she throws herself dramatically at Beltramo's feet.

Up until this point, I have provided textual examples of women who criticize men in indirect or direct discourse and in oblique or abusive language, as the case may be. I have not yet broached the issue of the women's class or social standing. That is because I believe that for the first third of the *Decameron*, while we are encouraged to believe that women who are truly classy will speak only in the most oblique of terms – witness, for example, the message sent by marchioness of Monferrato with her all-chicken banquet in *Decameron* 1.5 – we are not yet encouraged to believe that abusive language is a marker of the lower-class woman. Beginning with Day 4 of the *Decameron*, however, women of confirmed social standing do not criticize their husbands (or anybody else who is trying to act like a husband or even a prospective husband) in abusive language. If these women of the upper class criticize at all, as do Ghismonda in 4.1 (told by Fiammetta) and the wife of Guglielmo Rossiglione in 4.9 (told by Filostrato), they exit this life soon afterwards. Or, like Madonna Sismonda of 7.8 (told by Neifile), they benefit from the presence of a surrogate who can deliver a vituperative speech against the husband.[12] Or, like Monna Giovanna of 5.9 (told by Fiammetta), they pull their punches by blaming first (though not in direct discourse we could examine) and then offering extensive praise (granted, again, in indirect discourse).

The case of Federigo degli Alberighi and Monna Giovanna is worth a second look, even though they are not yet married when they exchange some crucial words. In the following passage, narrated by Fiammetta, Federigo degli Alberighi proves to Giovanna that she has indeed eaten his beloved falcon, which he has killed and served to her because he had nothing else to offer, and she responds to him:

> E questo detto, le penne e' piedi e 'l becco le fé in testimonianza di ciò gittare avanti. La qual cosa la donna vedendo e udendo, prima il biasimò d'aver per dar mangiare a una femina ucciso un tal falcone, e poi la grandezza dell'animo suo, la quale la povertà non avea potuto né potea rintuzzare, molto seco medesima commendò. (5.9.37)

> Having said this, he had the feathers and the feet and the beak thrown before her as proof. The woman, upon seeing and hearing this, blamed him at first for having killed such a falcon in order to give it to a mere female to eat, and then, to herself, she greatly praised the nobility of his soul, which poverty had not blunted and which it would never be able to blunt.

As we shall see, this passage is doing a good deal to bolster the courtesy and good manners of both Federigo degli Alberighi and Monna Giovanna.

A potential challenge to courtesy and good manners is presented by Federigo's gesture, which follows a most elegantly phrased justification for his being without a falcon that Giovanna now requests as a gift. Having the leftover body parts of his falcon thrown before her "as proof" seems openly aggressive but for the fact that the body parts stand as testimony to his just-concluded courteous statement. We would do well to ask how, exactly, the feathers and feet and beak "get thrown down." Does Federigo do it himself, and much more nicely, as Musa and Bondanella assert when they translate "And after he had said this, he laid the feathers, the feet, and beak of the bird before her as proof?"[13] Was it that he "caused the feathers, talons, and beak to be cast on the table before her," as McWilliam tells us?[14] If Federigo directs a servant to bring out the bird's remains, it seems improbable that a servant would, without specific orders from Federigo, choose to "throw" them before Monna Giovanna. But then, given what we know about Federigo, it also is hard for us to accept that Federigo would tell a servant "Have the feathers and the feet and beak thrown before her as proof of this" ("le penne e' piedi e 'l becco le farai in testimonianza di ciò gittare avanti"). Given contradictory bits of evidence, many readers will eliminate details that do not conform to their assumptions.

Another potential challenge to courtesy and good manners is posed by Monna Giovanna, whose first response is to blame. Multiple rhetorical features of this passage lead us to see her as justified in her attack on Federigo or as not really attacking him at all. First, if she is being excessive, perhaps it is only in response to Federigo's barely hidden aggression. Second, she denigrates herself as a "mere female" at the same time she blames Federigo. Third, as several other readers of this passage have pointed out to me, if we imagine Giovanna to have said something like "Really, you shouldn't have!", her reproach to Federigo could have the rhetorical force of a move to console him.[15] Finally, her blame is counterbalanced by what seems (particularly given the syntax and metrical rhythms of the Italian) a lengthy moment of praise.

What is most curious about this passage is that it encourages us to see the praise cancelling out any possible blame. This is true for Federigo, whose courteous speech, delivered in direct discourse just before he has pieces of his bird thrown before Monna Giovanna, seems to guarantee that readers will not look unkindly on him. For Federigo, it appears that words speak louder than actions, perhaps because the words were rendered at length in direct discourse. And we find that Monna Giovanna receives similar protection. She delivers a reproach but manages, thanks to a round of praise she does not even deliver out loud, to emerge untainted by the ungraciousness that can easily earn a woman harsh criticism, at least in the *Decameron*. For Monna Giovanna, it appears that mentally articulated words speak louder than words that are verbalized, perhaps because the mentally articulated words appear in a climactic moment of a lengthy sentence.

Once the *Decameron*'s narrators make sure that upper-class women have renounced any claim on the abusive language of Bartolomea and Catella, that abusive language becomes the inheritance of women from whom the frametale narrators can distance themselves. It is a language that belongs to a comic register such as we find in the stories of Calandrino. When Tessa, Calandrino's wife, finds him with another woman (Niccolosa) in 9.5, she gets her nails into his face and screams:

> Sozzo can vituperato, dunque mi fai tu questo? Vecchio impazzato, che maladetto sia il ben che io t'ho voluto: dunque non ti pare aver tanto a fare a casa tua, che ti vai innamorando per l'altrui? Ecco bello innamorato! Or non ti conoscì tu, tristo? Non ti conosci tu, dolente? che premendoti tutto, non uscirebbe tanto sugo che bastasse a una salsa. Alla fé di Dio, egli non era ora la Tessa quella che ti 'mpregnava, che Dio la faccia trista chiunque ella è, ché ella dee ben sicuramente esser cattiva cosa a aver vaghezza di così bella gioia come tu se'! (9.5.63–4)

> You dirty rotten dog, this is what you do to me? You crazy old fool – damn the love that I've felt for you! So you didn't think you had enough to do at home so you went around falling in love elsewhere! There's a fine lover boy! Now don't you see what you're doing, you twerp? You don't, you miserable creep? If you got squeezed dry, there wouldn't be enough juice to make a sauce. By God, it wasn't Tessa who got you pregnant, and god-dam whoever she is, because she really must be a piece of trash to take a fancy to a fine jewel like you!

Tessa seizes upon a vituperative language used by Bartolomea and Catella in private conversation with their husbands and showers it on Calandrino in a more public setting, where four other people (Niccolosa, Bruno, Buffalmacco, Filippo) serve as witnesses. As the four spectators laugh, open criticism of a husband is reinforced as a marker of lower-class behaviour.[16]

At the end of Day 10, there appears a twofold "solution" to the problems raised by the prospect of wives criticizing their husbands. The first solution is Panfilo's, and it appears in 10.9, the story of Messer Torello and his wife Adalieta (10.9), which can be seen as the first of two conclusions to the storytelling.[17] Panfilo renders Adalieta an exemplary wife to a husband who is above reproach.[18] At least when people behave in ways we recognize as exemplary, we can avoid instances where husbands act badly or wives speak badly about them.[19]

Then, in the very final story of the series, Dioneo offers a striking solution to the problem of critical wives. At a crucial moment in this novella, Griselda – the lower-class woman who has been cruelly tested by her upper-class husband, Gualtieri – is invited by him to comment on his new bride. Griselda offers a criticism that masks its status as criticism. Recognizing the superiority of her muted response, Gualtieri then reinstates her as a wife worthy of him. The passage reads as follows:

... in presenza d'ogni uomo sorridendo le disse: "Che ti par della nostra sposa?"

"Signor mio," rispose Griselda "a me ne par molto bene; e se così è savia come ella è bella, che 'l credo, io non dubito punto che voi non dobbiate con lei vivere il più consolato signor del mondo; ma quanto posso vi priego che quelle punture, le quale all'altra, che vostra fu, già deste, non diate a questa, ché appena che io creda che ella le potesse sostenere, sì perché più giovane è e sì ancora perché in dilicatezze è allevata, ove colei in continue fatiche da piccolina era stata."

Gualtieri, veggendo che ella fermamente credeva costei dovere esser sua moglie, né per ciò in alcuna cosa men che ben parlava, la si fece sedere allato e disse: "Griselda, tempo è omai che tu senta frutto della tua lunga pazienzia, e che coloro li quali me hanno reputato crudele e iniquo e bestiale conoscano che ciò che io faceva a antiveduto fine operava, volendoti insegnare d'esser moglie e a loro di saperla tenere, e a me partorire perpetua quiete mentre teco a vivere avessi ... (10.10.58–60)

... in the presence of all, he smiled and said, "What opinion do you have of our bride?"

"My lord," replied Griselda, "my opinion is very positive, and if she is as wise as she is beautiful, which I believe she is, I do not doubt at all that you will live with her as the happiest man in the world. But I beg you, as much as I can, that you not inflict on her the wounds you inflicted on that other woman, who was once yours, for I hardly believe that she would be able to bear them, because she is younger and also because she was brought up in great comfort, whereas the other woman had been in continuous hardship from the time she was a small child."

When Gualtieri saw that she firmly believed that the girl was to be his wife, and this notwithstanding, she said nothing but good, he had her sit beside him and said, "Griselda, it is now time that you should reap the fruit of your long patience, and it is time for those who have considered me cruel, unjust, and brutish to realize that what I did was directed toward a foreseen goal, given that I wanted to teach you how to be a wife, to show those other people how to handle a wife, and to create for myself perpetual serenity for as long as I should live with you ...

Griselda abstracts herself from her own material experience by speaking about herself in the third person. Thus, if there is any discontent to be registered, it is displaced onto that "other woman," and the offence to Griselda is unrecognizable. She is the lower-class woman *who shows the upper-class woman how to speak.*[20]

Or does she? Is Griselda (like Zinevra before her) put forward as a model of how women should respond to objectively blameworthy behaviour in their husbands? Or is she (like Zinevra before her) meant to show us what women (and like them, anyone who wields less power) end up having to tolerate?

Praise or blame? That is the question before us. It is a question that Boccaccio posed repeatedly throughout the *Decameron* and, indeed, throughout his career. It is a question we find ourselves grappling with repeatedly as we read the *Decameron* and other of Boccaccio's works. It is – as I have argued elsewhere – a question that threatens us with critical impasse, since we can find ourselves getting nowhere as we take sides about who to praise and who to blame.[21] So Petrarch and others in his wake found nothing but praise for Griselda's patience. Women today are likely to offer nothing but resistance to Griselda's example. Are we simply condemned to a cycle where, based on our own shifting values over time, we are destined to praise or blame the "virtuous wives" of the *Decameron*?

To attempt to answer this question, I would like to modulate our methodologically aware and critical voices towards a voice that overlaps more with the pronouncements of the *Decameron*'s non-analytic (and critical) wives.

In examining the story of Griselda, I have been struck by how much people seem to relish retelling it, and in particular how much they seem to relish retelling the scene I have just cited. I am referring not only to Petrarch, Chaucer, and other such writers, whose retellings can be found in the Rare Book rooms of our research libraries. I am referring also to people whose retellings can be found on personal websites and in other such arenas. Readers appear fascinated by a moment of "criticism and blame" that is barely recognizable as such. They assume the voices of Gualtieri and Griselda. They re-enact the scene. They editorialize. They explore motivation and intention. They appear to take considerable pleasure in doing so.

Here is one of the most engaging renditions I have found:

She's lost her children, remember: she thinks he murdered them. In fact, he merely took them away and had them raised secretly [*sic*] in Bologna, and now the boy is six and the daughter twelve, and he arranges it so the daughter, his daughter by Griselda, is brought ceremoniously into town as the young bride-to-be.

So Grisdelda's [sic] standing quietly by in her crummy rags and Gualtieri asks her what she thinks of his beautiful young thing, the next Mrs. Gualtieri.

... "Oh, my lord," she says. "She seems very beautiful to me. And if she is as wise as beautiful, I have no doubt that you will live with her as the happiest lord in the world."

And here she does get in a word. (Trumpets! stuffed with rags for mutes) She doesn't quite chide him, but she reflects so as to protect the young bride. Please don't treat this one as you did your last wife, she says. That woman (herself, in third person) was tough, raised tough from the start – a peasant after all. This lovely one is so young, and has obviously been brought up "... in a more delicate fashion."

The Marquis is so pleased now that he begins to fess up: Now's the time for you to reap the fruit of your long patience, he tells her. And for everyone to realize that he had always had a plan – he wasn't really cruel as some might think. "For I wanted to teach you how to be a wife, and to show these people how to know such a wife and how to choose and keep one, and to acquire for myself lasting tranquility for as long as I was to live with you." He's not a big risk-taker. At the very outset, he says, he was afraid she'd screw up his tranquility, so he tested her. And now she's passed with flying colors.

And then he has her reinstated, introduces her to her 12 year old daughter and 6 year old son, sets them straight on who she is, sets up her poor old dad in a manner he'd never dreamed of, and everyone is really, really happy.[22]

This passage is doing some very curious work. Adopting a complicit tone with us, the narrator sets out the details we need to remember as we witness the dialogue between Gualtieri and Griselda. Then the narrator pauses over three sections of the story: Griselda's statement, in which open acceptance and oblique criticism coexist; Gualtieri's response, in which open self-justification and oblique awareness coexist; and a speedy rush to the happiest of endings (lest such an ending escape us). It seems manifest that the narrator is on Griselda's side. S/he evokes sympathy for what we would imagine to be Griselda's emotions and her physical condition. S/he celebrates (if in muted fashion) any attempt on Griselda's part to stand up to Gualtieri. Gualtieri's assertions to the contrary, the narrator leads us to see him as both cruel and capricious.

A reader might object that it would now be relatively easy to create a space for an ironic reading of a character like Griselda. After all, haven't many readers in the last thirty years been insisting on precisely such ironic readings, ones that display the enormous lengths we have to go to in order to insist on the happy ending?[23]

This leads me to think about what might happen if we were to give the floor to a character like Madonna Zinevra, who continues to inspire admiration, even though some readers perceive her as an unserviceable exemplar. So here below, I reproduce the full text of a letter, under the signature of Madonna Zinevra, that was written in response to an assignment I gave my spring 2006 First-Year Writing Seminar ("The Craft of Storytelling: The *Decameron*") at Cornell University.[24] Zinevra's letter, authored by Nathan Peter Sell, Cornell '09, reads:[25]

My dear Abbot,

Firstly, I must congratulate you and Alessandro for finding each other and starting a beautiful marriage together. I also must commend you in your efforts of restoring the relatives of Alessandro to their previous wealth, the act being definite testimony to your undoubtedly firm devotion to your husband. From personal experience, I can tell you that loyalty and dedication to your loved one are the primary foundations of any marriage. My husband even tried to have me *killed*, but, I forgave him anyway, since he was impoverished and I couldn't just leave him like that.

But enough of me, I wanted to talk about a few things that you did while you were on your little pilgrimage. I did enjoy how you kept your true identity and purpose a secret even from the men following you on your journey. I know firsthand that this is no trivial task, as I was forced to parade around as a man for a number of years, all because my husband *tried to have me killed*, but that's neither here nor there. I think that you conducted yourself perfectly during your trip, and if I were in your shoes, I would have done just as you did. The way you directly but courteously addressed the Pope especially caught my attention, as you combined both your ambitious nature with your respect for proper authority. All of these facets of your character are truly laudable.

However, I do happen to disagree with the way that you went about introducing yourself to Alessandro. Now, my husband may be a bit hasty, jumps to conclusions, and isn't exactly perfect, but I know that at least he of all people would understand a decent approach from a woman, as opposed to an immoral proposal. I think you scared poor Alessandro half to death when you invited him to your bed and started to caress him while he was still under the impression that you were a man, thinking you were stuck "in the grip of some impure passion" (88). Then right there, on the spot, you ask him to take your hand in marriage. Now, I'm not the biggest fan of brash decisions, seeing as how one almost killed me (but of course all is forgiven!), but I cringed when you asked him to marry you just moments after revealing the fact that you are actually a woman. Imagine what the bewildered Alessandro must have been thinking! I understand that you were under a certain time constraint, but I still do believe that you could have exercised a bit more modesty.

In any case, I wish you all the best with Alessandro and the future that you two have before you. And if anyone ever asks you to hold a large trunk in your room, you say no to that person. I hope to hear from you soon!

Sincerely,

Zinevra

In this creative and nuanced response, Nate Sell does not limit himself to what a good many other readers can see, namely, the similarities between Zinevra and the abbot/princess (loyalty, respect for authority, intelligence, ambition) and the manifest divergence between them (the abbot/princess's forward sexual advances). Rather, his Madonna Zinevra struggles to suppress a terrible truth, only to have it peek through repeatedly: "My husband even tried to have me *killed* ... But enough of me ... I was forced to parade around as a man for a number of years, all because my husband *tried to have me killed*, but that's neither here nor there ... Now, I'm not the biggest fan of brash decisions, seeing as how one almost killed me (but of course all is forgiven!)." Remarkable for their sophistication are Sell's timing and his ability to vary the ways in which Zinevra keeps returning to the site of emotional trauma only to keep tamping down anything that would sound like open criticism of her husband. At less than 500 words, this letter from Madonna Zinevra provides insights into *Decameron* 2.9 that go far beyond what first-year university students are able to express in an analytic essay – indeed, it goes far beyond what most of us can express in the language and argumentation of academic discourse. It dramatizes the issue of control that is, I believe, at the heart of all of the instances of wifely criticism in the *Decameron*. It reminds us that a story like 2.9 poses questions like these: What are women allowed to say? What might they want to say? What can they get away with saying? It tells us that happy endings often require discarding unhappy and disturbing details. Above all, I believe, this letter reminds us what *literature* can do. Although this letter was written by a very young person – or perhaps precisely because of that – it shows us how creative and literary responses can expertly capture the delicate balance of enthusiasm and unease, of praise and blame, that hovers in the final reconciliation scene of a novella like 2.9.

And, I might as well just say it: That delicate balance of enthusiasm and unease is quite distinctively Boccaccian. In the *Decameron*, we hear praise that is not quite praise and blame that is not quite blame. That is why we have such difficulty agreeing, as we read Boccaccio's masterpiece, whether certain behaviours are the object of approbation or not. The *Decameron*, which steadfastly refuses to tell an uncompromised story about what to praise and what to blame, invites us to reflect on how we form our opinions. It describes for us situations that will elicit a range of responses (often contradictory ones), and then, as a great and innovative literary text, it invites us to examine how we might be encouraged by its own (often contradictory) rhetorical formulations to accept certain judgments and to discard others. From this we can derive a crucial lesson about our responsibility to think critically about the assumptions we make, the evidence we cite, the judgments we proffer.

7 He Ironizes, He Ironizes Not, He Ironizes …

"Everything in the *Decameron* hinges on the possibility inherent in irony, which leaves its readers room for independent perspectives toward the same phenomena or story." This fundamental observation comes from Timothy Kircher, who has studied how the *Decameron* "projects the *exemplum* tradition through the lens of irony."[1] Kircher sets out the cornerstone of his argument thus:

> Even as these narrators tell stories with "morals" or lessons, the reader is instantly challenged to assess their remarks, accept them or reject them, without recourse to clerical authority. A key support of medieval tradition, the theological and social status of the clergy, has been knocked away, and one is left to consider the worth of the tales in one's own terms: a liberating, anxious moment.[2]

By focusing on the reader, whom other scholars have not really taken into account as they study the *Decameron*'s irony, Kircher aligns himself with the theorists of irony – Linda Hutcheon and Stanley Fish principal among them – who have demonstrated how irony lies in the eye of the beholder.[3]

Taking up the lead that Kircher has offered, I would press forward: What happens, exactly, as readers of the *Decameron* grapple with texts that may (or may not) be infused with irony? What authorizes us to accept or to challenge a narrator's remarks? What might predispose us to see irony in certain places rather than others? What does Boccaccio's irony and our ability to perceive it (or not) have to do with what I have called the "ethical dimension" of the *Decameron*?

While Kircher's analysis focuses on Day 1 of the *Decameron*, to show how "the ten young story-tellers, in leaving the Dominican church of Santa Maria Novella and the diseased city, must create their own ethic,"[4]

I would like to turn to Day 10 of the *Decameron*, which is dedicated to the lofty themes of generosity and magnanimity. For it is one thing to be ironic about authorities, both spiritual and secular, as the young storytellers have placed themselves on the margins of society, and another to be ironic about magnanimity, that striving for the "greatness of soul" that Aristotle identified as "a sort of crown of the virtues" (*Nicomachean Ethics* 4.3.1124a1–2), and to be so as the storytellers are about to return to their home city of Florence. In fact, although Vittore Branca celebrates "literary ironization" as key to Boccaccio's masterful ability to renew literary traditions by turning them inside out, or more precisely, by directing a "subtle and resolute irony" at them, not a single example from Branca's study of the *Decameron*'s irony comes from Day 10.[5] At the end of the *Decameron*, expectations about the ultimate purpose of the work come into play, with readers tending to divide themselves into two clusters: A first group, with Vittore Branca as principal spokesperson, sees the *Decameron* as concluding with a "splendid crescendo"; a second group, whose position has been most articulately set out by Robert Hollander and Courtney Cahill, does not deny that magnanimity is a noble subject but "challeng[es] the notion that the *Decameron* concludes as a comedy and at its moral and aesthetic high point."[6]

Notable are the caution and restraint with which Hollander and Cahill advance their view of a "myth of order" in *Decameron* 10. Offering their work "without polemic ... in a spirit of inquiry and hoping that it will be read as openly as it is written," they go on to explain: "This is to say not that we are unconvinced by our arguments but that we are aware that others may not immediately (or perhaps ever) accept them, that there are issues here that resist simple solutions and readers who will find it difficult to leave behind a paradigm that seems both pleasing and sensible."[7]

Perhaps this caution is a requisite professional response to the professional standing of those scholars who have celebrated an optimistic reading of Day 10. Still, the deep-rootedness of the uplifting reading, which Hollander and Cahill acknowledge without resentment, may also tell us something about people's intolerance for mixing irony in with ethical and political discourses about how we should pursue happiness, virtue, and the good life.

Revelatory is an editorial titled "How to Live without Irony" by Christy Wampole, a scholar of French and Italian literature and thought.[8] Directing her critique at hipsters and lamenting the fact that an "ironic ethos can lead to a vacuity and vapidity of the individual and collective psyche," Wampole warns us that "historically, vacuums eventually have been filled by something – more often than not, a hazardous something. Fundamentalists are never ironists; dictators are never ironists; people who move things in the political landscape, regardless of the sides they choose, are never ironists."[9] Having evoked the possibility of fundamentalism (which presumably she sees as bad) and dictatorships (which we can pretty safely assume she considers bad), so that she can argue that irony brings about rigid thinking that could have deleterious consequences, Wampole adds that all civic actors, no matter what their persuasion, are irony-free. She evokes examples of "nonironic living" that are "pure" and "without dissimulation," and proclaims that "moving away from the ironic involves saying what you mean, meaning what you say and considering seriousness and forthrightness as expressive possibilities, despite the inherent risks."[10] In her conclusion, she states, "it is my firm conviction that [the ironic] mode of living is not viable and conceals within it many social and political risks. For such a large segment of the population to forfeit its civic voice through the pattern of negation I've described is to siphon energy from the cultural reserves of the community at large."[11]

Granted, Wampole's annoyance is directed at human beings in their daily lives, at the ironic construction of surroundings, at day-to-day ironization about values, and at irony as a refusal to engage with what she calls "the community at large." One would likely assume that she would still allow for irony in literature. But what happens when we expect literature to contribute to the ethical vision of the "community at large"?

Our expectations about an author's responsibility to the larger community inevitably colour our reading of the *Decameron*, and perhaps nowhere more than when the designated topics for storytelling offer positive communitarian messages – that is, in Day 5 (where "happy love" in marriage has been acclaimed a community good, *pace* the instances where happiness in marriage is entangled with violence against women) and in Day 10 (where "magnanimous liberality" has been acclaimed as a positive value, even though one might object, as have Hollander and Cahill, that Day 10 also shows the seamy underside of the so-called magnanimous characters).

In order to reflect on how willing we might be (or not) to adopt an ironic stance towards actions proclaimed as noble, I invite us to look to the story of Gentile de' Carisendi (10.4), told by Lauretta. Gentile enters the tomb of the pregnant married woman he loves, discovers she is alive, and spirits her away to his home, where she recovers and gives birth. Then, after an elaborate staged dinner at which he engages the woman's husband in a philosophical conversation that would justify his keeping the woman rather than giving her back to her husband, Gentile does indeed return the woman, together with the child. For this, he is acclaimed as munificent. Although multiple moments in this novella invite a tongue-in-cheek response, a good number of translators head the reader off at the pass before the reader can offer a snarky aside.

Let us take as a first example Messer Gentile's exclamation over Madonna Catalina's death, which I provide below in the original Italian followed by a selection of translations into English:

"Ecco, madonna Catalina, tu se' morta: io, mentre che vivesti, mai un solo sguardo da te aver non potei: per che, ora che difender non ti potrai, convien per certo che, così morta come tu se', io alcun bacio ti tolga." (10.4.8)

Deare Madame Catharina, I am not a little sorry for thy death, although (during thy life-time) I was scarcely worthy of one kind looke: Yet now being dead, thou canst not prohibite me, but I may robbe thee of a kisse. (Florio [?])[12]

"So, Madonna Catalina, you are dead! You never accorded me so much as a single glance when you were alive; but now that you are dead, and cannot reject my love, I am determined to steal a kiss or two from you." (McWilliam)[13]

"Well look, Caterina, you're dead now. I couldn't so much as catch your eye while you were still alive. Now that you're dead and no longer in a position to hold me off, I shall certainly help myself to a kiss or two." (Waldman)[14]

"There you are, Madonna Catalina, dead. While you were alive, I never received even as much as a single glance from you, and now that you are unable to defend yourself, dead as you are, I am determined to take a kiss or two." (Musa/Bondanella)[15]

There are many ways to read "tu sei morta" ("you are dead"). Depending on our assumptions about Gentile's state of mind – not to mention on our propensity for satire – one might deliver this line with the grief of an Orpheus lamenting the loss of Eurydice (think of Monteverdi), or with a certain matter-of-factness, or with masked glee. It is Florio who seems most unsettled by this line, so he has Gentile offer an apology as he speaks it. Waldman introduces a snippy irony of his own by translating "Ecco" as "Well look," although if Catalina is dead, she's not doing any looking at all. All of these translators except Musa and Bondanella attenuate Gentile's claim that Catalina can no longer "defend herself" ("difendere non ti potrai"), which draws attention to the violence of his sexual advances; they have her unable to "prohibit" him, unable to "reject [his] love," unable to "hold [him] off."

Things get even stickier as Messer Gentile puts his hand on the woman's breast and subsequently discovers she is alive:

> Vinto adunque da questo appetito le mise la mano in seno: e per alquanto spazio tenutalavi gli parve sentire alcuna cosa battere il cuore a costei. Il quale, poi che ogni paura ebbe cacciata da sé, con più sentimento cercando, trovò costei per certo non esser morta, quantunque poca e debole estimasse la vita... (10.4.11-12)

And so, overcome by this sudden longing, he placed his hand on the lady's bosom, and after keeping it there for some little time, he thought he could detect a faint heartbeat. Whereupon, subduing all his fears, he examined her more closely and discovered that she was in fact still alive, though the actual signs of life were minimal and very weak. (McWilliam)[16]

Yielding to the temptation, he placed a hand on her breast; after a while he fancied he felt a slight heartbeat. When he'd got over the shock, he felt more carefully and concluded that she was definitely not dead, even though she was only barely alive. (Waldman)[17]

Overcome, then, by this appetite, he placed his hand upon her breast: and having held it there for a while, he thought he felt a faint beating of her heart. When he recovered from his fear, he examined her more carefully and discovered that she was clearly not dead, though he thought the life left in her was weak and fading away. (Musa/Bondanella)[18]

... at length, laying his hands for some time upon her bosom, he thought he felt something beat, when throwing all fear aside, and attending more nicely to this circumstance, he was convinced she had a small spark of life remaining in her ... (Kelly)[19]

Overcome with this alluring appetite, gently he laid his hand upon her breast, with the like awefull respect, as if she were living, and holding it so an indifferent while: either he felt, or his imagination so perswaded him, the heart of the Lady to beate and pant. Casting off all fond feare, and the warmth of his increasing the motion: his inward soule assured him, that she was not dead utterly, but had some small sense of life remaining in her, whereof he would needs be further informed. (Florio [?])[20]

This is one of the creepiest parts of the story, and the translators have adopted several strategies for reducing the creepiness factor. McWilliam, evidently wishing to hold at bay the possibility that Gentile's move is premeditated, renders Gentile's longing a "sudden longing" even though this is not supported by the Italian original. Kelly has Gentile attending "nicely to this circumstance," and he gets rid of the problematic line where he would have to describe how Gentile is feeling Madonna Catalina's body. It is not at all clear how to render "con più sentimento cercando."[21] McWilliam and Musa and Bondanella rely on clinical language to ensure that Gentile will maintain his respectability; they eliminate any sense that there is feeling involved, and have Gentile examining her carefully. Waldman at least preserves the sense of close contact there, by having Gentile feel her "more carefully." In struggling with this line myself, I have opted for "he felt her with greater interest."

Several translators are especially careful to protect Messer Gentile's interests as he reports how he rescued Madonna Catalina. Gentile says, "da me fu ricolta e colla mia sollicitudine e opera delle mani la trassi alla morte: e Iddio, alla mia buona affezion riguardando, di corpo spaventevole così bella divenir me l'ha fatta" ("she was gathered up by me, and with my care and with the work of my hands I took her away from death. God, recognizing my good affectionate sensibility, transformed her for me from a horrifying body into such a beauty" [10.4.38]). When Gentile notes the "care" (*sollicitudine*) he showed towards Catalina, McWilliam nudges us towards an even more positive view by designating this as "*loving* care"; when Gentile speaks of his "buona affezion," which I would render as "consideration" or "kindness," McWilliam and Musa and Bondanella call this "pure affection," thus emphasizing innocent intentions.[22]

In translating Lauretta's summary of her story, the translators have a final occasion to redeem Gentile:

... non solo temperò onestamente il suo fuoco, ma liberalmente quello che egli soleva con tutto il pensier disiderare e cercar di rubare, avendolo, restituì. (10.4.48)

... [he] not only tempered his ardour with honour, but having that which with his whole soul he had long been bent on wresting from another, did with liberality restore it. (J.M. Rigg)[23]

... [he] not only kept his ardour under decent restraint, but on obtaining the object which he had coveted with his whole being for so long, generously surrendered it. (McWilliam)[24]

... he not only virtuously tempered his ardour but handed back what he actually possessed after he had sought to steal her with such passionate longing. (Waldman)[25]

... he not only virtuously tempered his passion, but he also generously returned, as soon as he possessed it, the thing he had always wanted and sought to steal with all his heart. (Musa/Bondanella)[26]

McWilliam comes to Gentile's rescue by eliminating any reference to theft and substituting covetousness instead. Musa and Bondanella admit that Gentile "sought to steal," but temper this by saying he returned it "*as soon as* he possessed it" (emphasis mine); this interpretation of the Italian "avendolo" is definitely in Gentile's favour. Likewise, Waldman reinforces Gentile's ownership when he reshapes the sentence and includes "avendolo" in the phrase "what he actually possessed." I would myself translate "avendolo" as "once he had it," which does not tell us anything about the amount of time it takes Gentile to return Catalina to her husband and relatives, and does not support Gentile's argument that Catalina is legitimately his.

In sum, many translators – apparently siding with Lauretta, who claims that her story offers a supreme example of generosity and nobility – encourage us to renounce irony and to accept an edifying lesson in virtue. The desire to uphold lofty ideals such as "love," "friendship," "generosity," and "magnanimity" is no doubt well-meaning. The problem arises when we try to protect these ideals by refusing to acknowledge breaches of ethical conduct.

At this point, I draw attention to the kind of pushback that readers of *Decameron* 10.4 might offer, and to do this, I cite a passage of commentary written by a college-age student:

Messer Gentile says that he is "determined to steal a kiss or two from [Catalina]." He visits her grave, kisses her "again and again," and after a bit, is "overcome by [a] sudden longing" to touch her breast. Upon doing so, he discovers that she is still alive, and removes her from the tomb so that he might revive her. Who knows what he would have done if he hadn't discovered a heartbeat? He might have had a "sudden longing" to do something more. However, Lauretta does not let the perverseness of this scene distract her audience. She cushions each strange moment with text that makes us sympathize with Gentile. Before he even goes to the tomb, she makes a big deal about how he is "distinguished for his valour and noble blood." When Gentile learns of Catalina's death, he is "*quite* overcome with sorrow" (emphasis mine). She also precedes the breast touching with a statement claiming that it is in his nature to want more: "But as every woman knows, no sooner does a man obtain one thing, especially if he happens to be in love, than he wants something else." Coincidentally (*ahem*), he only decides to touch Catalina's breast "just as [he] had made up his mind to [leave]." Once he leaves the tomb site, he goes quickly to his home, "riding without pause." So according to Lauretta, we are to believe that Gentile is a dedicated, honorable, and sensitive man (he does, after all, "[shed] tears profusely as he [kisses her]").[27]

Most striking in this passage are the flashes of ironic commentary. Textual citations are ambiguously positioned to be read either as "straight" or as scare quotes. To the mischievous rhetorical question "Who knows what he would have done if he hadn't discovered a heartbeat?", the student offers a sassy response: "He might have had a 'sudden longing' to do something more." A parenthetical *ahem* forces us to pause to think about how "coincidental" it is that Gentile thinks to feel Catalina up just as he decides to leave. And in the closing moment of the paragraph, the student positions himself both as defender and as critic of the narrator Lauretta, who portrays Gentile as considerate and caring even as she describes his violation of appropriate boundaries.

The rhetorical organization of this passage is, in my view, the result of a reader responding to the *Decameron* precisely as Boccaccio would have wanted readers to respond. The student has exposed the hybrid quality of the narrator's voice in *Decameron* 10.4, a voice that, depending on how we receive and process it, changes its timbre.

Of course, this brand of ironic commentary should be familiar to us, for it has been used to strong effect by modern political satire in the United States. Think, for example, of *The Colbert Report*, a satirical late night television program that, until recently, aired Monday through Thursday on the Comedy Channel. Think specifically of the segment titled "The Wørd," which featured comic routines on subjects such as "Truthiness" (17 October 2005), "Wikiality" (31 July 2006), and "Dumbocracy" (15 August 2006).[28]

"The Wørd" is relevant to our reading of the *Decameron* because it works on at least three diegetic levels: (1) information as reported verbally by Colbert; (2) verbal commentary by Colbert, presented as "straight" but in fact ironic; and (3) the (anonymous) ironic commentary that appears in writing on a separate lateral screen. That anonymous commentary offers the viewing audience possible models for their responses.

For those readers who don't like the idea of using Stephen Colbert as a model for ethical distancing, let me offer an acclaimed poet, Langston Hughes. His poem "World War," published in *Harlem Quarterly* in 1949–50, offers us a similar model:

WORLD WAR

What a grand time was the war!
    Oh, my, my!
What a grand time was the war!
    My, my, my!
In war time we had fun,
Sorry that old war is done!
What a grand time was the war!
    My, my!

Echo:

    Did
    Somebody
    Die?

The first stanza of this poem, with its grandiose statements punctuated by march and drumbeat rhythms, is reminiscent of the rhetoric the narrator Lauretta uses in *Decameron* 10.4. Lauretta's rhetoric has a similar over-the-top quality. The voice identified as "Echo," with its slow and solemn timing, punctuated by multiple appearances of the consonant D and the variations on did/dy/die at the end of each hollow-sounding verse, makes us pause in our tracks to ask, in effect, whether we have been told the entire story about war. When we supply our own Echo to Lauretta's grand statements, we see not only the magnanimity and munificence in Gentile's selfless act – my, my, my! – but also the abusive contours that should give us pause.

Readers who engage in ironic pushback remind us that if we slow down as we process information, we are able to ask whether we have been told the story in its entirety and whether we agree with the spin that has been put on the story. Authorized to include our own perspective, we are able to indicate approbation and/or disapproval. The method would seem clear. Especially when we disagree, we interject our commentary. This is likely what many active readers do in any case. It is liberating to have that space to respond.

"Liberating" is a word that Timothy Kircher uses in speaking about what happens when we respond independently to the *Decameron*. To be more precise, Kircher calls this a "liberating, *anxious* moment" (emphasis mine). The anxiety he identifies could well be the result of the sense of solitude and abandonment one might feel when one is on one's own. Here, however, I want to explore a form of anxiety that Kircher may or may not have intended: the anxiety that comes after we have offered our comments and other readers make assumptions about whether they are ironic or non-ironic. It is the anxiety that comes of the impossibility of knowing for sure how one's comments will be received. Not only might ironies fall on deaf ears, but non-ironic comments might be taken to be ironic. *He ironizes, he ironizes not, he ironizes …*

To explore this line of thought, I turn to the marginal comments offered by Francesco d'Amaretto Mannelli, who shows us that the tradition of snappy response to lines in the *Decameron* has a venerable origin. Mannelli was the copyist of the 1384 Codex Mannelli, a manuscript that provided the principal text for the *Decameron* until the Codex Hamilton 90 (datable to 1370) was identified as an autograph manuscript.[29] Mannelli's marginal notes are reproduced in large part in Vittore Branca's Einaudi edition of the *Decameron* and have been studied by Stefano Carrai and K.P. Clarke.[30]

Curiously, there is not always agreement about whether Mannelli's comments should be read as ironic. Commenting on the abbot/princess's claim that she wants to live honourably (2.3), Mannelli writes: "tu be · llo facesti quando Alexandro chiamasti nel leto tuo" ("You certainly did that when you called Alessandro into your bed"); Mannelli's comment is cited by Carrai, who draws attention to the irony, in my opinion correctly so.[31] Commenting on the wife of Mazzeo della Montagna, whose lover is of very questionable reputation but whom she prefers over other men (4.10), Mannelli writes: "Or lodati sieno i bendoni di San Gallo, che costei pur non prese il pegio come l'altre si dice che fanno" ("Well, praise be the hat straps of San Gallo, that she didn't get the worst of it the way they say other women do"). Here Carrai does not appear to grasp the irony.[32] Commenting on Madonna Filippa's question about whether she should throw her surplus sexuality to the dogs (6.7), Mannelli writes: "Monna Filippa, tu ài ragione! Che tanto tristo faccia Dio chi vi puose la vergogna, però che il danno è molto piccolo" ("Madonna Filippa, you're right! Goddamn whoever established this as shameful, because the damage is very minimal"). Carrai again appears to perceive as non-ironic a comment that I see as dripping with irony and sarcasm.[33]

Why would Carrai and I read these moments differently? It is because we have different assumptions about where Mannelli's sympathies lie. I am assuming that Mannelli is an advocate for female honour and chastity and that he would therefore look askance upon women who cherry-pick the moments in which to uphold their honour (the princess/abbot), whose choices are represented as honourable when they are questionable (the wife of Mazzeo della Montagna), and who downplay the problems that sexual excess creates for the established social system (Madonna Filippa).

Nor do we lack for other instances where people disagree about whether to hear irony. Consider how contemporary satirical messages are processed. We might think, for example, that we can be pretty sure where Randy Newman's irony is directed in his 1977 song "Short People," who, according to the lyrics, "got no reason to live" (i.e., the irony is directed at prejudiced people). Yet the song was interpreted by some people as deeply prejudicial.[34] We might think we can be pretty sure where Stephen Colbert's irony is directed, because we might think we can safely make assumptions about where his fictional persona's sympathies lie and what the "real" Stephen Colbert would want us to think. But in fact, as some researchers have shown, political ideology influences how we process ambiguous messages in late night comedy; the researchers found that "there was no significant difference between the groups in thinking Colbert was funny, but conservatives were more likely to report that Colbert only pretends to be joking and genuinely meant what he said while liberals were more likely to report that Colbert used satire and was not serious when offering political statements."[35]

If it is difficult to process ambiguous messages in the realm of popular culture, it appears to be even more difficult when the expectation is that speakers and writers will maintain a properly serious tone. The assumption is that satirists should stay satirists, and serious discussion banishes the ambiguities that satire imports. Thus, when on 24 September 2010, Stephen Colbert remained in character as he testified before the House Judiciary Subcommittee on Immigration, Citizenship, and Border Security regarding his day-long experience of working alongside migrant workers in upstate New York, his remarks produced considerable unease. And just as satirists do not import well into "serious" discussion and debate, it can be difficult to assess the objectives of serious people who resort to irony. An instructive example is provided by a passage from "Regulations for Literary Criticism in the 1990s," written by two well-known literary scholars, Michael Bérubé and Gerald Graff. This is the last part of "Regulation VII. *No Irony*":

> The lesson is clear. Employing irony, speaking tongue in cheek, talking wryly or self-mockingly – these smartass intellectual practices give our whole profession a bad name. If there's one thing calculated to alienate an otherwise friendly and helpful press, it's irony. As Dan Quayle once put it, irony is an ill wind that bites the hand that feeds our fashionable cynicism.
>
> We cannot mince words about irony. Knock it off, and knock it off now. In the first place, nobody understands your little ironies but you and your theorymongering friends. In the second place, even if someone *does* understand your ironies, they still won't translate into newsprint and you'll wind up looking foolish anyway. In the third place, great literature demands of us a high seriousness of purpose – not disrespectful laughter and clowning around. So just wipe that smirk off your face.[36]

Commenting on "Regulations for Literary Criticism in the 1990s," Linda Hutcheon notes that they were "intended to restore public confidence and sidestep further press attacks on the profession."[37] Jon Winokur, in *The Big Book of Irony*, introduces Regulation VII with this rubric: "In a bold effort to improve a flagging professional image, the Teachers for a Democratic Culture ironically try to outlaw irony."[38] Although Hutcheon says she has taken the injunction of Regulation VII "to [ironic] heart,"[39] in neither case am I fully convinced that these two readers of Regulation VII are seeing it as I would – as a smartass ironic response to half-literate politicians and to a critical press that prefers to reduce complex ideas to bland sound bites but still demands that literary scholars adhere only to genres deemed serious and proper. The Bérubé and Graff who authored this piece don't give a hoot about silly media reception – which is perhaps why the "Regulations" do not appear on Bérubé and Graff's online CVs.[40] Given that Hutcheon dedicates a significant portion of her book to moments when she interpreted messages as "straight" when those messages were evidently intended as ironic, one is led to wonder whether she has picked up on all of the ironies in Bérubé and Graff's composed outburst.

The various instances of ironic commentary I have cited – Stephen Colbert's "Wørd," Langston Hughes's Echo in his poem about the Second World War, select marginal comments offered by Mannelli in his manuscript of the *Decameron*, satirical music lyrics by Randy Newman, Bérubé and Graff's "Regulations for Literary Criticism in the 1990s" – all rely on a mechanism of assigning praise and blame that we must interpret. We will see irony present only if we judge that praise or blame has been wrongly assigned and only if we accept (as Linda Hutcheon has reminded us) that the topic, the audience, and the situation are appropriate for ironic commentary.[41]

Keeping in mind the lesson we have extracted – namely, that we will see irony present only if we judge that praise or blame has been wrongly assigned and only if we accept that the topic, the audience, and the situation are appropriate for ironic commentary – let us return to Day 10 of the *Decameron*. Critics inclined towards a reassuring teleological reading of the *Decameron* see the protagonists of Day 10 as "standard-bearers of social justice, knights in a new rationally based chivalry of generosity, self-denial, and moderation."[42] King Alfonso (10.1), the Abbot of Cluny (10.2), and the Saladin (10.9) are touted for their munificence; a cluster of characters at the centre of the day are praised for renouncing a love interest (Gentile de' Carisendi in 10.4, Messer Ansaldo in 10.5, King Charles of Anjou in 10.6, and King Peter of Aragon in 10.7), and two protagonists (Nathan in 10.3 and Titus in 10.8) demonstrate such radical generosity towards another that they are willing to place their lives on the line.

In the final accounting, the question "Does the *Decameron* promote the idea of the great-souled person, or not?", which has divided critics into the moralizing camp and a sceptical camp, functions much like a question to which I have previously objected: "Is the *Decameron* feminist or misogynist?"[43] Calculating a "virtue quotient" is as futile as calculating a "misogyny quotient." A more fruitful approach would be to identify the rhetorical strategies that encourage readers to view protagonists as generous rather than self-serving.

Decameron 10.4 offers an excellent opportunity to examine the techniques that are used to minimize bad behaviour and draw attention away from it, because that novella includes descriptions of behaviour that could justifiably be condemned yet is widely viewed as one of the most successful in Day 10.[44]

In what follows, I identify the rhetorical strategies that I see as central to the redemption of a protagonist such as Gentile de' Carisendi.

First of all, the behaviour must be "framed" as good. Successful framing can happen periodically throughout a story, but opening and closing statements provide the obvious occasions for casting an action as worthy, and these are used to great effect in *Decameron* 10.4, where the narrator bestows lavish praise on Gentile de' Carisendi. The praise must be plentiful enough to be memorable; and furthermore, it must be able to withstand a certain amount of questioning about whether it is actually warranted, given the circumstances.

Second: The framing operation can be exceptionally effective if it promotes love – and even better, if it shows that lust has been overcome and that the institution of marriage has been reaffirmed. This is because we still have very poor frameworks for recognizing genuine love.[45] Many readers – certainly the readers who occupy the moralizing camp – are quick to recognize when lust is masquerading as love but are not as quick to recognize controlling behaviour and abuse. For such readers, the reaffirmation of marriage, highlighted in the Day 10 novellas beginning with 10.4, legitimizes a variety of questionable behaviours.[46]

Third: Characters should be represented with specificity and should move in noble and courteous settings associated with upper-class families assumed to be genteel and courteous. Even better, the characters should be given names that speak to their nobility and gentility (as is the case with Gentile himself [10.4], whose name means "noble" or "genteel," and with Sofronia [10.8], whose name speaks to her wisdom and temperance).[47]

Fourth: Readers are encouraged to judge the "ends" as more important than the "means." In this regard, a surprising number of critics emphasize Gentile's turn away from sexual passion and his generosity as he renounces his "right" to retain Catalina as his own; they justify, whether explicitly or implicitly, his kissing and touching her without her consent, for these actions led to the preservation of her life and that of her child.[48]

Fifth: Indirect discourse is used to protect protagonists who have engaged in questionable behaviour. Gentile "tells all" about how he discovered that Madonna Catalina was alive: first to his mother (10.4.13), who takes it upon herself to revive Catalina; then to Catalina herself when she wakes up and wonders where she is (10.4.15); and later to Catalina's husband and the assembled gentlemen of Bologna (10.4.40).

Sixth: Characters who could question whether the act was aboveboard and/or truly generous do not object. Gentile's mother does not object when Gentile brings home a pregnant married woman; one would think that a mother deemed "wise and valiant" ("valorosa e savia" [10.4.13]) would comment on bad behaviour. Catalina's husband Niccoluccio – whose rhetorical abilities are repeatedly highlighted – does not object when Gentile stages a public banquet at which Gentile, by means of a sophistically posed question, gets Niccoluccio to concede that Gentile has a right to keep Catalina after he has found her, "abandoned" by her husband and her relatives. Indeed, readers – responding to the rhetorical dexterity of a narrator – even see Catalina's acceptance of what happens as proof of Gentile's generosity.

Seventh: Spectators who might be witness to bad behaviour are sidelined. A servant is left to wait outside while Gentile enters the tomb, presumably because Gentile is protecting his servant from what could be the fearful sight of a corpse; in fact, however, the narrator is also protecting Gentile so that his servant does not see him kissing (the presumably dead) Catalina.

Eighth: There is emphasis on munificence as a public act, one that can be witnessed and affirmed as such by internal audiences. As Michaela Paasche Grudin and Robert Grudin note, Day 10 "teems with society, as folks in substantial number watch, listen to, judge, wonder at, and appreciate the actions of central figures ... They set off the heroes as standard-bearers of social justice, knights in a new rationally based chivalry of generosity, self-denial, and moderation."[49] In contrast, behaviour that we might question tends to be relegated to the private sphere and to the internal thought processes of the protagonist. Or the behaviour seems a bit strange, but the narrator does not reveal what the protagonist is thinking or planning, so our ability to judge is circumscribed.

Ninth: Authoritative voices associated with exhortations to virtue and to civic duty can be called upon to bolster the sense of lofty purpose. The more that stories appear to channel the ethical writings of Aristotle and Cicero, and the more that they participate in reaffirming the uplifting vision to be found in works such as Dante's *Commedia*, the more likely they will be read as delivering an uplifting message, no matter how questionable isolated actions might appear. Thus, Grudin and Grudin, in their discussion of Day 10 of the *Decameron*, argue that

perhaps the best way to begin is to place Boccaccio in a tradition of which he has already repeatedly availed himself. Cicero, Brunetto, and Dante all conclude major works with a similar sense of uplift. Cicero concludes his

De re publica with Scipio's dream of a heavenly realm in which good deeds are rewarded, and when Brunetto breaks off his *Penitenza* at the end of the *Tesoretto*, his narrator has purified himself, and the spirit of Ptolemy is about to give a lecture on the heavens. Dante, writing under the influence of both Cicero and Brunetto, describes a similar form of geographic and spiritual ascent in the *Paradiso*, which itself shows Ciceronian influences. With Day X Boccaccio takes his place in this illustrious tradition. The understanding of human nature expressed in Days I–IX is now applied to a vision of an enlightened individual and a resurrected commonwealth.[50]

The principal successful technique, which I offer in tenth and final place, involves the rapid glossing over of potentially problematic moments in favour of representations that are balanced and harmonious. Attilio Momigliano, quoted later by Giorgio Cavallini, points out that the passage from sensual temptation to the discovery that the woman is still alive happens so rapidly that "the reader does not notice the repugnant element that there could be in this love for a cadaver."[51] Cavallini himself states that "contrary to what one might think, the scene is not macabre."[52] The "sleight-of-hand" necessary to achieve this effect is held up as evidence of Boccaccio's stylistic development and his supreme artistic achievement.

When we invite comparison with an earlier exploration of the moment of discovery in the tomb, we can see how much more fluid is the prose of the *Decameron*. Here is the relevant scene from the thirteenth question about love in the *Filocolo* (1336–9), where an unnamed knight explores the body of the (unnamed) dead married woman he loves:

> E dopo alquanto, non potendosi di baciare costei saziare, la cominciò a toccare e a mettere le mani nel gelato seno fra le fredde menne, e poi le segrete parti del corpo con quelle, divenuto ardito oltre al dovere, cominciò a cercare sotto i ricchi vestimenti: le quali andando tutte con timida mano tentando sopra lo stomaco la distese, e quivi con debole movimento sentì li deboli polsi muoversi alquanto. Divenne allora questi non poco pauroso, ma amore il facea ardito: e ricercando con più fidato sentimento, costei conobbe che morta non era ... (*Filocolo*, 4.67.7-8)[53]

And after a while, not being able to be satisfied with kissing her, he began to touch her and put his hands into the chilled bosom, onto her cold breasts; and then with those hands he began to seek out under her rich garments the secret parts of her body, becoming bolder than he should.

And as he was prodding them all with a timid hand, he reached over her stomach, and there he felt her weak pulse moving slightly with a frail motion. At this point he became quite alarmed, but love gave him boldness; and examining her more confidently he discovered that she was not dead.[54]

Between this passage and the *Decameron*, the description of a man feeling up a cold body will undergo a significant stylistic upgrade. The much cruder "fredde menne" (which the English translators have rendered as "cold breasts" but which I would render as "cold tits"), the "secret parts," and the "stomach" will disappear, allowing for a much lighter touch with a bosom (*seno*).[55] The passage in the *Filocolo* presents the knight as responding with considerable fear and then becoming bold thanks to love; the corresponding passage in the *Decameron* will mention Gentile's fear only in the moment that he has actively cast off his fears. Even the signs of life are given a somewhat more emotional character; the woman in the *Filocolo* has a "weak pulse," whereas it will be the heart of Madonna Catalina that appears to beat somewhat.

Boccaccio's increased stylistic control in the *Decameron* helps guarantee that readers will be convinced of Gentile de' Carisendi's magnanimity. Heightened musicality in the prose – created by the expert placement of sweet-sounding adverbs and the embedding of hendecasyllables – is crucial because readers perceive musicality as evidence of polished urbanity and impeccable sophistication.[56] The protagonist becomes "more noble," and his nobility is highlighted because the writer himself (using Lauretta as a narrator) is better able to make the case for magnanimity. This reminds us that our perceptions of magnanimity depend greatly on the rhetorical control exercised by the narrator.

When we become more aware of how a story about a protagonist's generosity and magnanimity can be constructed so as elicit such divergent views – affirmations of virtue on one hand, ironic responses on the other – we must also ask: Why did Boccaccio construct the storytelling of his *Decameron* to end in this way? That question continues to confound scholars writing about the multiple and often conflicting interpretations of the stories of Day 10. The answers might be grouped into several categories:

- The view advanced by Millicent Marcus, who maintains that Boccaccio's primary purpose is not to educate his readers about "virtue." Rather, he is trying to bring his readers to "entertain a plurality of perspectives" and to take responsibility for the fact that readers determine meaning.[57]

- Roberta Bruno Pagnamenta's argument that on Day 10, Boccaccio offers a series of stories that are "ethically" oriented even while emphasizing that the artistic and literary enterprise is just as important as ethics. She calls on Panfilo to support her argument, given that Panfilo emphasizes the importance of the act of storytelling as he introduces the Day 10 topic of magnanimous and generous deeds (see 9.Concl.4–5). Later, as he introduces his own Day 10 story, he distances himself from attempts to use storytelling as a political tool, reiterating that the point is not to "rectify the world's deficiencies or to denounce them" ("correggere i difetti mondani o pur per riprendergli" [10.9.4]).[58]

- Robert Hollander and Courtney Cahill's contention that Day 10 "is a critical examination of the myth of order and thus, in political terms, of the myth of law," a day in which "we witness … the destructive consequences that may result from upholding the law, particularly the rigid terms of contractual agreements."[59] Hollander and Cahill apply to the stories of Day 10 a label that they felicitously take from Michel de Montaigne: "supercelestial thoughts [in conjunction with] subterranean conduct." In the final accounting, they see Boccaccio taking up the mantle of the satirist.[60]

These critical positions reveal different emphases: Marcus focuses on the education of the reader, though her discussion also grants attention to artistic narration. Bruno Pagnamenta places more emphasis on artistic narration, though she acknowledges Marcus's points about the role readers play. Hollander and Cahill, perhaps because they would like the characters of Day 10 to be "objects of greater (and more analytical) scrutiny than they have been," and because they are the scholars to have sought most energetically to dislodge the uplifting reading, maintain the focus on the object studied (the representation of Day 10 characters and their deeds), though they attend to questions of narration and reading as well.

As my own analysis throughout this chapter indicates, my understanding of the configuration of these three components – readers, author/narrators, and textual representations – shares many features with those of the critics I have just cited but also departs from their conceptions in some key ways.

I believe we need to move beyond advocating exclusively for the reading that sees the *Decameron* ending on a triumphant note or the reading that sees only irony. Rather, as the title of my chapter suggests, we have to enter a loop where we constantly alternate: He ironizes, he ironizes not, he ironizes, he ironizes not... He refuses to teach, he teaches, he refuses to teach, he teaches ... Following Marcus's lead, we would have to accept "the arbitrariness and the fluidity of storytelling."[61] We would have to acknowledge, as Bruno Pagnamenta has, that Day 10 of the *Decameron* is "*ambiguously* suspended" between a conclusion that is "ethically oriented" and a conclusion that is involved in a "debunking operation."[62] We would have to concede, as Hollander and Cahill intimated when they expressed doubts as to whether the proponents of the uplifting reading would ever acknowledge the validity of the ironic reading, that depending on the evidence from Day 10 that we cite, we can arrive at widely divergent judgments. As discomfiting as it is to suspend oneself between the reassuring reading and the sceptical one, this is the best chance we have at accurately capturing the thrust of the stories of Day 10.

Consistent with what I argued earlier in chapter 4, I would emphasize that the stories of Day 10 interrogate us and test us, obliging us to reveal, even if fleetingly, what sort of moral and ethical vision we wish to embrace. Where do we set the bar for behaviour proclaimed virtuous? How much human imperfection, whether of intellect or of the will, are we willing to tolerate before we reject the notion that someone exhibits virtue? Do we think that a person considered ungenerous can perform a nobly generous deed? Are we willing to accept that someone of a different ideological persuasion could be virtuous?[63] How much self-interestedness will we accept as part and parcel of altruistic impulses? How much does it matter that luck may influence one's ability to develop virtue and to display it to others? The reader is hailed to answer these questions, revealing, in her assessment of what can be qualified as virtuous, her own standards of judgment. For some readers, evidence that a protagonist appears to have detached from the things of this world – whether these are material goods, love objects, or one's own life and one's own happiness – will secure a crown of virtue. In the final stories of the *Decameron*, they will see, as one scholar has, "a superior world molded by aware, responsible, and fundamentally good individuals actively involved in the creation of a better society."[64] For others (among whom I admit I include myself), it might be easier for a camel to get through a needle's eye than for the protagonists such as those in *Decameron* 10 to be recognized as truly worthy of praise. That is because I fully agree with Hollander and Cahill that, time and again, the characters of Day 10 reveal character weaknesses that make us wonder whether they are truly as noble of spirit as they are touted to be. The same individuals who perform deeds labelled noble can (in my view, as in Hollander and Cahill's) be self-interested, self-promoting, manipulative, foolhardy, power-mongering. A number of them are not free of sexual desire, even when that sexual desire appears highly inappropriate and misdirected. A number of them are not above using sophistic legal reasoning to shore up their own positions. Do those who see no irony here have a distorted sense of what it means to exhibit nobility of soul? Or do those who emphasize the ironic tinges possess a vision of virtue that is too uncompromising and idealistic, one that none of us humans could ever attain? These are the ethical questions with which Boccaccio leaves us as the storytelling comes to an end.

8   To Conclude: A Conclusion That Is Not One

In thinking about the ethical orientation of the Author of the *Decameron*, readers tend, as perhaps is to be expected, to follow the Author's lead and, thus, to focus on questions elicited by the Author's statements in his Proem, his defence of himself in the Introduction to Day 4, and the Author's Conclusion. He says he writes only for women in love – is that true? He offers his women readers delight and useful advice – does his book do for women what he claims? Is his a tenable ethical stance if he places responsibility on readers for what they find in this work? When, in the opening and closing lines, he states that his book is surnamed "Prince Gallehault" – a clear reference to Francesca da Rimini's label for the book she sees as responsible for her damnation in Dante's *Inferno* – are we to understand that the *Decameron* too could prove dangerous?

In the space provided by this closing of my book, I propose to explore how conclusions prove provisional, untrue to themselves. They invite us to ask what sorts of issues have been set to one side in order to produce the illusion of stability and finality. To do this, I shall first focus on two instances in which readers, responding to the Author's claims, illustrate the impossibility of ever concluding on a secure note, because elided questions and ambiguities demand further exploration. Then I shall turn my attention to the way the Author creates a persona that is not merely two-faced (something we could perhaps deal with) but *self-multiplyingly two-faced*, and the way he signals that each attempt to conclude will necessarily generate further occasions for discussion.

My first example comes from Robert Hollander's essay "*Utilità*," published as a chapter of his *Boccaccio's Dante and the Shaping Force of Satire*.[1] The moves in Hollander's argument illustrate the difficulties we experience as we struggle to determine what advice we extract from the *Decameron*, to what use we put this advice, and whether we are the kinds of readers for whom the *Decameron*'s advice is intended.

Hollander begins by revealing the Horatian and Ovidian subtexts behind the Author's promise of delight and useful advice ("diletto ... e utile consiglio" [*Proemio*, 14]) and his statement that the ladies for whom he writes will be able "to recognize what should be avoided and likewise what should be pursued" ("cognoscere quello che sia da fuggire e che sia similmente da seguitare" [*Proemio*, 14]).[2] Despite these classical references, Hollander argues, "the classical notion of 'utility' does not inform either the behavior of the characters or the attitudes of most of the narrators of the *Decameron*," and therefore the task of determining what is meant by "utility" is a difficult one.[3] Hollander then asks what the *Decameron*'s *utile consiglio* is and answers that the promised aid is "advice which is physically and morally helpful"; in this case, since the Author is the beneficiary of advice about "how to fall out of love," the beneficiaries of his advice will learn "how to follow reason and shun lust" (a lesson that, according to Hollander, many commentators have chosen to overlook because it does not sit well with their assumptions about the *Decameron*).[4] There follows an overview of the uses of the words *utile, utilità,* and *utilmente* that shows that *"utilità* has, then, little to do with wise or good counsel in the tales themselves."[5] Ultimately, Hollander argues, terms like "useful advice" (*utile consiglio*) mean different things to different readers, and the Author himself, despite having promised useful advice, makes clear that readers who wish to extract bad advice and evil actions will not be prevented from doing so.[6] The bottom line is that "the reader's moral predilections will govern his understanding."[7] Following some further marshalling of evidence from both the Author's Conclusion and Panfilo's commentary at the beginning of 10.9 about the purposes of the group's storytelling (i.e., not "to correct the defects of this world or to condemn them"), which Hollander includes because "Panfilo speaks to Boccaccio's purpose," Hollander closes his essay as follows:

> In the view of the *Decameron* sponsored here, Boccaccio is most concerned with our governance of our intellectual response to life. Unlike Dante, he does not wish to make us live or pray better; rather he wants to enable us to think more clearly about our human nature. About human behavior, he would seem to be saying, there is nothing to be done. The only attribute of human behavior explicitly approved of in the *Decameron* is thus *ingegno*, but not that wit which serves appetite so much as the one which is the

property of the minds of those who escape the social condition of human-kind in order to reflect upon the follies of the herd, the *ingegno* of the great solitary figures who appear in coruscating moments in this masterpiece of the depiction of human selfishness: Giotto, Cavalcanti, and Giovanni Boccaccio himself.[8]

Given the kinds of arguments I have made thus far in this book, it should be clear that I very much support Hollander's view that the def-inition of "good advice" depends on the reader and that it is the reader's ethical disposition that determines what the reader sees in the text. I also appreciate Hollander's awareness, expressed both in the essay on "*Utilità*" and elsewhere, of the way the *Decameron* generates widely divergent responses. With this in mind, I would like here to draw atten-tion to the major points of difference between Hollander's evaluation of Boccaccio's purposes and my own.

Most important to note is that Hollander appears to assume that the Author of the *Decameron* – the Author as he appears in the *Proemio*, the Introduction to Day 4, and the Author's Conclusion – is identical with Boccaccio. This was for a long time an operating assumption of Boccaccio scholarship, and it subtends much well-cited work in the field. It is crucial, in my view, that we reject this assumption, and that in our teaching and in our scholarship and even in our informal con-versations about Boccaccio, we present the Author of the *Decameron* as an authorial *persona*, to be examined and analysed and discussed as such. It is an ethical responsibility both to Boccaccio and to the text of the *Decameron* to maintain this distinction, even as we understand that there are quite a few points on which Boccaccio and the Author of the *Decameron* would agree.

Moreover, we need to be wary of thinking that what we might imagine to be the case is always supported by the text. According to Hollander, the *Decameron* provides a lesson in "how to follow reason and shun lust," because its Author has been the beneficiary of advice "about how to fall out of love" and now wishes to show his gratitude by providing the same sort of advice to those who are in need.[9] This strikes me as a projection onto a text that leaves room for speculation about what in fact the Author's friends did. What the Author says is: "In my distress, the pleasant conversation and the admirable expressions of comfort from certain of my friends brought me great relief, and I am firmly of the belief it is because of the comfort offered that I am not dead" ("Nella qual noia tanto rifrigerio già mi porsero i piacevoli ragionamenti d'alcuno amico e le sue laudevoli consolazioni, che io porto fermissima opinione per quelle essere avenuto che io non sia morto" [*Proemio*, 4]). Only in a subsequent moment does the Author describe how his love came to an end, thanks to the fact that God "established by immutable law that all earthly things should come to an end" ("diede per legge incommutabile a tutte le cose mondane aver fine" [*Proemio*, 5]). The passage from the *Proemio* does not support a reading that sees the Author receiving advice about "how to fall out of love." Furthermore, although the English translators have tended to attribute the relief the Author felt either to the intervention of his friends generally or to the combination of everything they did for him, the Italian text offers a different story. The Author stipulates, by means of the demonstrative pronoun *quelle*, which can refer back only to the *laudevoli consolazioni* ("admirable expressions of comfort"), that he believes he owes his life specifically to the *admirable expressions of comfort*, which in my view could be non-verbal as well as verbal and which are to be distinguished from pleasant conversations.

What this first example shows us is that we need to recognize who is speaking and to resist drawing firm conclusions when the speaker gives us only partial information.

My second example draws attention to mystifications the Author sets in place as he constructs his authorial persona with reference to father figures drawn from the poetry of Horace and Dante and invites us to see his project as a supremely ethical one. I am particularly interested in the way the Author of the *Decameron* splinters himself across a variety of subject positions, not all of which he can occupy simultaneously. Here I turn to an essay by Simone Marchesi, "*Sic me formabat puerum*: Horace's *Satire* I, 4 and Boccaccio's Defense of the *Decameron*."[10]

Intending to demonstrate that Boccaccio had Horace's *Satire* 1.4 in mind as he composed the Introduction to Day 4, Marchesi highlights the co-presence of key elements in Boccaccio and Horace's texts: commentary on the validity (or not) of the use of comedy; the claim of humility; ironic argumentation that depends on a reader's awareness of how the author is situating himself in relation to the literary canon; the foregrounding of critics' envy and the unjustified harshness of their attacks; the image of dust taken up by a whirlwind; the commentary on a father's method for instructing his son. Moreover, the positioning of the Author's defences (at the beginning of Day 4 and following Day 10) brings to mind Horace's first book of *Satires*, which are ten in number and which feature defences of Horace's poetry in the fourth and tenth of these.

Even as Marchesi urges us to recognize the Horatian subtext, he acknowledges the Dantean echoes that emerge throughout the Introduction to Day 4. When the Author refers to the "pleasures" and "base longings" ("diletti" and "corrotti appetiti" [4.Intro.42]) of his critics, Marchesi notes a possible echo of *Paradiso* 11.8 where Dante denounces the kind of person who is "wrapped up in the pleasures of the flesh" ("nel diletto della carne involto" [*Paradiso* 11.8]); Marchesi also advocates for hearing Horace's criticism of his detractors who declined to read satiric poetry because they would see in it the condemnation of their morals (*Satire* 1.4.24–33).[11] When the Author compares himself to dust that, caught up in a windstorm ("spirante turbo" [4.Intro.40]), either remains unmoved or rises upwards, Marchesi acknowledges the presence of Dante's phrase "come la rena quando turbo spira" ("like sand in a windstorm" [*Inferno* 3.60]), but he asks us also to hear Horace's description of the merchant caught up "like dust gathered up by a whirlwind" ("uti pulvis collectus turbine" [*Satire* 1.4.30]) in an all-consuming desire to hold on to what he has gained or accumulate more.[12] Commenting on a father's instructional methods in the incomplete novella of Filippo Balducci and his son, Marchesi first shows how Filippo Balducci's pedagogical method contrasts with that of Cacciaguida, who explains to Dante what Dante has been privileged to see, and tells him, "make manifest everything you have seen" ["tutta tua visïon fa manifesta" [*Paradiso* 17.128]); Marchesi then links Boccaccio's pedagogical method to that of Horace's father in *Satire* 1.4, who shapes his son's ethical stance by pointing out to him examples of others' reprehensible behaviour.[13]

The incomplete novella of Filippo Balducci and his son, which shows that "teaching based only on removal and repression is sooner or later destined to fail," assumes special weight in Marchesi's argument.[14] Marchesi argues that this story is "more concerned with commenting on different teaching strategies than with the subject matter of instruction *per se*. The point of the text is not to advance a new morality, but to comment on methods of instruction, not so much *what* should be taught, but rather *how* one should teach it."[15] The paternal "best practices" of Cacciaguida and Horace's father become for Marchesi the basis for Boccaccio's moral style in the *Decameron*. Marchesi concludes:

By following the model of Horace's father and rejecting the one embodied by Filippo Balducci – that is by choosing to represent reality and draw a difficult (but more solid) moral from it – the *Decameron* also launches into a teaching of morality through an exemplary mode, which is reminiscent (and, at the same time, subversive) of the medieval exemplary tradition.[16]

There are many things I admire about Marchesi's essay, principal among them Marchesi's ability to track Boccaccio's subtle use of textual sources. I agree with Marchesi that "Filippo Balducci ... insist[s] on *not showing* what his program of education should in truth be all about"; I also agree that Filippo Balducci relies on an "abstract, authority-based system of precepts."[17] I would like to explore, however, several questions that, in my view, Marchesi puts to rest too soon.

The first question regards what happens when we create analogies such as "the Author of the *Decameron* teaches as does Horace's father" or "the Author of the *Decameron* is like Horace, who has learned from Horace's father." I believe we have an ethical obligation to ask ourselves which questions we are putting aside in order to form analogies like these, and therefore I invite us to look at what Horace says about the way his father has taught him.

When Horace first introduces his father, it is to justify his own tendency to be blunt and to name things as they are: "If I shall say any thing too freely, if perhaps too ludicrously, you must favor me by your indulgence with this allowance. For my excellent father inured me to this custom, that by noting each particular vice I might avoid it by the example [of others]" (*Satire* 1.4.105–8).[18] Horace goes on to give specific examples:

When he exhorted me that I should live thriftily, frugally, and content with what he had provided for me; don't you see, [would he say,] how wretchedly the son of Albius lives? and how miserably Barrus? A strong lesson to hinder any one from squandering away his patrimony. When he would deter me from filthy fondness for a light woman: [take care, said he,] that you do not resemble Sectanus.

That I might not follow adulteresses, when I could enjoy a lawful amour: the character, cried he, of Trebonius, who was caught in the fact, is by no means creditable. The philosopher may tell you the reasons for what is better to be avoided, and what to be pursued. It is sufficient for me, if I can preserve the morality traditional from my forefathers, and keep your life and reputation inviolate, so long as you stand in need of a guardian: so soon as age shall have strengthened your limbs and mind, you will swim without cork. In this manner he formed me, as yet a boy: and whether he ordered me to do any particular thing: You have an authority for doing this:

[then] he instanced some one out of the select magistrates: or did he forbid me [any thing]; can you doubt, [says he,] whether this thing be dishonorable, and against your interest to be done, when this person and the other is become such a burning shame for his bad character [on these accounts]? As a neighboring funeral dispirits sick gluttons, and through fear of death forces them to have mercy upon themselves; so other men's disgraces often deter tender minds from vices. From this [method of education] I am clear from all such vices, as bring destruction along with them: by lighter foibles, and such as you may excuse, I am possessed. (*Satire* 1.4.109–32)

If we read this passage carefully, we have to subject Marchesi's binary categories to greater scrutiny. Horace's father does, as Marchesi notes, "[point] his young son in the direction of reality, not away from it, choosing to confront the examples (however negative they may be) of people worthy of blame, from the squanderer to the sex-addicted adulterer."[19] It is also patently evident that, in pointing out what he deems to be reprehensible financial and sexual conduct, Horace's father is commenting explicitly on his teaching methodology, which he distinguishes from that of the wise man or philosopher (*sapiens*). But we should resist Marchesi's too-neat distinction between a "reality-based" method (which Marchesi sees in Horace's father, in Horace, in Cacciaguida, and in Boccaccio himself) and an "abstract" and "authority-based" method (which Marchesi sees in the philosopher from whom Horace's father distinguishes himself, as well as in Filippo Balducci).[20] To create this distinction, Marchesi has to assume that the philosopher never deals with real-life examples and that "authority-based" means "based on bookish authority"; he also has to play down the significance of Horace's father's statement that it is "sufficient for me, if I can preserve the morality traditional from my forefathers, and keep your life and reputation inviolate" (*Satire* 1.4.116–19). These verses alert us that Horace's father does not appear to question the authority of the rule of their forefathers, nor does he appear to question the role the public plays in determining what is socially, ethically, and morally acceptable. If this privileged teaching method is based on what a public is able to see and what it understands to be acceptable, shouldn't we also ask whether the public can be deceived in its judgment? Should we be as concerned about upholding reputation and avoiding scandal as Horace's father is? Isn't it possible that the people's opinion of what is honourable and what is scandalous – an opinion that is the deciding factor in determining fame and reputation – can be wrong?

In asking these kinds of questions, we are set on a path where we must imagine a Boccaccio who is quite different from the one Marchesi offers. Marchesi's Boccaccio might say, in effect, "I teach, in content and style, as Horace learned to teach from his father, through reality-based examples; I also use the kinds of reality-based examples that one would find in Dante, though granted the content is quite different, and my style is humbler." My Boccaccio would speak differently, to say something like the following:

> As various scholars, including Simone Marchesi, have shown, because I refuse teaching methods based on removal and repression, I am not like Filippo Balducci. I am, however, very much like him (as Millicent Marcus has shown) in that a chief hallmark of my writing is the use of figurative language, which, as Filippo discovers, "can convey a truth with an efficacy superior to any equivalent literal expression."[21] I am like the father of whom Horace speaks in *Satire* 1.4 in that I offer examples of conduct that people consider reprehensible; unlike Horace's father, however, I do not believe that the codes according to which our forefathers lived should always be the most authoritative ones, and the examples of behavior I offer are not always clearly condemnable or worthy of praise. Moreover, let me remind you that, unlike Horace's father, I never indicate explicitly what sort of conduct I myself consider reprehensible.

Thus, the difference between Marchesi's and my views of Boccaccio comes down to this: that Marchesi's Boccaccio successfully integrates various influences (especially Horatian and Dantean influences) and emerges with a firm sense of authorial identity. This Boccaccio makes it clear whom he resembles and whom he does not, and there are no overlaps; his world has clear ethical parameters, and his reality-based teaching method can provide the basis for moral instruction. I would argue that the subject identity that Marchesi affirms for the Author of the *Decameron* is nowhere near as stable as Marchesi presents it. My Author of the *Decameron*, as I imagine him, has an authorial identity that is not as firm; his allegiances are more variegated, more discriminating; it is not always clear what his ethical parameters are; and his reality-based teaching method might or might not provide the basis for moral instruction.

It is worth pausing over how Marchesi treats the matter of allegiances and authorial identity. Marchesi allows for the possibility that the Author of the *Decameron* can acknowledge two literary fathers (Dante and Horace), just as Marchesi himself can recognize two professorial fathers (Robert Hollander and Alessandro Barchiesi) as having played crucial roles in his own scholarly formation; thanking Hollander and Barchiesi, Marchesi writes: "Of them I might truly say, with Horace, that 'sic me formaba*n*t puerum.'"[22] A Boccaccian acceptance of a double-influence is not surprising given Boccaccio's tendency, throughout his life, towards hybridity and double-allegiances of various sorts. Nevertheless, this acceptance of a double-allegiance merits further attention, for it stands in marked contrast to the positions put forth by Horace and Dante. When Horace foregrounds the lessons provided by his biological father and makes his biological father the source of his poetical lessons, he manages, as Catherine Schlegel has shown, to displace two men who could have been seen as poetical fathers (i.e., his predecessor in satire, Lucilius, and his patron Maecenas).[23] Dante, as he accepts the paternal guidance of his great-grandfather Cacciaguida, rejects previous father figures he has encountered, among them Virgil and Brunetto Latini.[24]

To create a stable authorial identity, one that can be the source of edifying moral instruction, Marchesi has to overlook the ways in which Boccaccio is using Horace and Dante to send contradictory messages about who he is as Author, who is guilty of moral and ethical failings, and what claims can legitimately be made about his work.

It is important to revisit the Author's closing argument in the Introduction to Day 4:

E volendo per questa volta assai aver risposto, dico che dall'aiuto di Dio e dal vostro, gentilissime donne, nel quale io spero, armato, e di buona pazienza, con esso procederò avanti, dando le spalle a questo vento e lasciandol soffiar: per ciò che io non veggo che di me altro possa avvenire che quello che della minuta polvere avviene, la quale, spirante turbo, o egli di terra non la muove, o se la muove la porta in alto e spesse volte sopra le teste degli uomini, sopra le corone dei re e degl'imperadori, e talvolta sopra gli alti palagi e sopra le eccelse torri la lascia; delle quali se ella cade, più giù andar non può che il luogo onde levata fu. E se mai con tutta la mia forza a dovervi in cosa alcuna compiacere mi disposi, ora più che mai mi vi disporrò, per ciò che io conosco che altra cosa dir non potrà alcuno con ragione, se non che gli altri e io, che v'amiamo, naturalmente operiamo; alle cui leggi, cioè della natura, voler contrastare troppo gran forze bisognano, e spesse volte non solamente invano ma con grandissimo danno del faticante s'adoperano. Le quali forze io confesso che io non l'ho né d'averle disidero in questo; e se io l'avessi, più tosto a altrui le presterei che io per me l'adoperassi. Per che tacciansi i morditori, e se essi riscaldar non si possono assiderati si vivano: e ne' lor diletti, anzi appetiti corrotti standosi, me nel mio, questa brieve vita che posta n'è, lascino stare. (4.Intro.40–2)

Letting this suffice as my reply for the moment, I will say, most gentle ladies, that armed with the assistance that I hope God and you will provide me, I shall proceed very patiently, turning my back on this wind and letting it blow, for I don't see how anything can happen to me other than what happens to fine dust in a whirlwind: either the winds do not move it from the ground, or if they do move it, they carry it on high, many times leaving it on the heads of men, the crowns of kings and emperors, and occasionally on high palaces and lofty towers; if it falls from there it cannot go any lower than the place from which it was lifted up. And if in the past I readied myself to please you in some way, I shall now ready myself to do this even more, for I realize that a reasonable person can not but state that other people and I who love you conduct ourselves according to what is natural. To oppose the laws of nature one would need incredible strength, and often, that strength is used not only in vain but with enormous harm to the person who is expending such great effort. I confess that I do not have that strength nor do I desire to have it in this case. If I did have it, I would sooner lend it to others than use it myself. So let my detractors be silent, and if they are unable to turn warm, let them live icily benumbed. In this short lifetime that is given to us, let them stay with their pleasures, actually their perverse longings, and leave me to my own.

Let us accept Marchesi's argument that behind the image of the dust gathered up by the whirlwind lie both the whirling dust of *Inferno* 3.60 and that of Horace's *Satire* 1.4.32. Let us also notice, however, that Boccaccio scholars do not comment on *why* the Author of the *Decameron* would have compared himself to the Dantean image of dust gathered up by the whirlwind. My best surmise is that they are inclined to think that, at least in this case, Boccaccio simply liked Dante's images and phrasings, so he drew on them as he pleased, without particular attention to context. Marchesi does choose to comment on why Boccaccio would have marshalled Horace's reference to the whirling dust. He concludes that Horace's criticism of the merchant "rush[ing] headlong, like dust gathered up by a whirlwind" is directed at the kinds of profit-seeking people who complain that the Author of the *Decameron* should focus on making a gainful living rather than writing nonsense; and to support this argument, he reminds readers of the presence in the *Decameron* of merchants like Landolfo Rufolo (2.4) who are engaged in "the same frantic, incessant and senseless activism of Horace's merchant."[25] Yet this explanation too leaves questions open. If the Author is applying the image of dust to himself, why would he use a Horatian image of the mercantile man caught up in a whirlwind of dust, given that this image would be better applied to the kinds of profit-seeking men who would criticize the Author rather than to the Author himself?

Neither of these subtexts puts the Author of the *Decameron* into the good light in which he would prefer to be seen. The recall of Horace's man caught up in a whirlwind of senseless activity, when applied to the Author, reminds us there are multiple ways to be caught up in pointless activity; the winds of indirection can sweep up the profit-seekers, but they can also sweep up those who deal with words and ideas. That possibility is nudged to the side by the image of the dust that is borne on high, landing even on the crowns of kings and emperors and on high palaces and towers; here Boccaccio is aligning his Author's voice with that of Dante, to whom it is promised that his outcry, like the wind, will strike the highest peaks and be no little source of honour to him.[26] But as we recall this image from the *Paradiso* that asserts authorial honour, we have to remember that with the phrase "spirante turbo" Boccaccio is very clearly echoing a verse describing the landscape in *Inferno* 3, a canto wherein are punished cowards and neutrals who lived "without blame and without praise" ("sanza 'nfamia e sanza lodo" [*Inferno* 3.36]).[27] I would contend that Boccaccio wanted us to consider whether the Author of the *Decameron* was himself guilty of such cowardice, given that in a later moment, the Author will abdicate responsibility for what the *Decameron* contains, choosing instead to see his readers as fully answerable for what they choose to see in his work. Moreover, I believe he would have wanted us to ask: Is the Author making an honourable statement against high-status people, or is he just stirring up a lot of dust?

Nor would Boccaccio have wanted readers to stop here, so before he concludes his defence at the beginning of Day 4, he makes statements that invite readers to consider the perspective that Dante would have offered. When the Author of the *Decameron* claims that he and others who love women are following the laws of nature, and that to oppose the laws of nature would require incredible strength that could do violence to a person struggling against nature, Dante would have begged to differ. As a champion of charitable love and as someone who recognized the violence that charitable love does to human nature,

Dante might well have responded by citing Thomas Aquinas, who reminds us that individuals cannot be charitable thanks to human nature alone:

> ... charity is a friendship of man for God, founded upon the fellowship of everlasting happiness. Now this fellowship is in respect, not of natural, but of gratuitous gifts, for, according to Rom. 6:23, "the grace of God is life everlasting": wherefore charity itself surpasses our natural faculties. Now that which surpasses the faculty of nature, cannot be natural or acquired by the natural powers, since a natural effect does not transcend its cause.
>
> Therefore charity can be in us neither naturally, nor through acquisition by the natural powers, but by the infusion of the Holy Ghost, Who is the love of the Father and the Son, and the participation of Whom in us is created charity, as stated above.[28]

Thus, when in *Purgatorio* 13 and 14 Dante affirms the virtue of charitable love in opposition to envy, he represents charity as a violent force: a whip, a scourge, a hard bit, and a bridle to be applied with force. That is because, as I have argued elsewhere, Dante views charity as doing beneficent and necessary violence to human nature by forcing humans to turn towards God and take on another, more perfect, nature.[29]

This is a violence rejected by the Author of the *Decameron*. He chooses to follow the laws of nature and to love women. We ourselves will have to decide whether we sign on to the Author's embrace of human nature. Whether we do or not will depend not only on how much attention we pay to what Marchesi has called "the *Decameron*'s insistence on the intrinsic dangers that lie in adopting an unconditionally hedonistic ethics (and a literalistic poetics)" but also on how open we are to hearing, as a counterweight to the Author's pronouncements about the impossibility of resisting love for women, a Dante-inflected voice that proclaims the necessity of a discipline of love.[30]

The Author ends with a line about his critics that Marchesi has justifiably found truly puzzling: "ne' lor diletti, anzi appetiti corrotti standosi, me nel mio, questa brieve vita che posta n'è, lascino stare ("in this short lifetime that is given to us, let them stay with their pleasures, actually their perverse longings, and leave me to my own"). Marchesi writes:

> If it is clear that the pleasure, which the author wants to prolong, coincides with his traditional, Ovidian *servitium amoris* (his "duty of pleasing" his

female audience), what are the pleasures – that Boccaccio immediately qualifies as "corrupted appetites" – in which the detractors of the *Decameron* are immersed? The text of the Introduction to Day IV has provided the reader with no hint as to what they might be.[31]

To explain them, Marchesi cites Horace, who in *Satire* 1.4 accuses his detractors of not wishing to read satire because they will recognize criticism of their vices. This is of course possible; Marchesi has convincingly shown that Boccaccio had *Satire* 1.4 in mind when he composed the Introduction to Day 4. Nevertheless, it seems quite clear that Boccaccio wanted us to struggle with this line and to make us pause over the ways in which he distinguishes himself from his detractors. Rather than focus only on the phrase that draws Marchesi's attention, I would include the hypothetical clause that precedes it: *"and if they are unable to turn warm, let them live icily benumbed: in this short lifetime that is given to us, let them stay with their pleasures, actually their perverse longings, and leave me to my own"* (*"e se essi riscaldar non·si possono assiderati si vivano*: e ne' lor diletti, anzi appetiti corrotti standosi, me nel mio, questa brieve vita che posta n'è, lascino stare" [emphasis mine]). Why call attention to the critics' warmth or lack of it?

In translating this line, Musa and Bondanella correctly, in my view, decline to specify the source of the Author's pleasure and desire; they do, however, intervene to specify the critics' failing: "So let those critics of mine be silent, and if they cannot warm up to my work, let them live numbed with the chill of their own pleasures, or rather with their corrupt desires, and let me go on enjoying my own for this short lifetime granted to us."[32] To translate "se essi riscaldar non si possono" as "if they cannot warm up to my work" is tricky, because the Italian text contains no such reference to the Author's work. Given that the Author has already told women that his critics are people who "do not love you and do not wish to be loved by you" and who "neither feel nor know the pleasures and the power of natural affection" ("non v'ama e da voi non disidera d'esser amato, sì come persona che i piaceri né la vertù della natural affezione né sente né conosce" [4.Intro.32]), it seems reasonable to assume that the critics' lack of warmth derives not from their inability to warm up to the Author's work but from their inability to understand, whether emotionally or intellectually, natural affection for women.

So the Author has made a choice, and it is a choice for women. Ultimately, in my view, his response to his critics is hinging on the kinds of deliberative choices people make. Admittedly, I am inclined to read the passage in this way because I give particular weight to the echo of *Inferno* 3 that appeared earlier when the Author compared himself to the dust that is caught up in the whirlwind. To the ante-Inferno in *Inferno* 3 are relegated the cowards and the neutrals who shunned making a choice either for good or for evil; neither heaven nor hell deigns to accept them. For Boccaccio, who commented on this canto in his *Esposizioni sopra la Commedia* (*Expositions on Dante's "Comedy"*), circularity – which is to say, continued movement without a fixed objective – is an important element in Dante's representation of those who refused to make the choices that would bring them praise or blame. Also important, however, is the frigidity that makes it impossible to choose to act. Writing about the vice of inertia, punished in *Inferno* 3, Boccaccio states:

> Pare adunque questo vizio consistere in una freddeza d'animo, la quale, occupate non solamente le potenzie intellettive, ma eziandio le sensitive, tiene coloro, ne' quali esso dimora, del tutto oziosi, in tanto che, brievemente, niuna oportunità pare che muover gli possa ad alcuno atto operativo: e per questo non come uomini, ma come bruti animali, anzi come vermini putridi e fastidiosi, menano la vita loro.
>
> Ed in questo pare loro, per quel che comprender si possa, sentire alcun diletto, il quale, per ciò che da viziosa cagione è preso, senza colpa esser non puote. (3.all.7–8)[33]

It is evident, then, that this sin is accompanied by a mental frigidity that, after taking control of both the cognitive and sensitive faculties of sinners, so tightly clutches those who sluggishly persist in their sinfulness that they are soon rendered incapable of being moved toward any action by anything whatsoever. Therefore, they carry out their lives not like men, but like brutish beasts. Indeed, they are like putrid, disgusting worms.

For this aspect, for as much as can be understood here, they seem to feel a sort of pleasure that, being derived from sinfulness, cannot subsist without guilt.

In this allegorical exposition of *Inferno* 3, Boccaccio draws distinctions between those who are moved towards action and those who are not, between those who do not suffer mental frigidity and those who do, and ultimately between those who are men and those who are brutish beasts. And when, in the Introduction to *Decameron* 4, the Author sets out the differences between himself and his critics, he will draw on these categories. His critics may accuse him of otiose activity, but *he* is the one who militantly serves women, and *they* are the ones who fail to hear the call; he has indicated his choice, no matter the consequences, and he remains on the side of warmth; his critics can be left in the cold, given that they are intellectually and emotionally incapable of choosing this sort of love. He has exercised his choice, no matter what; his critics appear characterized by the enmeshed pleasures and corrupted desires that are proper to those who refuse to exercise their choice either for what is good or for what is evil.

And yet, even as the Author mobilizes these defences, encouraging the reader to side with him, the conclusion that he is in the right depends very much on the particular lens we apply. The Author has chosen to take responsibility for his love for women; but there remain many other instances in which he declines to take a stand for one side or another and in which he deflects responsibility for a choice. Boccaccio presents us with an Author who asks us to side with him; yet at the same time, the Author's affirmations open up breaches, showing us that we cannot assume this Author speaks in one voice, we cannot assume there is but a single perspective, and we therefore cannot assume there is but a single lesson to be learned.

What my analysis of Marchesi's argument shows us is that in weighing what the Author says in the *Decameron*, we need to pay studied attention to the way Boccaccio draws on subtexts not only to help clarify his authorial project but also to show us that when we formulate conclusions about the thrust of this project, we may well privilege a certain perspective or certain perspectives over others, and we may well marginalize information that strikes us as contradictory. In weighing the Author's statements, we are thrown off balance at every turn, because for every analogy we create or refuse (such as "the Author is like Horace's father" or "the Author is not like Filippo Balducci"), we also have to acknowledge the imperfect application of such analogies. Analogies prove simultaneously relevant and not relevant. Conclusions come to the fore, and conclusions dissolve. Of the Author, we would have to say: He is/isn't like Dante. He is/isn't like Filippo Balducci. He is/isn't like Filippo Balducci's son. He is/isn't like Horace's father. He is/isn't like Horace. He is/isn't like those who refused to take a side, to choose either good or evil. And one could continue: He is/isn't like the historical Giovanni Boccaccio. He is/isn't like Prince Gallehault. And so on and so forth. The effect of this is to show that any conclusions we draw are conditional, based on our perspective and on the weight we give to the evidence we adduce. The Author of the *Decameron* – and by extension the text of the *Decameron* itself – is never stable and fixed, but rather always floating and mutable.

The Author, never stable, never fixed (except when he is). That, of course, is the message that is clearly transmitted by the Author's Conclusion. I would like to keep our focus on this mutability and to take under consideration the mutability and instability in the Author's Conclusion to the *Decameron*.

Readings of the Author's Conclusion tend to highlight the moments that might be used to help readers face the language and the contents of a text that is highly slippery. These moments include: his justification for the use of language and content that might be considered inappropriate; his shifting responsibility onto readers for what they find in his work; his noting that he has not conceived of these stories but is merely the vehicle of transmission; his claim that the stories do not demand to be read and that, in any case, he has provided for means by which the reader can make an informed decision about what will be found in them.

Scholars who have commented on the Author's Conclusion remain aware that the authorial persona constructed here is highly complex and mutable. Many of them have understood this mutability as stylistic variation (in Latin, *variatio*) that reflects appropriately the richness of content in the *Decameron*, and for which, understandably, Boccaccio has been lauded.[34] Classical and medieval rhetoricians, guardians of the Italian canon such as Francesco Petrarca and Pietro Bembo, and acclaimed literary critics and historians are called upon to justify and sing the praises of Boccaccio's variation and mixing of stylistic registers.[35] The mutability is not limited to language, of course, and David Wallace has called attention to the "egregiously complex persona" that Boccaccio develops.[36] Gregory Stone, who provides the most sustained close reading of the Author's Conclusion and who teases out its hermeneutic complexities, views this mutability as crucial to Boccaccio's project of communicating how readers should and shouldn't read.[37] Presenting Boccaccio's case against a philological mode of reading, whose "primary aim is to *say what Boccaccio said*," Stone writes:

> But what Boccaccio said is that Boccaccio himself cannot properly say what Boccaccio said ... Boccaccio himself cannot say what he said, since all things, including his *lingua*, are subject to constant mutability. If the philologist is to remain honest to his task, if he is to say precisely what

Boccaccio said, then he must say that he cannot say what Boccaccio said, since what Boccaccio said is that he cannot say what he said.[38]

In addressing the question of variation, mutability, and difference in the Author's Conclusion, I would like to foreground a passage from Boccaccio's *De casibus virorum illustrium* that I have previously identified as crucial to the understanding of Boccaccio's work.[39] The narrator of the *De casibus* comments on Theseus's excessive credulity, which brought about his downfall:

Et cum ita sit, omnesne putabis uno eodemque animo verba proferre? Nil profecto hac existimatione stolidius. Circumspecti quidem viri atque constantis est negligere neminem, sed numquenque pro meritis pendere, et, ne posit de incognitos precipiti sententia falli, se in se ipsum colligere, et, quasi e specula mentis librato iudicio, intueri quis verba faciens, quod ob meritum, quis in quem facta, quo in loco, quo in tempore, iratus an quietus animo, hostis an amicus, infamis aut honestus homo sit.[40]

Do you believe that there is but one point of view behind all statements? Certainly nothing is more foolish than to think so. The man who judges carefully ignores no one's ideas, but rather weighs each according to its merits, then considers the matter carefully so that he does not make a mistake by coming to too hasty a conclusion concerning things with which he is not familiar. In the watchtower of his mind, he uses balanced judgment as he observes who is speaking and to what end; he wants to know who speaks against whom, where things took place, when they happened, whether the speaker is angry or calm, enemy or friend, infamous or honorable.

This passage draws attention, obviously, to the existence of multiple points of view and to the fact that privileging one person's point of view over those of others could be risky. The vigilant interpreter will "[judge] carefully" by evaluating all possible points of view. The passage encourages one to think it is indeed possible (assuming that we examine enough points of view and possess a mind's watchtower that is sufficiently lofty) not only to determine the who, what, when, where, how, and why but also to determine the disposition of the speaker. The passage invites us to believe that philological interpretation is possible – that when one desires to know the who, what, when, where, how, and why, one will be able to arrive at the answers to those questions if one weighs matters carefully and mobilizes all the forces of the watchtower of one's mind. It suggests that mutability can be managed and controlled. If there are multiple interpretive possibilities, the man of careful judgment will presumably know how to get to the bottom of the matter and sort things out.

What do we do, however, if the speaker cannot be classified as *either* "angry or calm, enemy or friend, infamous or honorable"? What if the speaker is *"both* angry *and* calm, enemy *and* friend, infamous *and* honorable"? That is the case, I shall argue, with the Author of the *Decameron*, and most especially with the authorial persona as he emerges in the Author's Conclusion. We like to think we know whose side he is on. Even though we understand that his persona is strikingly complex, it is tempting to think that at least his allegiance to women is unshakeable, given his repeated claims to that effect.

As he begins his Conclusion, the Author takes care to frame his argument by reminding the women to whom he addresses himself that they are most worthy, that he has laboured to provide for their solace, that he relies on their merciful prayers and divine grace rather than his own merits in order to accomplish what he is doing, and that he will let his pen and his hand rest after thanking first God and then the ladies themselves for having brought him to complete his task. The Author then switches genres, transitioning from the genre of the "acknowledgments page" to a defence of his work. He announces that he intends to respond briefly to "a few small things" ("alcune cosette") that perhaps someone among the women or various other people might say (*Concl. Autore*, 2). The Author's allegiance to women appears intact, since the designation of the potential criticisms as trifling may not yet be a veiled criticism of the women; after all, the Author states that these possible criticisms might stem from a lone woman or from people not even included among the women he addresses.

Delaying the moment when he will concede rest to his pen and to his hand, the Author sets about subtly undermining the very women whose merits he sang in the opening sentence of his Conclusion. He aims sniping comments at anyone who might articulate an objection. Among the women who might not agree are the bigoted, who are more inclined to pay attention to words than to deeds and who are more concerned about seeking to appear to be good ("spigolistra donna ... le quali più le parole pesan che' fatti e più d'apparer s'ingegnan d'esser buone" [*Concl. Autore*, 5]). Then there are the people who are reciting paternosters and baking home goods for their spiritual directors – yet they "say and even do little things when the occasion presents itself" ("dicono e anche fanno delle cosette otta per vicenda" [*Concl. Autore*, 15]). Characterizing his audience as "simple young girls, as the majority of you are" ("semplici giovinette, come voi il più siete [*Concl. Autore*, 18]), he underscores that he is writing for women who are "idle" ("oziose" [*Concl. Autore*, 20]) and for women who don't "make profitable use of time" ("utilmente adoperare il tempo" [*Concl. Autore*, 21]), the way that men dedicated to study do. In defending the length of his stories, he doesn't just content himself with referring back to his female audience's idleness; he also raises interest in what they are doing when they are not reading, as he tells the women that "you have all that leftover time that you don't dedicate to amorous pleasures" ("tanto del tempo avanza quanto negli amorosi piaceri non ispendete" [*Concl. Autore*, 21]). Noting also that the women he addresses will never study in Athens, Bologna, and Paris, he claims that to women one must direct a lengthier speech than one would direct towards those who "have, through their studies, sharpened their wits" ("quegli che hanno negli studii gl'ingegni assottigliati" [*Concl. Autore*, 21]). And all this before the Author begins a tawdry series of sexual innuendoes, vaunting how valiantly he has used his lingual abilities, how he has been "weighed," and how much a neighbour lady of his has appreciated him (*Concl. Autore*, 27).

The shifting tonalities of the Author's Conclusion are challenging to grasp. When this Author speaks, his offerings can be uncertain, ambiguous, discordant, contradictory. The defence of his work, which began with a gracious nod to the most noble ladies and an acknowledgment of how they merit his thanks, now appears to have become an underhanded misogynist offensive against women.

How we understand the Author's mutability is paramount. Gregory Stone provides a crucial point of entry by focusing on the Author's use of the word *lingua* in the following passage:

Confesso nondimeno le cose di questo mondo non avere stabilità alcuna, ma sempre essere in mutamento, e così potrebbe della mia lingua esser intervenuto; la qual, non credendo io al mio giudicio, il quale a mio potere io fuggo nelle mie cose, non ha guari mi disse una mia vicina che io l'aveva la migliore e la più dolce del mondo: e in verità quando questo fu, egli erano poche a scrivere delle soprascritte novelle. (*Concl. Autore*, 27)

Nevertheless, I confess that the things of this world have no stability whatsoever, but are subject to constant change. This may have happened to my lingual abilities [*lingua*]. Speaking of which, given that I avoid placing credence in my own judgment regarding matters concerning me, a woman who is a neighbor of mine told me that I had the best and the sweetest lingual abilities in the world; and to tell the truth, when she said this, there were not many novellas yet to write.

Identifying this passage as "itself a perfect example of the linguistic mutability that is its explicit theme," Stone writes:

> At first, *lingua* is a metaphor, a linguistically improper usage meaning not the physical *lingua* but rather "language." Boccaccio says that his *lingua*, his language, may have already changed. And, indeed, we witness this change right here, as the neighbor lady, who seems to praise, for its sexual prowess, Boccaccio's "tongue," thereby restores *lingua* to its proper, literal, physical sense. Boccaccio, a cunning linguist, splits his tongue in two: the first sense of *lingua* (language) is linguistically improper, metaphorical, yet morally proper, weighty, serious, honest; the second sense of *lingua* (tongue) is linguistically proper, literal, yet morally improper, frivolous, bawdy. Boccaccio's tongue, when it says "tongue," says something other than what it says.[41]

In Stone's view, the shuttling between two usages is between metaphorical and literal, between proper and improper. This view is consistent with David Wallace's view of the Author's Conclusion as an "extraordinary mixture of bookishness and sexual innuendo" and of the Author as "author, literary theorist, seducer, and midnight rambler."[42] These readings capture the widely accepted understanding of the Author's mutability; they emphasize, by turn, the Author's intellectual accomplishments and his sexual ones, and the tension between them.

Still, whether the Author is seen in a more bookish or in a more erotic light, readers have accepted as an operative fiction that he, with his *Decameron* as a kind of Prince Gallehault, can bring pleasure and solace to his imagined female readers, even if he does so within certain limits. Thus, in a concluding line about the Author's Conclusion, Wallace can write: "The two-faced text imagines itself, finally, as a surrogate for its masculine author, slipping his way into the houses of Florence and exercising his tongue for the pleasure and solace of women who cannot cross their own doorways and so take part in the greater political world."[43]

But just when we think we have a handle on the Author's two-facedness, we may find, if we train our attention on an alternative moment, that other ways of being two-faced have escaped our notice. In this alternative moment – what we might call another "perfect example" if we were not aware that yet more perfect examples may remain to be found – the Author is not describing his own abilities, lingual or otherwise – he is describing his female audience: "a avere a favellare a semplici giovinette, come voi il più siete, sciocchezza sarebbe stata l'andar cercando e faticandosi in trovar cose molte esquisite, e gran cura porre di molto misuratamente parlare" ("in having to speak to simple girls, as the majority of you are, it would have been silly to go seeking out and laboring over stylishly refined things, and to put a lot of effort into weighing my words" [*Concl. Autore*, 18]).

The Author's description of his female audience as "semplici giovinette, come voi il più siete (*Concl. Autore*, 18), which I have translated as "simple girls, as the majority of you are," reveals a kind of two-facedness that readers appear hesitant to acknowledge, especially if they feel secure in their conclusion that the Author is a champion for women.

To begin: How much condescension do we register in the diminutive *giovinette*? If *giovani* is to be understood as "young ladies" when the Author addresses his audience as "Nobilissime giovani" ("Most noble young ladies") at the very opening of his Author's Conclusion, how are we to understand the diminutive suffix that he now tacks onto the women? In a concession to the Author, translators tend to render *giovinette* the same way they would render *giovani*, that is, as "young ladies."[44] Yet to do so is to expunge the potentially disparaging colouring of the term. *Giovinetta* appears for the first time in the *Decameron* when Dioneo uses it to describe the nameless young girl whom the monk sees in 1.4 and with whom he and the abbot then have sex (1.4.5); the naive Alibech is a *giovinetta* (3.10.12); the two very young nuns who first have sex with Masetto are *giovinette* (3.1.21); Giletta di Narbona is a *giovinetta* when she falls in love with Beltramo in a way that appears inappropriate for her age (3.9.5); Griselda, identified by Gualtieri as a possible wife who will not disturb his tranquility, is twice called a *giovinetta* (10.10.9; 10.10.14); and lest we forget what *giovinetta* means, Fiammetta insistently (seven times!) labels as *giovinette* the very young girls, approximately fifteen years of age, with whom King Charles inappropriately falls in love (10.6 at 11, 13, 18, 21, 25, 36, and 36).

Furthermore, what are we to make of the fact that the Author characterizes the majority of his audience as <u>semplici</u> giovinette? Is *semplici* to be understood as a standard term to be applied to females, to indicate their widely accepted secondary status with respect to men?

Or, given that *semplice* is the adjective applied to less ably-minded figures such as Ferondo (3.8.6), Alibech (3.10.11), and Calandrino (8.3.4; 8.3.18), should it be given a much more critical thrust, and should we therefore understand it to mean something more like "naive," or "ingenuous," or "unsophisticated"? (As far as I know, no translators have dared to try out "naive" or "ingenuous" as possibilities, though Guido Waldman allows for a whiff of condescension when he renders "semplici giovinette" as "unsophisticated young lasses" [684]). Would we go as far as does Rhiannon Daniels when, in parsing this line, she states that these are the not very intelligent women ("donne poco intelligenti") from whom Boccaccio sought to distinguish Fiammetta in the dedication to his *Teseida*?[45] Or should we instead prefer the reading of those translators who soften the term by presenting the women as "unaffected" or "unassuming" or "unpretentious"?[46] In weighing this one adjective – and certainly in translating it into English – we discover that we are being asked to decide how snidely hostile or friendly or ambivalently friendly we believe the Author is towards women. We have to ask why this characterization of the majority of the female audience as *semplici* seems to be functioning as fine print that most readers tend to ignore, preferring the Author's prominently placed labels instead (i.e., "most noble young women" ["nobilissime giovani"], "most charming women" [graziosis-sime donne"], "dearest women" ["carissime donne"]). Most important, we have to admit that, in drawing conclusions about the exact colouring of a label like *semplici giovinette* – applied not to all of the audience, just to the greater part of it – the language we have proves inadequate to the task. These terms mutate as we, in interpreting them, decide which values and which contexts to privilege. Each such decision is a conclusion, fated to be fragmentary and unfinished, because the Author is not a champion of *all* women, because the audience is not composed *only* of simple young girls, and because – as is clear from the variations in the English translations – terms like *semplici* and *giovinette* can be read both *in bono* and *in malo*, depending on the spin we place on them.

Giovanni Boccaccio, by leaving us with these constructions of the Author and his audience in his Conclusion, and by using a language that is bound to be interpreted variously by different constituents who weigh its nuances, virtually guarantees that discussion will endure. Perhaps the most principled response to his efforts would be to refuse to say "The End," and instead to extend the invitation to dialogue about the ethical dimension of the *Decameron*, and to promise, "To be continued ..."

Notes

Introduction

1 Solomon, *Ethics and Excellence*, 4.
2 Hollander first made this argument in the chapter titled "The Book as Galeotto" in his *Boccaccio's Two Venuses*; he reiterates and expands on his views in his *Boccaccio's Dante and the Shaping Force of Satire*, 4, 15, 100.
3 Hollander, *Boccaccio's Dante*, 100.
4 Hollander, *Boccaccio's Dante*, 97–100.
5 Hollander, *Boccaccio's Dante*, 98.
6 Migiel, *A Rhetoric of the "Decameron."*
7 Hastings, "To Teach or Not to Teach."
8 Hastings, "To Teach or Not to Teach."
9 Hastings, "To Teach or Not to Teach," 20–2.
10 Hastings, "To Teach or Not to Teach," 23–5, as he discusses Olson, *Literature as Recreation*.
11 Kirkham, "Morale"; Kirkham, *The Sign of Reason*.
12 Kirkham, "Morale," 259, 261–2.
13 Kirkham, "Morale," 260–3.
14 Kirkham, "Morale," 266–8.
15 Kirkham, "Morale," 268.
16 Hollander, *Boccaccio's Dante*, 73.
17 Smarr, *"Decameron,"* ch. 8 of *Boccaccio and Fiammetta*.
18 Hastings, *Nature and Reason in the "Decameron,"* 5–6.
19 Hastings, *Nature and Reason in the "Decameron."*
20 Hastings, *Nature and Reason in the "Decameron,"* 107.
21 Baratto, "Orientamenti morali del Boccaccio," in *Realtà e stile nel "Decameron,"* 49–68 at 54.

22 Baratto, *Realtà e stile nel "Decameron,"* 65–8.
23 Marcus, *An Allegory of Form*, 8.
24 Marcus, *An Allegory of Form*, 9.
25 Marcus, *An Allegory of Form*, 9.
26 Marcus, *An Allegory of Form*, 9.
27 Hollander, *Boccaccio's Dante*, 71–2.
28 Hollander, *Boccaccio's Dante*, 115.
29 Flasch, *Poesia dopo la peste*, 36.
30 Flasch, *Poesia dopo la peste*, 36, my translation of the following: "Pensava a una filosofia che, come quella dei sapienti greci più antichi, fosse al tempo stesso insegnamento di vita, e quindi etica, politica, poesia e teologia." Flasch adds: "Chi parlava così, si rifiutava di apprendere il proprio concetto di filosofia nelle aule delle università" (A person who speaks like this was refusing to develop his personal understanding of philosophy within university classrooms).
31 Flasch, *Poesia dopo la peste*, 11.
32 Flasch first describes his prejudices (*Poesia dopo la peste*, 4) and subsequently goes on to show how, in the course of his reading of the *Decameron*, these prejudices fell away.
33 Carroll, "Art and Ethical Criticism," reviews and responds to the objections to ethical criticism.
34 Kircher, "The Modality of Moral Communication."
35 Kircher, "The Modality of Moral Communication," 1044.
36 Kircher, "The Modality of Moral Communication," 1044, 1037.
37 Kircher, "The Modality of Moral Communication," 1038.
38 Grudin and Grudin, *Boccaccio's "Decameron" and the Ciceronian Renaissance*, 4.
39 Grudin and Grudin, *Boccaccio's "Decameron" and the Ciceronian Renaissance*, 1.
40 It is important to clarify here that my primary interest is neither in translation theory nor in the history of translations of the *Decameron*. These are valid areas for exploration that I leave to other scholars. Guyda Armstrong, for example, has provided a masterful study of the way that textual and translation studies can help us understand Boccaccio's place in anglophone reading culture; see her *The English Boccaccio*. Significantly, Armstrong limits her study to translations of the *Decameron* that precede 1932, partly because of practical considerations that have to do with what is possible in a single monograph and partly because of the epistemological and ethical challenges that one would face in assessing translations completed after the 1930s. Armstrong notes that "much work still needs to be done on the post-war scholarly translations of Boccaccio, for example, which have made such an important contribution to the academic study of the author in universities

around the world, but perhaps we need to wait a generation or two more so that their contribution can be appreciated at its fullest" (17).

41 For the view of the *Corbaccio* as an ironic fiction, see Barricelli, "Satire of Satire"; Hollander, *Boccaccio's Last Fiction*; Psaki, "The Play of Genre and Voicing"; Armstrong, "Boccaccio and the Infernal Body"; and Migiel, "Boccaccio and Women."

42 Migiel, *A Rhetoric of the "Decameron,"* 164.

Chapter One

1 Victoria Kirkham is one of the staunchest proponents of a Boccaccio interested in moral and ethical matters. See Kirkham, "Morale." Another crucial scholarly voice (and one whose contribution to the debate has been unfortunately overlooked) is Flasch, *Poesia dopo la peste*. Flasch argues, among other things, that the *Decameron* offers "filosofia morale per le donne, piacevole e concretamente percepibile" (moral philosophy for women, a moral philosophy that is pleasurable and that can be grasped in its particulars [26]).

2 De Sanctis, *Storia della letteratura italiana*, ch. 9, s. 16; see 1: 359.

3 De Sanctis, *Storia della letteratura italiana*, ch. 9, s. 16; see 1: 359.

4 As Timothy Kircher would put it, the *Decameron* emphasizes the "contingent, subjective apprehension of moral truth." See his "The Modality of Moral Communication," 1035.

5 See Boccaccio, *Decameron*, trans. McWilliam, 2nd rev. ed.; Boccaccio, *The Decameron*, trans. Musa and Bondanella; Boccaccio, *Decameron*, trans. Waldman. Note that McWilliam's translation, first published by Penguin Books in 1972, was republished in 1995 with minor revisions to the translation and with an updated introduction. Hereafter, in referring to these translations, I will use the translators' names.

6 Daniel Tonozzi brought this instance of direct discourse to my attention.

7 The autograph manuscript of this text (which includes the Latin translation of Aristotle's *Nicomachean Ethics*) is housed in the Biblioteca Ambrosiana in Milan as codex Ambrosiano A 204 Inf. For an informative overview of the debates regarding the dating of this manuscript (to 1339–40 or to the early 1340s), see Barsella, "The Myth of Prometheus," 40n.

8 *Nichomachean Ethics*, Book 10, Chapter 6, at 1176a30–1177a11, in Thomas Aquinas, *Commentary on Aristotle's Nicomachean Ethics*, 618–19.

9 I like Musa and Bondanella's earlier choice, "Dioneo, you speak very well," which Martinez also uses, and I would consider this acceptable. Musa and Bondanella's alternative appears in the collection of twenty-one novellas that they translated for the Norton Critical Edition; see Boccaccio,

The Decameron: A New Translation, 15. For Martinez's translation, see Martinez, "The Tale of the Monk and His Abbot," 114.

10 Jonathan Usher does not translate this line when he cites it in his essay "Boccaccio's *Ars Moriendi*," but based on what he says about the "delicate serenity" and the "judicious admixture of reason and pleasure" (623), I believe he would likely agree with me.

11 Filomena recognizes Dioneo as "sollazzevole e festevole" (1.Concl.14) when she is about to grant him his privilege. McWilliam translates this as "jovial and entertaining" (68), Musa and Bondanella as "entertaining and jovial" (70), and Waldman as "the life and soul of the party" (62).

12 Elissa is "tutta festevole" when she begins her story of the king of Cyprus and the lady of Gascony (1.9.2). McWilliam writes that she begins "all merrily" (61), Musa/Bondanella "most joyously" (63), Waldman "merrily" (57).

13 This takes us back to a question I have raised previously: Does the *Decameron* distinguish between male and female laughter? Arguing against Giulio Savelli, I have claimed that it does. See Migiel, *A Rhetoric of the "Decameron,"* 139–42.

14 McWilliam, 20; Musa/Bondanella, 21; Waldman, 20.

15 Note that Pampinea's "senza modo" follows upon the description of excessive behaviour in the Author's description of the plague, Day 1.Intro.21: "Altri, in contraria opinion tratti, affermavano il bere assai e il godere e l'andar cantando a torno e sollazzando e il sodisfare d'ogni cosa all'appetito che si potesse e di ciò che avveniva ridersi e beffarsi esser medicina certissima a tanto male: e così come il dicevano il mettevano in opera a lor potere, il giorno e la notte ora a quella taverna ora a quella altra andando, bevendo *senza modo* e senza misura, e molto più" (Others, drawn to the opposite belief, maintained that there was an absolutely certain remedy to this atrocious situation: drinking a lot and enjoying oneself and going around singing and having fun and satisfying all the desires one could and laughing about what was happening and joking. They put their words into action as much as they could, day and night going from one tavern to another, drinking disproportionately and *to excess*, and that wasn't all either [emphasis mine]). Other instances include the description of ser Cepparello's swift decline at 1.1.81 ("peggiorando senza modo" [taking a terrible turn for the worse), the women unable to control their laughter in 2.2.2 following the story of Martellino ("senza modo risero le donne"), Pericone who is extremely pained ("dolente senza modo") that he and Alibech do not understand each other's language in 2.7.22, the description of Zima in 3.5.4 as "extremely avaricious" ("avarissimo senza modo"), the extreme crudeness of Ferondo in 3.8.5 ("uomo materiale

e grosso senza modo"), Cimone who is extremely distressed in 5.1.42 ("senza modo dolente"), and the extreme anguish of the widow in 8.7.143 ("dolorosa senza modo").

16 McWilliam, 20; Musa and Bondanella, 20–1; Waldman, 20.

17 Harold Bloom identified *clinamen* as a key revisionary ratio that allowed writers to deal with the anxiety of influence. See Bloom, *The Anxiety of Influence*, 14.

18 McWilliam, 20; Musa and Bondanella, 21; Waldman, 20.

19 Interestingly, in their first translation, published in the Norton Critical Edition of selected *Decameron* stories, Musa and Bondanella translated "pensieri" simply as "thoughts," the way I do, and only subsequently, with the publication of the full translation, decided to opt for "troubled thoughts" instead. See Boccaccio, *The Decameron: A New Translation*, 14.

20 Musa and Bondanella, 21.

21 Musa and Bondanella use the expression "only thought" (21), while McWilliam opts for "sole concern" (20) and Waldman for "entire concern" (20).

Chapter Two

1 Migiel, *A Rhetoric of the "Decameron,"* ch. 6, "Men, Women, and Figurative Language in the *Decameron*."

2 Although the tendency is most marked in as yet inexperienced readers, I do not mean to make sweeping generalizations. Readers even younger than undergraduates are indeed capable of reading carefully and precisely, as I discovered during a Telluride Association Summer Program for rising high school seniors ("He Said, She Said: The Battle of the Sexes in Medieval and Renaissance Writing") that Kathleen Long and I taught during the summer of 2004. Jennifer Green, one of our students in that seminar, was immediately able to articulate the terms of Maestro Alberto's metaphor for me, and I had no indication that any of the other fifteen students in the room would have given a different answer.

3 Some translators restyle Maestro Alberto's response, changing the degree of pleasure that he would appear to offer women. Maestro Alberto states that "come che nel porro niuna cosa sia buona, pur men reo e più piacevole alla bocca è il capo di quello" (1.10.17). For this, I would offer the following translation: "while no part of the leek is good, the head of it is, however, less objectionable and more pleasing to the palate." Mark Musa and Peter Bondanella render this as "while no part of the leek is truly good, its root part happens to be less distasteful and more pleasing to the palate"; see *The Decameron*, trans. Musa and Bondanella, 67. In doing so,

they shield us from the original, which tells us that *no part of the leek is good*. Apparently, to Musa and Bondanella, "if no part of the leek is truly good," then there might at least be a part that would *appear* to be good. These translators also domesticate the meal by substituting "lentils and leeks" for the lupini beans and leeks of the original. That path of argumentation seems to be the one that, along a slippery slope, leads even Millicent Marcus to talk about the "savoury white head" (222) and the "tasty white head" (230); see Marcus, "The Tale of Maestro Alberto (I.10)," 222, 230.

4 Picone, "Le 'merende' di maestro Alberto."
5 Picone, "Le 'merende' di maestro Alberto," 102.
6 Boccaccio and Busi, *Decamerone da un italiano all'altro*, 1: 75.
7 Boccaccio and Busi, *Decamerone da un italiano all'altro*, 1: 75.
8 Marcus, "The Tale of Maestro Alberto (I.10)," 222.
9 Marcus, "The Tale of Maestro Alberto (I.10)," 230.
10 Russo, "Maestro Alberto da Bologna (I, 10)," in *Letture critiche del "Decameron,"* 136–9; Baratto, *Realtà e stile nel "Decameron,"* 333–5.
11 Picone, "Le 'merende' di maestro Alberto," 106–7.
12 Marcus, "The Tale of Maestro Alberto (I.10)," 231, 227.
13 Migiel, *A Rhetoric of the "Decameron,"* 117: "It is not that Madonna Malgherida lacks the instruments to speak effectively; it is that she does not respect the rule of male superiority."
14 Picone, "Le 'merende' di maestro Alberto (I.10)," 107, 110.
15 Dante Alighieri, *Inferno*.
16 For yet another reading of Maestro Alberto's situation, see the passage in Italo Svevo's *La coscienza di Zeno* (1923), found at "15 maggio 1915" (in Part VIII, "Psico-analisi"), where the elderly Zeno, infatuated with a young girl named Teresina, represents his own bumbling courtship of her in light of the novella of Maestro Alberto. Svevo's handling of this moment reveals, once again, that the situation need not be resolved in favour of the elderly male lover. Indeed, a closer look at the passage suggests that we might not necessarily be convinced by Pampinea's exhortation to side with Maestro Alberto, who, after all, does not achieve his desired goal. That is what Zeno notes when he considers how he might be able to use the force of Maestro Alberto's rhetoric to try to get the girl he wants: "Avrei voluto dare una lezioncina a Teresina e cercai di ricordarmi come da Boccaccio «Maestro Alberto da Bologna onestamente fa vergognare una donna la quale lui d'esser di lei innamorato voleva far vergognare». Ma il ragionamento di Maestro Alberto non ebbe il suo effetto perché Madonna Malgherida de' Ghisolieri gli disse: «Il vostro amor m'è caro sí come di savio e valente uomo esser dee; e per ciò, *salva la mia onestà*, come a cosa

vostra ogni vostro piacere imponete sicuramente»" (I would have liked to teach Teresina a little lesson. I tried to remember how in Boccaccio, "Maestro Alberto da Bologna justly shames a woman who tried to shame him because he was in love with her." But Maestro Alberto didn't succeed because Madonna Malgherida de' Ghisolieri said to him, "Your love is as dear to me as the love of a wise and worthy man should be; and so, *provided that my honor is secure*, you may seek your every pleasure from me as if I were your own"). The Italian text is taken from Svevo, *La coscienza di Zeno*, 2: 943.

17 The text and translation of the *Vita Nuova* are taken from the translation by Cervigni and Vasta, 78–80.

18 Migiel, *A Rhetoric of the "Decameron,"* 164.

Chapter Three

1 Readers might wonder why I opt for an apparently vague term like "the man in question" and why, unlike other translators, I do not substitute "the stablehand" or "the groom" for at least some of the personal pronouns in this passage. I believe that the use of apparently vague terminology is deliberate here. Such terminology puts us in the subject position of the king, who does not know the status or the condition of the man he has marked, though it is true that the king knows that the man is a member of his household.

2 See Thomas Aquinas, *Commentary on Aristotle's "Nicomachean Ethics,"* Book 6, Lecture 10, 1272, at 400. Here Aquinas, in discussing "an operative principle called shrewdness, as it were a certain ingenuity or skillfulness," writes that "when the intention is good, ingenuity of this sort deserves praise, but when the intention is bad, it is called craftiness, which implies evil as prudence implies good." The Litzinger translation, dating to 1964, is based on the Marietti edition, which precedes by several years the critical edition available in Thomas Aquinas, *Sententia libri Ethicorum*, ed. Dominican Fathers and introduced by R.A. Gauthier, OP, vol. 47 of *Opera Omnia* (Rome: Leonine Commission, 1968).

3 Boccaccio, *Decameron*, translation attributed to John Florio: "The Querry, who partly saw, but felt what was done to him; perceived plainely (being a subtill ingenious fellow) for what intent he was thus marked."

4 Boccaccio, *Decameron*, trans. Payne, 137: "The culprit, who had felt all this, like a shrewd fellow as he was, understood plainly enough why he had been thus marked."

5 Boccaccio, *Decameron*, trans. McWilliam, 204; Boccaccio and Busi, *Decamerone da un italiano all'altro*, 1: 207; Boccaccio, *Decameron*, trans. Waldman, 180.

6 Dante Alighieri, *Inferno*, 4.102.
7 Boccaccio, *Decameron*, trans. Rigg.
8 Boccaccio, *Decameron*, trans. Payne, 137.
9 Boccaccio, *Decameron*, trans. Musa and Bondanella, 205.
10 Boccaccio, *Decameron*, trans. McWilliam, 204.
11 Boccaccio, *Decameron*, trans. Waldman, 81.
12 Boccaccio and Busi, *Decamerone*, 1: 207.
13 Boccaccio, *Decameron*, trans. Florio [?].
14 Boccaccio, *Decameron*, trans. Rigg: "who was discreet enough never to reveal the secret as long as the King lived, or again to stake his life on such a venture." Boccaccio, *Decameron*, trans. Payne, 137: "he, like a wise man, never, during Agilulf's lifetime, discovered the matter nor ever again committed his life to the hazard of such a venture."
15 Boccaccio, *Decameron*, trans. Waldman, 181.
16 Herbert McCabe OP makes the argument that Aquinas's *prudentia*, which is misrepresented by English words such as "prudence," finds a near perfect translation in Jane Austen's "good sense." See his "Aquinas on Good Sense," 152–65.
17 Boccaccio, *Decameron*, trans. McWilliam, 205.
18 Boccaccio, *The Decameron*, trans. Musa and Bondanella, 206.
19 Boccaccio and Busi, *Decamerone*, 1: 208.
20 Boccaccio, *Decameron*, trans. Florio.
21 Boccaccio, *Decameron*, trans. Rigg.
22 Boccaccio, *Decameron*, trans. Payne, 134.
23 Boccaccio, *Decameron*, trans. McWilliam, 200.
24 Boccaccio, *Decameron*, trans. Musa and Bondanella, 201.
25 Boccaccio, *Decameron*, trans. Waldman, 177.
26 Boccaccio, *Décaméron*, traduction nouvelle de Dozon et al., 240.
27 Boccaccio, *Decameron*, ed. Branca, 1: 339n.
28 These days, philology sometimes gets a bad rap in some circles devoted to theory – as if one could divorce philology from theoretical reflection! – but the examples I adduce here stand as yet more proof that precise philological work is part and parcel of the precise metacritical investigations that good scholars try to foster. For another fascinating example of scholarship attentive to the metacritical implications of philological decisions, see Giulio Lepschy's discussion of hermeneutical and translation challenges in "*La Veniexiana*: A Venetian Play of the Renaissance," 97–117, and in particular the section on "Feminism and Philology" at 107–17.
29 For an analysis of how the rubrics of the *Decameron* tend toward the privileging of the protagonist, see Usher, "Le rubriche del *Decameron*."

30 See Valian, *Why So Slow?*

31 Valian, *Why So Slow?*, 3.

32 For the original Latin text, see Thomas Aquinas, *Opera Omnia*, available on the World Wide Web at Corpus Thomisticum, http://www. corpusthomisticum.org/iopera.html. The English translation is taken from the New Advent website, http://www.newadvent.org/summa.

33 Thomas Aquinas, *Commentary on Aristotle's "Nicomachean Ethics,"* Book 6, Lecture 7, 1196, at 381.

34 Aristotle, *Nicomachean Ethics.*

35 Pertile, "Dante, Boccaccio, e l'intelligenza."

36 Pertile, "Dante, Boccaccio, e l'intelligenza," 62.

37 Pertile, "Dante, Boccaccio, e l'intelligenza," 64. For a critique of this assumption that because Boccaccio describes ser Cepparello's expert self-fashioning, he also exalts human intelligence and artistic imagination that are completely free of moral underpinnings, see Flasch, *Poesia dopo la peste*, 121.

38 Pertile, "Dante, Boccaccio, e l'intelligenza," 65: "Nel primo gruppo [...] il protagonista viene a trovarsi in una situazione critica e riesce ad uscirne solo grazie a un impiego dell'intelligenza del tutto incurante di regole morali o fede religiosa" (In the first group ... the protagonists find themselves in a predicament and manage to extricate themselves from this predicament thanks solely to a use of intelligence that completely disregards moral rules or religious faith).

39 On page 65, Pertile says that in this second group, "la molla che fa scattare l'intelligenza non viene attivata dalla necessità di superare una situazione critica, ma dal bisogno insopprimibile di soddisfare gli istinti naturali [...] L'intelligenza ha allora il compito di trovare il modo di appagare l'istinto senza infrangere apertamente le convenzioni sociali, senza dar scandalo" (intelligence is not activated by the need to overcome a predicament, but by the unsuppressable need to satisfy natural instincts ... Intelligence thus is responsible for finding a way to fulfill these instincts without openly transgressing social conventions and without giving cause for scandal).

40 Examples include stories like 1.5 (the marchioness of Monferrato), 1.6 (the rich man and the inquisitor), 1.7 (Bergamino), 1.8 (Guglielmo Borsiere), 1.9 (the woman of Gascony), 2.9 (Madonna Zinevra), 3.9 (Giletta da Narbona), 6.1 (Madonna Oretta), 6.2 (Cisti the Baker), 6.3 (monna Nonna de' Pulci), and 9.1 (Madonna Francesca). Pertile also excludes 8.4, the story of the trick played on the rector of Fiesole by Madonna Piccarda, who aims at defending her chastity but does so by relying on less than honourable tactics. One could include more examples if one did not limit oneself to the named protagonist; in such cases we might include the abbot princess

of 2.3; the sensible servant who counsels Andreola against suicide in 4.6 and the loving father of the same novella; the good husband in 4.8; Ruggero di Lauria, who intervenes to stop the execution of two lovers in 5.6; and Minuccio d'Arezzo, who comes to Lisa's aid in 10.7.

41 Pertile, "Dante, Boccaccio, e l'intelligenza," 71: "D'altra parte non c'è dubbio che in questi personaggi spregiudicati si riconoscano volentieri i lettori del *Decameron*, quelli del Trecento come quelli d'oggi" (On the other hand, there is no doubt that readers of the *Decameron*, whether in the fourteenth century or today, willingly recognize themselves in these unscrupulous characters). Pertile goes on to say that it is beyond question that Boccaccio's sympathetic attachment to an ideological endorsement of this intelligence is contagious ("È indubbio insomma che quell'uso dell'intelligenza ha tanto spazio nel libro solo in forza della simpatia, della partecipazione, dell'adesione ideologica dell'autore alla sua materia: simpatia e partecipazione che sono contagiose, se il libro le comunica a noi attraverso i secoli" (In short, it is without a doubt that such a use of intelligence has such reign in this book thanks to the author's sympathy for, participation in, and ideological adherence to his subject; his sympathy and participation are contagious, as the book communicates these feelings to us across the centuries [72]).

42 Imagining Guido da Montefeltro as a character in the *Decameron*, Pertile declares that such a character "becomes in our eyes a positive hero, an extreme example of a human ability to prevail even in the most difficult trials" (diverrà così ai nostri occhi eroe positivo, estremo esempio della capacità umana di superare anche le prove più ardue [62]). Speaking about Cepparello, the character from the *Decameron* who most clearly inherits Guido's legacy, Pertile asserts that "si finisce anche noi per ammirare Cepparello" (we too end up admiring Cepparello [64]).

43 See Pertile, "Dante, Boccaccio, e l'intelligenza," 67–8, for his discussion of *Decameron* 3.2.

44 See Pertile, "Dante, Boccaccio, e l'intelligenza," 65–7 and again on 70–1.

45 Ferme, "*Ingegno* and Morality in the New Social Order." Ferme, who writes in English, resolutely does not translate key words from the original Italian. Figuring prominently among these are *ingegno* and *beffa*, with *diletto*, *utile consiglio*, *danno*, and *motto* adding to the list of richly evocative terms.

46 Pertile, "Dante, Boccaccio, e l'intelligenza," 64 and 65, respectively.

47 Pertile, "Dante, Boccaccio, e l'intelligenza," 65.

48 Pertile, "Dante, Boccaccio, e l'intelligenza," 67.

Chapter Four

1 See Baratto, *Realtà e stile nel "Decameron,"* esp. 305–9; Cottino-Jones, "Desire and the Fantastic in the *Decameron*"; Bruni, *Boccaccio*, 314–17, 384–5; Celati, "Lo spirito della novella."

2 Martin Eisner has also considered the question of truth in *Decameron* 3.8, though he does so by focusing on the relation between Dante and Boccaccio. See his "The Tale of Ferondo's Purgatory."

3 Boccaccio and Busi, *Decamerone da un italiano a un altro*.

4 Boccaccio, *Decameron*, trans. Musa and Bondanella, 255.

5 Boccaccio, *Decameron*, trans. Waldman, 223.

6 This is a case where two-valued Boolean logic, dealing only with the states of "true" or "false," "off" or "on," or "black" and "white," proves insufficient to deal with shades of grey, and where we must rely instead on fuzzy logic, which is an extension of many-valued logic. See Bennett, *Logic Made Easy*, ch. 11, "Fuzzy Logic, Fallacies, and Paradoxes."

7 Here, between Ferondo and Lauretta, we witness the linguistic symbiosis that is crucial to the *Decameron*'s plurilinguism and to its irony. Lauretta quotes Ferondo's language and then expands on it as if she herself were reproducing his clumsy repetition. She achieves a number of things: She draws attention to Ferondo's stylistic infelicities; and she shows that one can use such a stylistic infelicity to show one's conscious distancing from a character who uses it unconsciously.

8 This is an attitude that we see also in the pilgrim Dante in *Paradiso* 2, when he turns quickly from the praise of God that Beatrice has encouraged him to express to a curiosity-filled question about his surroundings.

9 Syntax seems to create the challenge for translators. The modern Spanish translation does the best job of communicating the wariness of the Italian text. Given the similarity of Italian and Spanish syntax, the Spanish translation is able to track the Italian original closely: "y Ferondo, que por sus celos había recibido muchas palizas, según la promesa que el abad había hecho a la mujer, dejó de ser celoso de allí en adelante, con lo que, contenta la mujer, honestamente como solía con él vivió aunque, cuando convenientemente podía, de buen grado se encontraba con el santo abad que bien y diligentemente en sus mayores necesidades la había servido." See Boccaccio, *El Decamerón*.

10 Boccaccio and Busi, *Decamerone da un italiano a un altro*, 1: 272–3.

11 Boccaccio, *Decameron*, trans. McWilliam, 264.

12 Boccaccio, *Decameron*, trans. Musa and Bondanella, 265.

13 Boccaccio, *Decameron*, trans. Waldman, 231.

14 See "Du Vilain de Bailluel," 223–49, with the critical edition of the text at 246–9.
15 The storyline of this fabliau would make it an obvious choice for the topic of Day 7, where adulterous wives play tricks on their husbands either out of love or in order to save themselves. Francesco Bruni discusses the similarity among 3.8, 7.9, and "Du Vilain de Bailluel" in his *Boccaccio*, 316n.
16 Hardly anyone seems to have noticed this. Perhaps that is because many readers seem to think they know what women in the *Decameron* want. Or perhaps that is because, early in the novella, we receive ample information about the desires, abilities, and thought processes of the abbot; we know he has a weakness for women, that he passionately desires Ferondo's beautiful wife, and that he is a clever schemer. There is never much question about what drives him to act as he does. As for what makes Ferondo tick, we get the same information the abbot has, namely, that Ferondo guards his wife vigilantly and has limited intellective capacities. Of these things, the narrator is careful to provide confirmation: The wife confirms that Ferondo is controlling, and the lengthy direct citations of Ferondo's speech give us some sense of his interests and his thought processes.
17 Boccaccio, *Decameron*, trans. Payne, 170.
18 Boccaccio, *Decameron*, trans. McWilliam, 255.
19 Boccaccio, *Decameron*, trans. Waldman, 224.
20 Boccaccio, *Decameron*, trans. Musa and Bondanella, 256.
21 Boccaccio, *Decameron*, trans. Musa and Bondanella, 255.
22 Boccaccio, *Decameron*, trans. McWilliam, 254.
23 Boccaccio, *Decameron*, trans. Waldman, 223.
24 Boccaccio, *Decameron*, trans. attributed to Florio (1620).
25 The translation by Rigg is available on the *Decameron Web*, http://www.brown.edu/Departments/Italian_Studies/dweb/texts/DecIndex.php?lang=eng.
26 Boccaccio, *Decameron*, trans. Payne, 169.
27 Boccaccio, *Decameron*, trans. Payne, 169n.

Chapter Five

1 Tolan, *Petrus Alfonsi*, 156.
2 Douglas Radcliff-Umstead sees the affirmation of a "Renaissance love ethic" in this story; see his "Boccaccio's Adaptation," 179. Aldo Scaglione also reaffirms the primacy of Love; see his *Nature and Love in the Middle Ages*, 91.
3 "Nemo est qui se a mulieris ingenio custodire possit, nisi quem Deus custodierit, et haec talis narratio, ne ducam uxorem, est magna dehortatio." See Petrus Alfonsi, *Petri Alfonsi Disciplina Clericalis*, 20.

4 "Non debes credere omnes mulieres esse tales" (You shouldn't believe that all women are like that). This brings the student to ask if his teacher has ever heard of a woman who dedicated her wits to promoting the good. When the teacher says he has heard of such a woman, the student asks the teacher to tell him about her, since this will be a new and unusual thing ("Refer mihi de illa, quia videtur mihi res nova!"). See Petrus Alfonsi, *Petri Alfonsi Disciplina Clericalis*, 20.

5 See *Il libro dei sette savi*.

6 Boccaccio, *Il Decamerone di m. Giovanni Boccaccio di nuovo emendato secondo gli antichi essemplari ...*, 319. Exemplar consulted in Milan, Biblioteca Ambrosiana, S.N. # A. VIII. 1.

7 Note the emphasis on the women's strategies as extraordinary and victorious in the following passage from Wallace, *Boccaccio: Decameron*, 78–9: "The women of the seventh day demonstrate an extraordinary range of stratagems for securing or recovering such control; three winning formulas are offered by the fourth, fifth and sixth *novelle*, set in the mid-peninsula cities of Arezzo, Rimini, and Florence."

8 Tateo, *Boccaccio*, 172–3; and Wallace, *Boccaccio: Decameron*, 82–3.

9 Wallace, *Boccaccio: Decameron*, 82–3.

10 Rigg translates "for what cause he knew not"; and Payne, seconded by Cormac Ó Cuilleanáin, translates "and without knowing why, he quickly became jealous of her." See Boccaccio, *Decameron*, trans. Ó Cuilleanáin, 483.

11 Boccaccio, *Decameron*, translation attributed to John Florio.

12 Boccaccio, *Decameron*, ed. Vittore Branca, 2: 815: "'In senso psicologico: *crepare, schiattare*' (Marti)."

13 Petrus Alfonsi, *Petrus Alfonsi Disciplina clericalis*, 19.

14 There is some precedent for this kind of wordplay in the exemplum from the *Disciplina clericalis*, though in that text, it is organized around the paronomastic couple of *puteo* (well) and *putans* (believing), which is impossible to render in English translation. Here is the prime example: "Mulier vero plena arte et calliditate sumpsit lapidem, quem proiecit in *puteum* hac intentione ut vir suus audito sonitu lapidis in *puteum* ruentis *putaret* sese in *puteum* cecidisse. Et hoc peracto mulier post *puteum* se abscondit. Vir simplex atque insipiens audito sonitu lapidis in *puteum* ruentis mox et absque mora de domo egrediens celeri cursu ad *puteum* venit, *putans* verum esse quod mulierem audisset cecidisse." (So the wife, full of craftiness and guile, picked up a stone and threw it into the well with the intent of making her husband think, when he heard the stone fall into the well, that she had fallen in. When she had done this, the wife hid herself behind the well. The husband being simple-hearted and

foolish and unknowing, when he heard the stone falling into the well, immediately rushed out of the house, and ran to the well, being really convinced that he had heard his wife fall in). For the Latin, see Petrus Alfonsi, *Petri Alfonsi Disciplina Clericalis*, 19–20, and for the English translation, see Petrus Alfonsi, *The Disciplina clericalis of Petrus Alfonsi*, 127.

15 For this translation, I am indebted to anonymous Reader A of my manuscript, who offered a better solution than the one I had originally chosen.

16 Boccaccio, *Decameron*, trans. Payne, 335.

17 Boccaccio, *Decameron*, trans. Rigg.

18 Boccaccio, *Decameron*, trans. Aldington, 354.

19 Boccaccio, *Decameron*, trans. Winwar, 408.

20 Boccaccio, *Decameron*, trans. Ó Cuilleanáin, 487.

21 Boccaccio, *Decameron*, trans. Musa and Bondanella, 507.

22 Boccaccio, *Decameron*, trans. McWilliam, 505.

23 Boccaccio, *Decameron*, trans. Waldman, 434.

24 Scrivano, *Una certa idea del comico*, 61.

25 Tateo, *Boccaccio*, 149.

26 Lodovico Branca and Maria Grazia Ciardi Dupré Dal Poggetto document an edition that eliminates the final line of 7.4; see their "Lodovico di Salvesto Ceffini copista del *Decameron*," 148. The 1620 English translation attributed to John Florio also eliminates this line; see Boccaccio, *Decameron*, trans. Florio (attributed).

27 In 8.1.5, Neifile introduces "un tedesco al soldo" (a German mercenary soldier).

28 This is consistent with Vittore Branca's footnote to this line, where he states,"Oggi diremmo: *e crepi l'avarizia*" (These days we would say: *and down with avarice*). See Boccaccio, *Decameron*, 2: 820n.

29 The phrase is Vittore Branca's. See Boccaccio, *Decameron*, 2: 820n.

30 Marafioti, "Boccaccio's Lauretta."

31 Marafioti, "Boccaccio's Lauretta," 15.

32 See Vittore Branca's note in Boccaccio, *Decameron*, 2: 821n, and the more extended analysis in Tateo, *Boccaccio*, 172–3.

33 Dante Alighieri, *Purgatorio*. Subsequent references appear in the text.

34 Tateo, *Boccaccio*, 172–3.

35 Vallicella, "On Wasting Time With Philosophy." In his biography on this website, Vallicella describes himself as a "recovering academician" who "taught philosophy at various universities in the USA and abroad before abandoning a tenured position to live the eremitic life of the independent philosopher in the Sonoran desert."

Chapter Six

1 Zinevra's rhetorical skill is evident not only in the succinctness and the moral pointedness of this denunciation but also in the material vocalizing of her pain. Her self-identification is broadened by two adjectives preceding her name ("io sono la *misera sventurata* Zinevra") and by the series of wailing "ah" sounds that characterize both this revelation of her name and the adjectival modifying phrase that follows it ("sei **anni** an**data** tapi**nando** in forma d'uom per lo mondo"). The open wail is rendered even more stunning by the alternately accented morpheme AN, which suggests that Zinevra is swept away by repeated waves that overpower her. We could visualize this as follows. The first accented "AN" is followed by a non-accented (and therefore muted) "an," making us think that the pain might have receded, only to return, after a warning "DA ta ta," in a third accented AN: **sei AN**ni an**DA**ta tapi**NAN**do.

2 Boccaccio, *The Decameron*, trans. Waldman, 156.

3 Boccaccio, *The Decameron*, trans. McWilliam, 177.

4 Boccaccio, *Decameron*, trans. Musa and Bondanella, 177.

5 See the footnote to this passage, in Boccaccio, *Decameron*, ed. Branca, 1: 300.

6 Some other editions add a comma that could alter our reading: "E, fattili venire onorevolissimi vestimenti femminili e donne che compagnia le tenessero, secondo la dimanda fatta da lei, a Bernabò perdonò la meritata morte." (See, for example, Boccaccio, *Decameron*, ed. Fanfani.) The comma makes it less certain that Madonna Zinevra's request regards Bernabò's fate. Her request may refer just as easily to the clothes and the attendant women, which the Sultan has just provided.

7 *Il Decamerone di Giovanni Boccaccio novamente corretto con tre novelle aggiunte*, 71. The passage can also be found in *Il Decamerone di M. Giovanni Boccaccio Di nuovo emendato secondo gli Antichi essemplari …* 116. In the Deputati edition, the relevant portion of the passage reads "domandando perdonanza, la quale ella (quantunque egli mal degno ne fosse) benignamente gli diede"(*Il Decameron di Messer Giovanni Boccaccio*, 129).

8 See Boccaccio, *Decameron*, ed. Branca, 1: 387.

9 Migiel, *A Rhetoric of the "Decameron,"* especially the Introduction and Conclusion, and also Migiel, "The Untidy Business of Gender Studies."

10 On the identified sources and analogues for 3.6, see Lee, *The "Decameron,"* 79–91.

11 Yet, listening to the text, I wonder if it is not alerting us to the incomplete resolution this silence offers. In the Italian, I register an insistent turn toward nouns that end in –*menti* (*congiugnimenti, abbracciamenti*) and adverbs that

end in *–mente*: (*affettuosissimamente, solamente, segretamente, diligentemente*). This persistent refrain announces "you lie!" (*menti*), "she lies!" (*mente*).

12 Playing the part of the virtuous wife, Madonna Sismonda does not criticize her husband, who claims to have beaten her and cut her hair. Since the acerbic criticism comes instead from her mother, Madonna Sismonda remains above reproach. For this observation, I am indebted to Kathleen Long (conversation on 31 August 2005).

13 Boccaccio, *Decameron*, trans. Musa and Bondanella, 430–1.

14 Boccaccio, *Decameron*, trans. McWilliam, 431.

15 This reading was advanced by John Najemy and seconded by Kathleen Long at a department colloquium where I presented my current work on the *Decameron* (19 October 2006).

16 I would emphasize here that I am not saying that upper-class women characters in the *Decameron* never use what is marked as "lower-class" speech; my claim is instead that, as the *Decameron* progresses, *open criticism of a husband is reinforced as a marker of lower-class behaviour*.

17 Although Franco Fido does not explicitly make this claim, his reading of 10.9 leads us to recognize this story as a privileged endpoint of the frametale narrators' interests. See his "Il sorriso di messer Torello," in *Il regime delle simmetrie imperfette*, 11–35.

18 Adalieta, as Irene Eibenstein-Alvisi has argued, is a "perfect wife" who functions as a viable model for the genteel women narrators of the *Decameron*. See Eibenstein-Alvisi, "The Dialogic Construction of Woman in the Italian Renaissance," ch. 5, "The *Decameron*'s Perfect Wives."

19 Panfilo may be preparing for this solution, I believe, as he tells 9.6, a story in which he revises the fabliau sources so that the husband is not a thief and so that the wife never has occasion to confront the husband for blameworthy behaviour. For a summary of the possible sources and analogues for 9.6, see Lee, *The "Decameron,"* 281–7.

20 This passage would merit further analysis, particularly for the way it forces us to re-evaluate our view of a husband, Bernabò, whom we might have been content to define as foolish rather than bestial. When Gualtieri states that others have marked him as "crudele e iniquo e bestiale" (cruel, unjust, and brutish), we must remember that these are the very words applied earlier to Bernabò. Zinevra had referred to her husband as "crudele e iniquo" (cruel and unjust [2.9.69]). Dioneo had highlighted Bernabò's "bestialità" [asinine stupidity [2.10.3]). The women of the group had all agreed with Dioneo that Bernabò had been a "bestia" (fool, or ass [2.Concl.1]). Thanks to an overlay from Dante's "mad bestiality" (*matta bestialitade*), which Dioneo recalls at the very beginning of the novella

of Griselda, Bernabò's foolishness begins to look more like Gualtieri's bestiality and brutishness. (For this particular observation about how the moral and emotional charge of *bestialità* can change over the course of the *Decameron*, I am indebted to Michael Papio, who drew our attention to this during the discussion following my presentation of an earlier version of this chapter at the University of Wisconsin–Madison.)

21 Both in my book *A Rhetoric of the "Decameron"* and in my essay "The Untidy Business of Gender Studies," I have argued that the debate about whether the *Decameron* is misogynist or philogynist has produced an impasse in our thinking.

22 Unfortunately, I no longer know who authored this. My notes show that I had found this passage at a website titled "Patient Griselda" (date of access 21 January 2006), but the website is no longer available, and the professor I believed to be the author has told me that she is not.

23 Shirley S. Allen is representative of the readers who believe that Boccaccio must want us to read 10.10 ironically. See her "The Griselda Tale."

24 For Assignment 1d (part of an assignment sequence focused on 2.9), I had instructed students to assume Zinevra's voice and to write a letter to either the abbot/princess (2.3) or Bartolomea of Pisa (2.10).

25 I have reproduced the assignment exactly as it was submitted to me, including with the one textual citation from page 88 of McWilliam's translation of the *Decameron*.

Chapter Seven

1 Kircher, "The Modality of Moral Communication," 1037.

2 Kircher, "The Modality of Moral Communication," 1037–8.

3 Carlo Delcorno makes a number of very fine observations about the *Decameron*'s irony, but his focus, which is mainly on the ironies created by single words or by various diegetic levels within the *Decameron*, does not bring the reader into the picture; see his "Ironia/parodia." For views of irony that are more compelling, see Hutcheon, *Irony's Edge;* and Fish, "Short People Got No Reason to Live."

4 Kircher, "The Modality of Moral Communication," 1071.

5 Branca, "Ironizzazione letteraria come rinnovamento di tradizioni," in *Boccaccio medievale e nuovi studi*, 335–46, esp. 337.

6 Robert Hollander, with Courtney Cahill, "Day Ten of the *Decameron* and the Myth of Order," in Hollander, *Boccaccio's Dante*, 111.

7 Hollander and Cahill, "Day Ten of the *Decameron* and the Myth of Order," 109.

8 Wampole, "How to Live without Irony," 1, 5.

9 Wampole, "How to Live without Irony," 5.
10 Wampole, "How to Live without Irony," 5.
11 Wampole, "How to Live without Irony," 5. Wampole's diatribe brings to mind what Linda Hutcheon has said about the "considerable punch" that irony packs: "People do not usually get upset about metaphor or synecdoche, but they certainly do get worked up about irony ... Sometimes, as we all know well, people get upset because they are the targets or victims of irony. Sometimes, though, anger erupts at the seeming inappropriateness of irony in certain situations." See Hutcheon and Valdés, "Irony, Nostalgia, and the Postmodern: A Dialogue," 21.
12 Boccaccio, *Decameron*, trans. Florio (?).
13 Boccaccio, *Decameron*, trans. McWilliam, 720.
14 Boccaccio, *Decameron*, trans. Waldman, 613.
15 Boccaccio, *Decameron*, trans. Musa and Bondanella, 723.
16 Boccaccio, *Decameron*, trans. McWilliam, 720.
17 Boccaccio, *Decameron*, trans. Waldman, 613.
18 Boccaccio, *Decameron*, trans. Musa and Bondanella, 723–4.
19 Boccaccio, trans. Kelly, 487.
20 Boccaccio, *Decameron*, trans. Florio (?).
21 For evidence of this, see "sentimento" in the *Vocabolario degli Accademici della Crusca*.
22 Boccaccio, *Decameron*, trans. McWilliam, 724; trans. Musa and Bondanella, 728.
23 Boccaccio, *Decameron*, trans. Rigg.
24 Boccaccio, *Decameron*, trans. McWilliam, 726.
25 Boccaccio, *Decameron*, trans. Waldman, 618.
26 Boccaccio, *Decameron*, trans. Musa and Bondanella, 729.
27 Mark Thomas (Cornell '10) wrote this for a first-year writing seminar, "Life in an Age of Moral Complexity," that I taught during the summer of 2006. The quotations are taken from Boccaccio, *Decameron*, trans. McWilliam, 719–20.
28 For "Truthiness" (17 October 2005), http://thecolbertreport.cc.com/videos/63ite2/the-word---truthiness. For "Wikiality" (31 July 2006), http://thecolbertreport.cc.com/videos/z1aahs/the-word---wikiality. For "Dumb-ocracy" (15 August 2006), http://thecolbertreport.cc.com/videos/6qb0k5/the-word---dumb-ocracy.
29 The 1384 Codex Mannelli is housed in the Biblioteca Medicea Laurenziana as MS Plut. XLII, 1.
30 For the critical studies, see Carrai, "Di chi sono le postille recenziori"; Carrai, "La prima ricezione del *Decameron*"; Clarke, "Leggere il *Decameron*"; and Clarke, "Reading/Writing Griselda."

31 Carrai, "La prima ricezione del *Decameron*," 107, commenting on Codex Mannelli, 23r.
32 Carrai, "La prima ricezione del *Decameron*," 107, commenting on Codex Mannelli, 78r.
33 Carrai, "La prima ricezione del *Decameron*," 107, commenting on Codex Mannelli 101r.
34 Fish, "Short People Got No Reason to Live."
35 LaMarre, Landreville, and Beam, "The Irony of Satire."
36 Bérubé and Graff, "Regulations for Literary Criticism in the 1990s."
37 Hutcheon, *Irony's Edge*, 7.
38 Winokur, *The Big Book of Irony*, 61.
39 Hutcheon, *Irony's Edge*, 7.
40 Bérubé's CV is available at his home page (http://english.la.psu.edu/faculty-staff/mfb12). Graff's CV and list of publications can be found at http://tigger.uic.edu/~ggraff/home.html. Date of access 26 January 2014.
41 Hutcheon, *Irony's Edge*, 15.
42 Grudin and Grudin, *Boccaccio's "Decameron,"* 134.
43 Migiel, "The Untidy Business of Gender Studies"; Migiel, "Boccaccio and Women."
44 See, for example, Cavallini, *La decima giornata del "Decameron,"* 76, who describes this novella as "ricca di situazioni suggestive e di risvolti psicologici" (rich in its suggestive possibilities and psychological implications) and who then proclaims it one of the most successful novellas of the Tenth Day and perhaps the entire *Decameron*.
45 bell hooks has made this argument with specific reference to American culture in *All About Love*.
46 As I noted earlier in this chapter, the edifying readings of Day 5, dedicated to love that ends happily, are related to the edifying readings of Day 10, as all of the stories of Day 5 and the final seven stories of Day 10 affirm marriage. Victoria Kirkham's response to Dioneo's story about Alibech and Rustico (3.10) is instructive. Commenting on Dioneo's invitation to his female companions to learn to "put the devil back into hell, because this is highly pleasing to God and pleasurable for the parties involved, and because much good can be born from it subsequently" (apparate a rimettere il diavolo in inferno, per ciò che egli è forte a grado a Dio e piacere delle parti, e molto bene ne può nascere e seguire [3.10.35]), Kirkham takes her distance: "Needless to say, God is not served, nor are souls saved, by humbling the sort of proud devil that happened to be tempting Rustico. Worse still, to sanction lust in the name of the Lord and the vocabulary of Christian piety is blatant sacrilege" (see Kirkham, "Love's Labors Rewarded and Paradise Lost

(*Decameron* III 10)," in *The Sign of Reason in Boccaccio's Fiction*, 199). Kirkham then offers an alternative way to see Dioneo's story as edifying; she argues that it functions within the larger frameworks of the *Decameron* – and indeed of Boccaccio's work as a whole – to show us that "for if we now ask where the adultery and fornication of the Third Day lead in the *Decameron*, we find a pattern that recalls thematic motifs of Boccaccio's earlier works. Carnal desire (III), while humanly natural (Intro. IV), leads to tragedy and death (IV) unless legitimized by the life-affirming institution of matrimony (V)" (209, emphasis hers).

47 Francesco Bausi comments on Sofronia's name, citing also what Victoria Kirkham and Giuseppe Mazzotta have said about it; see his "Gli spiriti magni," 250.

48 See Branca, *Boccaccio medievale e nuovi studi*, 176; Cavallini, *La decima giornata del "Decameron*," 66–7, 74; Novajra, "Dalla pratica della virtù all'esercizio del potere: X Giornata," 173–4; Barolini, "The Wheel of the *Decameron*," 532; Kirkham, *The Sign of Reason in Boccaccio's Fiction*, 160–1.

49 Grudin and Grudin, *Boccaccio's "Decameron*," 133–4.

50 Grudin and Grudin, *Boccaccio's "Decameron*," 130.

51 Cavallini, *La decima giornata del "Decameron*," 64: "Il trapasso dalla tentazione sensuale alla scoperta che la donna è ancora viva avviene così rapidamente che il lettore non avverte quello che di ripugnante vi potrebbe essere in questo amore per un cadavere" (The movement from fleshly temptation to the discovery that the woman is still alive happens so quickly that the reader does not notice the repugnance that could be part of this love for a corpse).

52 Cavallini, "La decima giornata del *Decameron*," 63: "La scena non è macabra come si potrebbe pensare" (One might think that this scene would be macabre, but it is not).

53 Boccaccio, *Filocolo*.

54 Boccaccio, *Il Filocolo*, trans. Cheney, 295.

55 Christopher Kleinhenz defines the "menne / de lo petto" (which appear in a poem attributed to Giacomino Pugliese) as "capezzoli" (nipples); see his "Erotismo e carnalità nella poesia del Due e Trecento," 304. The *Grande dizionario della lingua italiana*, however, defines *menna* as "mammella" (breast), which I would select as the preferred translation, especially given that Boccaccio, in *Filocolo*, 3.11, clearly uses *menna* in this sense.

56 Cavallini repeatedly calls attention to the musicality and the stylistic sophistication of the prose, both in 10.4 and in other novellas of Day 10. See his *La decima giornata del "Decameron*," esp. 57, 64, 111, 145.

57 Marcus, *An Allegory of Form*, 108–9.

58 Bruno Pagnamenta, *Il "Decameron": L'ambiguità come strategia narrativa*, 124–5.
59 Hollander and Cahill, "Day Ten of the *Decameron* and the Myth of Order," 114.
60 Hollander and Cahill, "Day Ten of the *Decameron* and the Myth of Order," 115, 159–63.
61 Marcus, *An Allegory of Form*, 107.
62 Bruno Pagnamenta, *Il "Decameron": L'ambiguità come strategia narrativa*, 120.
63 This, of course, is the problem Boccaccio presents to us when, following Fiammetta's tale of King Carlo (10.6), a Guelph, he has the Ghibelline woman from among the narrators refuse to praise a Guelph ruler, and when, following Pampinea's tale of the Ghibelline King Piero (10.7), he has that same Ghibelline lady express enthusiastic praise.
64 Cottino-Jones, *Order from Chaos*, 170.

Chapter Eight

1 Hollander, *Boccaccio's Dante*, 69–88.
2 Hollander, *Boccaccio's Dante*, 69–71.
3 Hollander, *Boccaccio's Dante*, 71.
4 Hollander, *Boccaccio's Dante*, 72–3.
5 Hollander, *Boccaccio's Dante*, 74–83. As Hollander notes, even when *utile* is used "as a moralist would warrant" in the Author's story of Filippo Balducci, it appears in order to demonstrate that traditional morality is a "foolish intrusion upon the preserve of human reality" (75–6).
6 Hollander, *Boccaccio's Dante*, 83–4.
7 Hollander, *Boccaccio's Dante*, 83–4 at 84.
8 Hollander, *Boccaccio's Dante*, 85–6.
9 Hollander, *Boccaccio's Dante*, 85–6.
10 Marchesi, *"Sic me formabat puerum."*
11 Marchesi, *"Sic me formabat puerum,"* 14–16.
12 Marchesi, *"Sic me formabat puerum,"* 16–17.
13 Marchesi, *"Sic me formabat puerum,"* 23–6.
14 Marchesi, *"Sic me formabat puerum,"* 23.
15 Marchesi, *"Sic me formabat puerum,"* 20.
16 Marchesi, *"Sic me formabat puerum,"* 27.
17 Marchesi, *"Sic me formabat puerum,"* 25.
18 Horace, *The Works*. Subsequent citations appear in the text.
19 Marchesi, *"Sic me formabat puerum,"* 26.
20 Marchesi, *"Sic me formabat puerum,"* 25–6.
21 Marcus, *An Allegory of Form*, 51. See also Marcus at 63, when she comments on the turn away from tragedy as a literary mode: "Henceforth the language

of the *Decameron* will be that of nightingales, *papere*, and devils in Hell – not that of hearts which bleed real blood."

22 Marchesi, *"Sic me formabat puerum,"* 29n.

23 Schlegel, *Satire and the Threat of Speech*, ch. 2, "Horace and His Fathers: *Satires* I, 4 and I, 6."

24 The idea of Cacciaguida as the "true father," widely accepted in Dante studies, is commented on by Marchesi (*"Sic me formabat puerum,"* 24). One of the most insightful analyses of the polarity Cacciaguida–Brunetto Latini remains Freccero, "The Eternal Image of the Father," 62–76.

25 Marchesi, *"Sic me formabat puerum,"* 16n (for the quotation from Horace) and 16.

26 In *Paradiso* 17.133–5, Cacciaguida predicts for Dante that "Questo tuo grido farà come vento, / che le più alte cime più percuote; / e ciò non fa d'onor poco argumento" (Your outcry will be like the wind, / Which strikes the highest peaks, / And this is no small cause for honor"). The English translation is mine. Marchesi notes, as does Branca, that Boccaccio had Cacciaguida's speech in mind when he wrote about the winds of envy striking the highest peaks in *Decameron* 4.Intro.1; see Marchesi, *"Sic me formabat puerum,"* 23–4 and the relevant note in Branca's edition of the *Decameron*.

27 Dante Alighieri, *Inferno*.

28 Thomas Aquinas, *Summa Theologica*, II–II, Q. 24, A. 2, in *Summa Theologica*, trans. Fathers of the English Dominican Province.

29 Migiel, "The Signs of Power in Dante's Theology," 89–90.

30 Marchesi, *"Sic me formabat puerum,"* 19.

31 Marchesi, *"Sic me formabat puerum,"* 2.

32 Boccaccio, *The Decameron*, trans. Musa and Bondanella, 293.

33 The texts referred to here and subsequently are Boccaccio, *Esposizioni sopra la Comedia*; and Boccaccio, *Boccaccio's Expositions on Dante's "Comedy."*

34 Baratto, *Realtà e stile nel "Decameron,"* 13–15; Andrea Battistini, "Retorica," 320–43, esp. 336–8.

35 Particularly concentrated examples of this can be found in Battistini, "Retorica," 336–8.

36 Wallace, *Boccaccio: "Decameron,"* 107.

37 Stone, *The Ethics of Nature in the Middle Ages*, ch. 9, "Two Ways Not to Read (And Going Both Ways)," esp. 177–86.

38 Stone, *The Ethics of Nature in the Middle Ages*, 184.

39 See Migiel, "Boccaccio and Women."

40 Boccaccio, *De casibus virorum illustrium*, I, xi, 3–5.

41 Stone, *The Ethics of Nature in the Middle Ages*, 185.

42 Wallace, *Boccaccio: "Decameron,"* 107.

43 Wallace, *Boccaccio: "Decameron,"* 107.

44 Boccaccio, *The Decameron*, trans. Musa and Bondanella, 805; trans. McWilliam, 801; trans. Nichols, 653.

45 Daniels, *Boccaccio and the Book*, 5.

46 McWilliam opts for "unaffected" (801), Musa and Bondanella for "unassuming" (805), and Nichols for "unpretentious" (653).

Works Cited

Alighieri, Dante. *Inferno*. Ed. Anna Maria Chiavacci Leonardi. 7th ed. Milan:
  Mondadori, 2004.
_____. *Paradiso*. Ed. Anna Maria Chiavacci Leonardi. 6th ed. Milan:
  Mondadori, 2004.
_____. *Purgatorio*. Ed. Anna Maria Chiavacci Leonardi. 5th ed. Milan:
  Mondadori, 2004.
_____. *Vita Nuova*. Italian text with facing English translation by Dino S.
  Cervigni and Edward Vasta. Notre Dame: University of Notre Dame Press,
  1995.
Allen, Shirley S. "The Griselda Tale and the Portrayal of Women in the
  Decameron." *Philological Quarterly* 56 (1977): 1–13.
Aquinas, Thomas. *Commentary on Aristotle's Nicomachean Ethics*. Trans. C.I.
  Litzinger. Foreword by Ralph McInerney. Notre Dame: Dumb Ox Books,
  1964.
_____. *Sententia libri Ethicorum*. Ed. Dominican Fathers and introduced by
  R.A. Gauthier, O.P. Vol. 47 of *Opera Omnia*. Rome: Leonine Commission, 1968.
_____. *Summa Theologica*. In *Opera Omnia*. Available on the World Wide
  Web at Corpus Thomisticum. http://www.corpusthomisticum.org/iopera.
  html. Date of access 10 January 2014.
_____. *Summa Theologica*. Trans. Fathers of the English Dominican Province.
  3 vols. New York: Benziger Brothers, 1947–8.
_____. *Summa Theologica*. Trans. Fathers of the English Dominican Province.
  2nd rev. ed. Available on the World Wide Web at *New Advent* (online edition
  of 2008). http://www.newadvent.org/summa. Date of access 7 January 2014.
Aristotle. *Nicomachean Ethics*. Trans. W.D. Ross. Available on the World Wide
  Web at http://classics.mit.edu/Aristotle/nicomachaen.html. Date of access
  10 January 2014.

Armstrong, Guyda. "Boccaccio and the Infernal Body: The Widow as Wilderness." In *Boccaccio and Feminist Criticism*. Ed. F. Regina Psaki and Thomas C. Stillinger. 83–104. Chapel Hill: Annali d'Italianistica, 2006.

_____. *The English Boccaccio: A History in Books*. Toronto: University of Toronto Press, 2013.

Baratto, Mario. *Realtà e stile nel "Decameron."* 2nd ed. Rome: Editori Riuniti, 1993 [1984].

Barolini, Teodolinda. "The Wheel of the *Decameron*." *Romance Philology* 36 (1983): 521–40.

Barricelli, Gian Piero. "Satire of Satire: Boccaccio's *Corbaccio*." *Italian Quarterly* 18 (1975): 95–111.

Barsella, Susanna. "The Myth of Prometheus in Boccaccio's *Decameron*." *MLN* 119: Supplement (2004): 120–41.

Battistini, Andrea. "Retorica." In *Lessico critico decameroniano*. Ed. Renzo Bragantini and Pier Massimo Forni. 320–43. Turin: Bollati Boringhieri, 1995.

Bausi, Francesco. "Gli spiriti magni: Filigrane aristoteliche e tomistiche nella Decima Giornata del *Decameron*." *Studi sul Boccaccio* 27 (1999): 205–53.

Bennett, Deborah J. *Logic Made Easy: How to Know When Language Deceives You*. New York: W.W. Norton, 2004.

Bérubé, Michael, and Gerald Graff. "Regulations for Literary Criticism in the 1990s." *Democratic Culture: Newsletter of Teachers for a Democratic Culture* 2.2 (1993): 2–3.

Bloom, Harold. *The Anxiety of Influence: A Theory of Poetry*. 2nd ed. Oxford: Oxford University Press, 1997.

Boccaccio, Giovanni. *Boccaccio's Expositions on Dante's "Comedy."* Trans. Michael Papio. Toronto: University of Toronto Press, 2009.

_____. *De casibus virorum illustrium*. Ed. Pier Giorgio Ricci and Vittorio Zaccaria. Vol. 9 of *Tutte le opere di Giovanni Boccaccio*. Milan: Mondadori, 1983.

_____. *Il Decamerone di Giovanni Boccaccio novamente corretto con tre novelle aggiunte*. Venice: Aldo Romano e Andrea Asolano, 1522.

_____. *Il Decameron*. Venice: Gabriel Giolito de Ferrari, 1550.

_____. *Il Decamerone di m. Giovanni Boccaccio di nuovo emendato secondo gli antichi essemplari, per giudicio et diligenza di più autori con la diversità di molti testi posta per ordine in margine, & nel fine con gli epiteti dell'autore, con la espositione de proverbi et luoghi difficili, che nell'opera si contengono, con tavole & altre cose notabili & molto utili alli studiosi della lingua volgare*. Venice: Gabriel Giolito de Ferrari, 1550.

_____. *Il Decameron di Messer Giovanni Boccaccio Cittadino Fiorentino, Ricorretto in Roma, et Emendato secondo l'ordine del Sacro Conc. Di Trento, Et riscontrato in Firenze con Testi Antichi & alla sua vera lezione ridotto da' Deputati di loro Alt. Ser.* Florence: Giunti, 1573.

_____. *Decameron.* Translation attributed to John Florio (1620). *Decameron Web.* http://www.brown.edu/Departments/Italian_Studies/dweb/texts/florio/index.php. Date of access 28 June 2014.

_____. *The Decameron or Ten Days' Entertainment.* Trans. W.K. Kelly. London: Bohn, 1855.

_____. *Decameron.* Ed. Pietro Fanfani. 2 vols. Florence: Le Monnier, 1857.

_____. *Decameron.* Trans. J.M. Rigg. *Decameron Web.* http://www.brown.edu/Departments/Italian_Studies/dweb/texts/DecIndex.php?lang=eng.

_____. *Decameron.* Trans. Richard Aldington. Illustrated by Rockwell Kent. Garden City: Garden City Books, 1949 [1930].

_____. *Decameron.* Trans. Frances Winwar. New York Random House, 1955 [1930].

_____. *Decameron.* Trans. John Payne. New York: Blue Ribbon Books, 1931.

_____. *The Decameron: A New Translation (21 Novelle, Contemporary Reactions, Modern Criticism).* Trans. and ed. Mark Musa and Peter Bondanella. New York: W.W. Norton, 1977.

_____. *Decameron.* Trans. Mark Musa and Peter Bondanella. New York: New American Library (Signet Classics), 2002 [1982].

_____. *Decameron.* Ed. Vittore Branca. 2 vols. Turin: Einaudi, 1992.

_____. *Decameron.* Trans. Guido Waldman. Oxford: Oxford University Press, 1993.

_____. *Decameron.* Trans. G.H. McWilliam. 2nd ed. New York: Penguin Books, 1995.

_____. *Decameron.* Trans. Cormac Ó Cuilleanáin (based on John Payne's 1886 translation). Ware, Hertfordshire: Wordsworth Editions, 2004.

_____. *Decameron.* Trans. J.G. Nichols. New York: Everyman's Library, 2009.

_____. *Décaméron.* Trans. Marthe Dozon, Catherine Guimbard, and Marc Scialom, under the direction of Christian Bec. Paris: Bibliothèque classique, 1994.

_____. *El Decamerón.* First online edition, May 2008. In Chantal López y Omar Cortés, *Biblioteca Virtual Antorcha.* http://www.antorcha.net/biblioteca_virtual/literatura/decameron/tercera8.html.

_____. *Esposizioni sopra la Comedia.* Ed. Giorgio Padoan. 2 vols. Milan: Mondadori, 1994 [1965].

_____. *Filocolo.* Ed. Antonio Enzo Quaglio. Milan: Mondadori, 1998.

_____. *Il Filocolo.* Trans. Donald Cheney, with the collaboration of Thomas Bergin. New York: Garland Publishing, 1985.

Boccaccio, Giovanni, and Aldo Busi. *Decamerone da un italiano a un altro*. 2 vols. Milan: Rizzoli, 1990.

Branca, Lodovico, and Maria Grazia Ciardi Dupré Dal Poggetto. "Lodovico di Salvesto Ceffini copista del *Decameron*: L'illustrazione del codice Ceffini." *Studi sul Boccaccio* 22 (1994): 135–96.

Branca, Vittore. *Boccaccio medievale e nuovi studi sul "Decameron."* Florence: Sansoni, 1990.

Bruni, Francesco. *Boccaccio: L'invenzione della letteratura mezzana*. Bologna: Il Mulino, 1990.

Bruno Pagnamenta, Roberta. *Il "Decameron": L'ambiguità come strategia narrativa*. Ravenna: Longo, 1999.

Carrai, Stefano. "Di chi sono le postille recenziori nel codice Mannelli?" *Studi sul Boccaccio* 30 (2002): 159–68.

_____. "La prima ricezione del *Decameron* nelle postille di Francesco Mannelli." In *Autori e lettori di Boccaccio*. Atti del Convegno internazionale di Certaldo (20–2 settembre 2001). Ed. Michelangelo Picone. 99–111. Florence: Cesati, 2002.

Carroll, Noel. "Art and Ethical Criticism: An Overview of Recent Directions of Research." *Ethics* 110.2 (January 2000): 350–87.

Cavallini, Giorgio. *La decima giornata del "Decameron."* Rome: Bulzoni, 1980.

Celati, Gianni. "Lo spirito della novella." *Griseldaonline* 6 (2006–7). Published on 21 March 2007. http://www.griseldaonline.it/temi/rifiuti-scarti-esuberi/lo-spirito-della-novella.html. Date of access 13 March 2015.

Clarke, K.P. "Leggere il *Decameron* a margine del codice Mannelli." In *Boccaccio e i suoi lettori: Una lunga ricezione*. Ed. Gian Mario Anselmi, Giovanni Baffetti, Carlo Delcorno, and Sebastiana Nobili. 195–207. Bologna: Il Mulino, 2013.

_____. "Reading/Writing Griselda: A Fourteenth-Century Response (Florence, Biblioteca Medicea Laurenziana, MS Plut. 42,1)." In *On Allegory: Some Medieval Aspects and Approaches*. Ed. Mary Carr, K.P. Clarke, and Marco Nievergelt. 183–208. Newcastle: Cambridge Scholars, 2008.

Colbert, Stephen. "Dumb-ocracy" (15 August 2006). http://thecolbertreport.cc.com/videos/6qb0k5/the-word---dumb-ocracy. Date of access 28 June 2014.

_____. "Truthiness." (17 October 2005). http://thecolbertreport.cc.com/videos/63ite2/the-word---truthiness. Date of access 28 June 2014.

_____. "Wikiality" (31 July 2006). http://thecolbertreport.cc.com/videos/z1aahs/the-word---wikiality. Date of access 28 June 2014.

Cottino-Jones, Marga. "Desire and the Fantastic in the *Decameron*: The Third Day." *Italica* 70 (1993): 1–18.

_____. *Order from Chaos: Social and Aesthetic Harmonies in Boccaccio's "Decameron."* Washington, D.C.: University Press of America, 1982.

Daniels, Rhiannon. *Boccaccio and the Book: Production and Reading in Italy 1340–1520*. London: Legenda, 2009.

Delcorno, Carlo. "Ironia/parodia." In *Lessico critico decameroniano*. Ed. Renzo Bragantini and Pier Massimo Forni. 162–91. Turin: Bollati Boringhieri, 1995.

De Sanctis, Francesco. *Storia della letteratura italiana*. Ed. Niccolò Gallo. 2 vols. Turin: Einaudi, 1975.

"Du Vilain de Bailluel." In *Nouveau recueil complet des fabliaux* (NRCF). Ed. Willem Noomen and Nico Van Den Boogaard. Vol. 5. 223–49. Assen/Maastricht: Van Gorcum, 1990.

Eibenstein-Alvisi, Irene. "The Dialogic Construction of Woman in the Italian Renaissance." PhD diss., Cornell University, 2003.

Eisner, Martin. "The Tale of Ferondo's Purgatory." In *The "Decameron" Third Day in Perspective*. Ed. Pier Massimo Forni and Francesco Ciabattoni. 150–69. Toronto: University of Toronto Press, 2014.

Ferme, Valerio C. "*Ingegno* and Morality in the New Social Order: The Role of the *Beffa* in Boccaccio's *Decameron*." *Romance Languages Annual* 4 (1992): 248–55.

Fido, Franco. *Il regime delle simmetrie imperfette: Studi sul "Decameron."* Milan: Franco Angeli, 1988.

Fish, Stanley. "Short People Got No Reason to Live: Reading Irony." *Daedalus* 112.1 (Winter 1983): 175–91. Later included in *Doing What Comes Naturally: Change, Rhetoric, and the Practice of Theory in Literary and Legal Studies*. Durham: Duke University Press, 1989.

Flasch, Kurt. *Poesia dopo la peste: Saggio su Boccaccio*. Trans. Rosa Taliani. Bari: Laterza, 1995.

Freccero, John. "The Eternal Image of the Father." In *The Poetry of Allusion: Virgil and Ovid in Dante's "Commedia."* Ed. Rachel Jacoff and Jeffrey T. Schnapp. 62–76. Stanford: Stanford University Press, 1991.

Grande dizionario della lingua italiana. Dir. Salvatore Battaglia. Turin: UTET, 1962–.

Grudin, Michaela Paasche, and Robert Grudin. *Boccaccio's "Decameron" and the Ciceronian Renaissance*. New York: Palgrave Macmillan, 2012.

Hastings, R.W. [R. Hastings]. *Nature and Reason in the "Decameron."* Manchester: Manchester University Press, 1975.

_____. "To Teach or Not to Teach: The Moral Dimension of the *Decameron* Reconsidered." *Italian Studies* 44 (1989): 19–40.

Hollander, Robert. *Boccaccio's Dante and the Shaping Force of Satire*. Ann Arbor: University of Michigan Press, 1997.

_____. *Boccaccio's Last Fiction: "Il Corbaccio."* Philadelphia: University of Pennsylvania Press, 1988.

_____. *Boccaccio's Two Venuses*. New York: Columbia University Press, 1977.

_____. "Why Did Dante Write the *Comedy*?" *Dante Studies* 111 (1993): 19–25.

hooks, bell. *All About Love: New Visions*. New York: William Morrow, 2000.

Horace. *The Works of Horace*. Trans. C. Smart. Revised by Theodore Alois Buckley. New York: Harper & Brothers, 1863. Available on the World Wide Web at the Perseus Digital Library. www.perseus.tufts.edu/hopper. Date of access 29 May 2014.

Hughes, Langston. "World War." *Harlem Quarterly* (1949-50): 9.

Hutcheon, Linda. *Irony's Edge: The Theory and Politics of Irony*. London: Routledge, 1994.

Hutcheon, Linda, and Mario J. Valdés. "Irony, Nostalgia, and the Postmodern: A Dialogue." *Poligrafías. Revista de Literatura Comparada* 3 (1998–2000): 18–41.

Kircher, Timothy. "The Modality of Moral Communication in the *Decameron*'s First Day, in Contrast to the Mirror of the Exemplum." *Renaissance Quarterly* 54 (2001): 1035–73.

Kirkham, Victoria. "Morale." In *Lessico critico decameroniano*. Ed. Renzo Bragantini and Pier Massimo Forni. 249–68. Turin: Bollati Boringhieri, 1995.

_____. *The Sign of Reason in Boccaccio's Fiction*. Firenze: Olschki, 1993.

Kleinhenz, Christopher. "Erotismo e carnalità nella poesia del Due e Trecento." In *"Por le soie amisté": Essays in Honor of Norris J. Lacy*. Ed. Keith Busby and Catherine M. Jones. 293–310. Amsterdam: Rodopi, 2000.

LaMarre, Heather L., Kristen D. Landreville, and Michael A. Beam. "The Irony of Satire: Political Ideology and the Motivation to See What You Want to See in *The Colbert Report*." *International Journal of Press/Politics* 14 (April 2009): 212–31.

Lee, A.C. *The "Decameron": Its Sources and Analogues*. 1909 rpt. New York: Haskell House Publishers, 1972.

Lepschy, Giulio. "*La Veniexiana*: A Venetian Play of the Renaissance." In *Mother Tongues and Other Reflections on the Italian Language*. 97–117. Toronto: University of Toronto Press, 2002.

Il libro dei sette savi. In *Biblioteca dei Classici Italiani* di Giuseppe Bonghi. http://www.classicitaliani.it/trecento/libro_sette_savi_prosa.htm. Date of access 28 August 2009.

Marafioti, Martin. "Boccaccio's Lauretta: The *brigata*'s Bearer of Bad News." *Italian Culture* 19.2 (2001): 7–18.

Marchesi, Simone. "*Sic me formabat puerum*: Horace's *Satire* I, 4 and Boccaccio's Defense of the *Decameron*." *MLN* 116.1 (2001): 1–29.

Marcus, Millicent J. *An Allegory of Form: Literary Self-Consciousness in the "Decameron."* Saratoga: Anma Libri, 1979.

_____. "The Tale of Maestro Alberto (I.10)." In *The "Decameron" First Day in Perspective*. Ed. Elissa B. Weaver. 222–40. Toronto: University of Toronto Press, 2004.

Martinez, Ronald. "The Tale of the Monk and His Abbot (I.4)." In *The "Decameron" First Day in Perspective*. Ed. Elissa Weaver. 113–34. Toronto: University of Toronto Press, 2004.

McCabe, Herbert, OP. "Aquinas on Good Sense." In *God Still Matters*. Foreword by Alasdair MacIntyre. Ed. and introduced by Brian Davies OP. 152–65. London: Continuum, 2002.

Migiel, Marilyn. "Boccaccio and Women." In *The Cambridge Companion to Boccaccio*. Ed. Guyda Armstrong, Rhiannon Daniels, and Stephen Milner. 171-84. Cambridge: Cambridge University Press, 2015.

_____. *A Rhetoric of the "Decameron."* Toronto: University of Toronto Press, 2003.

_____. "The Signs of Power in Dante's Theology: *Purgatorio* X–XXVII." PhD diss., Yale University, 1981.

_____. "The Untidy Business of Gender Studies: Or, Why It's Almost Useless to Ask if the *Decameron* Is Feminist." In *Boccaccio and Feminist Criticism*. Ed. F. Regina Psaki and Thomas C. Stillinger. 217–33. Chapel Hill: Annali d'Italianistica, 2006.

Novajra, Ada. "Dalla pratica della virtù all'esercizio del potere: X Giornata." In *Prospettive sul "Decameron."* Ed. Giorgio Bàrberi-Squarotti. 165–92. Turin: Tirrenia, 1989.

Olson, Glending. *Literature as Recreation in the Later Middle Ages*. Ithaca: Cornell University Press, 1982.

Paden, Michael. "Elissa: La ghibellina del *Decameron*." *Rivista di studi italiani* 11 (1993): 1–12, and also in *Studi sul Boccaccio* 21 (1993): 39–50.

Pertile, Lino. "Dante, Boccaccio, e l'intelligenza." *Italian Studies* 43 (1988): 60–74.

Petrus Alfonsi. *The Disciplina clericalis of Petrus Alfonsi*. Trans. and ed. Eberhard Hermes. London: Routledge & Kegan Paul, 1977.

_____. *Petri Alfonsi Disciplina Clericalis*. Ed. Alfons Hilka and Werner Söderhjelm. Vol. 1, *Lateinischer Text*. In *Acta Societatis Scientiarum Fennicæ* 38/4 (1911): 20. Available on the World Wide Web at *The Latin Library*. http://www.thelatinlibrary.com/alfonsi.disciplina.html.

Picone, Michelangelo. "Le 'merende' di maestro Alberto (*Decameron* I.10)." *Rassegna europea di letteratura italiana* 16 (2000): 99–110.

Psaki, F. Regina. "The Play of Genre and Voicing in Boccaccio's *Corbaccio*." *Italiana* 5 (1993): 41–54.

Radcliff-Umstead, Douglas. "Boccaccio's Adaptation of Some Latin Sources for the *Decameron*." *Italica* 45 (1968): 171–94.

Richardson, Brian. "The 'Ghibelline' Narrator in the *Decameron*." *Italian Studies* 33 (1978): 20–8.

Russo, Luigi. *Letture critiche del "Decameron."* Bari: Laterza, 1967.

Scaglione, Aldo. *Nature and Love in the Middle Ages*. Berkeley: University of
    California Press, 1963.
Schlegel, Catherine M. *Satire and the Threat of Speech: Horace's "Satires" Book I*.
    Madison: University of Wisconsin Press, 2005.
Scrivano, Fabrizio. *Una certa idea del comico: Retorica e riso nella cultura del
    Seicento*. Pisa: Pacini, 2002.
Smarr, Janet Levarie. *Boccaccio and Fiammetta: The Narrator as Lover*. Urbana:
    University of Illinois Press, 1986.
Solomon, Robert C. *Ethics and Excellence: Cooperation and Integrity in Business*.
    Oxford: Oxford University Press, 1993.
Stone, Gregory B. *The Ethics of Nature in the Middle Ages: On Boccaccio's
    Poetaphysics*. New York: St Martin's Press, 1998.
Svevo, Italo. *La coscienza di Zeno*. In *Romanzi*. Vol. 2 of *Opera Omnia*. Ed. Bruno
    Maier. Milan: dall'Oglio, 1969.
Tateo, Francesco. *Boccaccio*. 2nd ed. Bari: Laterza, 1998.
Tolan, John Victor. *Petrus Alfonsi and His Medieval Readers*. Gainesville:
    University Press of Florida, 1993.
Usher, Jonathan. "Boccaccio's *Ars Moriendi* in the *Decameron*." *Modern
    Language Review* 81.3 (1986): 621–32.
_____. "Le rubriche del *Decameron*." *Medioevo romanzo* 10 (1985): 391–418.
Valian, Virginia. *Why So Slow? The Advancement of Women*. Cambridge,
    MA: MIT Press, 1998.
Vallicella, Bill. "On Wasting Time with Philosophy (and a Jab at Pascal)."
    Maverick Philosopher. Posted 22 August 2009. http://maverickphilosopher.
    typepad.com/maverick_philosopher/2009/08/on-wasting-time-with-
    philosophy-and-a-jab-at-pascal.html. Date of access 5 October 2009.
Vocabolario degli Accademici della Crusca. Venice: Giovanni Alberti, 1612.
    http://vocabolario.sns.it/html/index.html. Date of access 23 June 2014.
Wallace, David. *Giovanni Boccaccio: "Decameron"*. Cambridge: Cambridge
    University Press, 1991.
Wampole, Christy. "How to Live without Irony." *New York Times*. 17
    November 2012. Sunday Review section, 1, 5.
Winokur, Jon. *The Big Book of Irony*. New York: St. Martin's Press, 2007.

Index